OUR OWN PEOPLE

OUR OWN PEOPLE

A Memoir of 'Ignace Reiss'
and His Friends

ELISABETH K. PORETSKY

Ann Arbor

THE UNIVERSITY OF MICHIGAN PRESS

First published in English by Oxford University Press, London 1969
© Elisabeth K. Poretsky 1969
All rights reserved
SBN 472-73500-4
Library of Congress Catalog Card No. 73-107978
Published in the United States of America by
The University of Michigan Press 1970
Manufactured in the United States of America

Contents

PREFACE by F. W. D. Deakin   vii

*To the Central Committee of the Communist Party of
the U.S.S.R., 17 July 1937*   1

I   A Small Town in Galicia   5

II   The Polish Party   27

III   First Assignment: Lwow   37

IV   Berlin and Vienna   53

V   Prague and Amsterdam   72

VI   Moscow, 1929–1932   86

VII   Europe in the Thirties   130

VIII   Moscow, 1937   156

IX   Paris   208

X   Switzerland   227

XI   Aftermath: Amsterdam and Paris   243

EPILOGUE: The United States   271

INDEX   275

253631

Preface

In the years preceding the First World War, six schoolboys grew up in a small town on the frontier of Austrian Galicia and Imperial Russia. They formed, in their early youth, a secret bond of friendship, which not only was to hold fast throughout the course of their lives, but exercised a sustaining influence on their fate. By separate but converging paths, each of these young men, in the halcyon years following on the October Revolution, was to enter the service of the Soviet State, as pioneer members of its military intelligence and security services; and each was to die a violent death by execution at the hands of its agents—or by suicide.

This book is the odyssey of these men, and essentially of one of them, Ignace Poretsky. It is written by his widow after more than thirty years of withdrawal and reflection. The account possesses a special haunting quality. The author has for long been the only survivor of this small group, who symbolize, with a grim completeness, the intensity of the faith of the revolutionary European youth of the generation of 1917 in the future of the World Revolution under the leadership of Lenin and the Russian Bolshevik party; generating a fervour, which was fated to be matched for most of them, unendurably, by the slow shared erosion of that belief.

This is the stark and precise testimonial to their broken dreams, distilled with controlled emotion; a meditation, historical and deeply human, on the fate of all those who were trapped in similar fashion; and a cool analysis of the stages of this destruction.

The conspiratorial career of Ignace Poretsky is the illustration of a process. By early 1919 he was a member of the new and illegal Polish Communist Party (his native province now

forming an integral part of the recently re-created Republic of
Poland): that summer he had been called, by one of his childhood friends, to Vienna, where, as in Berlin, young revolutionaries were being collected from the parties and groups from all
over Europe which had recently joined together, at the initiative of Lenin, to found the Third International—the Comintern
—as the general staff of the coming World Revolution.

To these young men and women, their course was very
simply identifiable with the future and security of the Soviet
State, already menaced by the collapse of revolution in
Central and Eastern Europe, and the spread of Civil War in
Russia itself. It was but a short step, hardly discernible, from
working in the Comintern agencies in Vienna in the field of
revolutionary propaganda to entering into the Soviet security
services, and in the case of Ignace Poretsky, known hencefor-
ward under his cover name of 'Ludwik', into the military
intelligence apparatus—the so-called Fourth Department of the
General Staff.

These agencies were in their infancy, improvised by a handful of trusted and experienced conspirators—some of them
personal comrades of Lenin—but desperately short of sub-
ordinates with a flair for such work, and with a knowledge of
political conditions outside Russia. Inevitably, the core of recruitment lay in the cadres of the European Communist parties;
in particular, the Germans, Austrians, Poles, and Hungarians.

To many such men, among them 'Ludwik' himself, the work
of a Soviet agent, which he had become already by 1922,
was but a logical, and temporary, extension of a dedicated
revolutionary task. They were unaware of taking any irrevocable step. Once the state of emergency, which threatened the
Soviet Union in the early 1920s, had passed, 'Ludwik' and
those engaged with him would return to their own parties, and
to the local work of promoting their national communist
revolutions.

But the emergency did not end, and there was no return.
Each recruit was caught up in the apparatus, cut off by strict
and essential security measures from any contact with party
comrades and their work at home, and confined into an
isolated anonymous frame.

For six years 'Ludwik' served the Fourth Department in Western Europe, and returned to Moscow in 1927 to receive the Order of the Red Banner for his special services to the Soviet Union. The cause and ideals, however, for which he, and many like him, had fought, had already seeped away, at first almost imperceptibly. Stalin registered by stages his victory over Trotsky and his opponents by the obliteration of the first generation of revolutionaries, not only in the Bolshevik party, but among the leadership and ranks of all Communist parties grouped in the Comintern, and in the international agencies serving the Soviet Union.

'Ludwik' was not alone in his agonizing hesitations in comprehending the real nature of the new tyranny, and the mounting signs of the total destruction of all for which he had struggled and sacrificed his existence as a normal human being. The final revelation came during his stay in Moscow in 1929–1932. He had been shelved with some embarrassment by his Department, which was already exposed to the first signs of the purges of its 'foreign' non-Russian specialists. He was offered a nominal post in the Polish section of the Comintern, which theoretically meant party work. His wife 'reminded him of his wish to return to such work, but he merely said, "Party work? What party work? What party for that matter?" '

But one more assignment abroad would mean the immediate protection of his family, and the last faint chance to reflect on the manner of wrenching himself free. 'Ludwik' was posted to Paris as a member of the foreign section of the N.K.V.D. His new colleagues were alien and suspicious. The dedicated idealists of the 1917 generation of European revolutionaries were now expendable, and being replaced by the faceless Russian technicians of the Stalinist training schools. When, at the height of the purges in 1936, 'Ludwik' was invited back from Paris to Moscow by his superiors, his wife persuaded him to let her go in his stead.

Her description of the smell of fear pervading every flat and room in the Soviet capital, in the streets, in the corridors in every office, is conveyed with a sad perception in the form of dialogues with the friends of her husband, who, like him, had followed the same path of no return from the small town in

Galicia to the rootless anonymity of the life of Soviet agents, their revolutionary faith extinguished, trapped at the centre of the machine of despotism, awaiting an inescapable end.

All that was left was the loyalty to each other, which held against all pressures.

Shortly after his wife's return to Paris 'Ludwik' decided to end the torment of his inner conflict. He composed an open letter to the Central Committee of the Communist Party of the Soviet Union, distilling the accumulated bitterness and horror of the last years. In a final gesture of defiance, 'Ludwik' dispatched to the Soviet Embassy in Paris the original copy, wrapped in the Order of the Red Banner, together with his secret mandate from the Polish Communist Party in 1919—his fatal passport of entry into Soviet service. He then withdrew, with his wife and child, to a village in Switzerland.

It was not in his nature to seek police protection in a Western country: such an act would have been to him a final humiliation. Liberated from the burden of the past, there could be no future. One never resigned from the service of a Soviet agency. On 4 September 1937 an unidentified body was found by the Swiss police near Lausanne. The case of 'Ludwik' was closed, according to the rules of the sinister game.

In the following months, his friends in Moscow disappeared without trace. The only survivor of the group, Walter Krivitsky, remained, for a space, at his post in Western Europe. He then sought apparent safety, in contrast to 'Ludwik', by flight to the West. He wrote down, in friendless isolation, his own experiences before seeking oblivion in suicide in a Washington hotel.

It has remained to the widow of 'Ludwik' to compose this memorial to a generation of revolutionaries, adding to the understanding of their hopes, and lighting up the history of their seduction and destruction. As the author was leaving Moscow in 1937, the eldest member of the group said, 'Never come back, not under any circumstances. Perhaps one of you will live to tell about us.'

This book is the response.

1969   F. W. D. Deakin

To the Central Committee of the Communist Party of the U.S.S.R.

I should have written the letter I am writing you today a long time ago, on that day when the Sixteen[1] were massacred in the cellars of the Lubianka on the orders of the 'Father of the People'.

I kept quiet then and I did not raise my voice at the murders that followed, and as a result I bear a heavy responsibility. My guilt is grave, but I will try to repair it, to repair it promptly and thus ease my conscience.

Up to this moment I marched alongside you. Now I will not take another step. Our paths diverge! He who now keeps quiet becomes Stalin's accomplice, betrays the working class, betrays socialism.

I have been fighting for socialism since my twentieth year. Now on the threshold of my fortieth I do not want to live off the favours of a Yezhov.[2] I have sixteen years of illegal work behind me. That is not little, but I have enough strength left to begin all over again. For it will indeed be necessary to begin everything all over again to save socialism. That fight began a long time ago and I want to take my part in it.

The noise that is made about the deeds of pilots flying over the Pole is supposed to drown out the moans and the cries of the victims tortured in the cellars of the Lubianka, in Svobodnaia, in Minsk, in Kiev, in Leningrad, in Tiflis. It will not succeed. The voice of truth is stronger than the noise of the most powerful engines.

It is quite true that the records of the pilots will affect the hearts of American ladies and of the youth of two continents intoxicated by sports, much more easily than we will succeed in conquering international opinion and affecting the conscience of the world. But make no mistake, truth will find a way and the day of judgement is much nearer than those in the Kremlin think. The day when international socialism will judge

[1] The 16 old Bolsheviks tried in Moscow in August 1936 and subsequently executed.

[2] N. I. Yezhov was People's Commissar for Internal Affairs from September 1936. See chapter IX, p. 219.

the crimes committed in the past ten years is not far off. Nothing will be forgotten and nothing will be forgiven. History is harsh. 'The leader of genius', 'the Father of the People', 'the Sun of Socialism' will have to account for what he has done. He will have to account for the defeated Chinese revolution, for the red plebiscite in Germany, for the defeat of the German proletariat, for social fascism, for the things told to Mr. Howard[1], *for his flattery of M. Laval—all acts of genius.*

This trial will take place in the open and many a living and dead witness will attend it. All will speak and this time will tell the truth, all the truth. All will testify—those who were slandered and those who were shot though innocent—and the international workers' movement will rehabilitate them, the Kamenevs, the Mrachkovskys, the Smirnovs and the Muralovs, the Drobnis, Serebriakovs, Mdivanis, and Okudzhavas, Rakovskys, and Andreas Nins[2]*—'the spies and enemy agents, the saboteurs and Gestapo agents'!*

The working class must defeat Stalin and Stalinism so that the U.S.S.R. and the international workers' movement do not succumb to fascism and counter-revolution. This mixture of the worst of opportunism, devoid of principles, and of lies and blood threatens to poison the world and the last forces of the working class.

What is needed today is a fight without mercy against Stalinism! The class struggle and not the popular front, workers' intervention in the Spanish revolution as opposed to the action of committees.

Down with the lie of socialism in one country! Return to Lenin's international!

Neither the Second nor the Third International can carry out this historical mission. Corrupt and dislocated, all they can do is to prevent the working class from fighting. They can only be the policemen at the service of the bourgeoisie. The irony of history! In the past the bourgeoisie provided its own Cavaignacs and Gallifets, its Trepovs and Wrangels. Today, under the glorious leadership of the two Internationals, it is the proletarians themselves who have become the executioners of their comrades. The bourgeoisie can attend quietly to its own business: order and

---

[1] The American Roy Howard, who interviewed Stalin in 1935.

[2] Kamenev, Mrachkovsky, and Smirnov were tried and executed in August 1936, Muralov, Drobnis, and Serebriakov in January 1937, and Mdivani and Okudzhava in Georgia in July 1937, Rakovsky, arrested at the end of 1936, was not tried until 1938. Nin, political secretary of P.O.U.M., was arrested in Spain in June 1937, and may have died under interrogation.

peace rule. There are still Noskes and Yezhovs, Negrins and Diazs. Stalin is their leader and Feuchtwanger[1] their Homer.

No. I cannot stand it any longer. I take my freedom of action. I return to Lenin, to his doctrine, to his acts.

I intend to devote my feeble forces to the cause of Lenin. I want to continue the fight, for only our victory—that of the proletarian revolution—will free humanity of capitalism and the U.S.S.R. of Stalinism.

Forward to new struggles! For the Fourth International!

LUDWIK

1th July 1937

P.S. *In 1928 I was awarded the Order of the Red Banner for services to the proletarian revolution. I am enclosing the decoration. It would be beneath my dignity to wear an order also worn by the executioners of the best men of the working class in Russia. (In the last two weeks* Izvestiia *has published the names of those who have received the award. Their achievements have been discreetly kept quiet: they are the men who have carried out the death sentences on the old Bolsheviks.)*

[1] See chapter VIII, pp. 176ff.

CHAPTER I

A Small Town in Galicia

This book will tell the story of six men who came from a small town in the province of Galicia, on the border of the Austro-Hungarian empire. The public only learned of the existence of some of these men from the manner in which they died; this will be a record of the lives of the six, and of others who shared their fate, from the outbreak of the First World War through the Russian revolution, which for a short while put them on the stage of history and whose decline led to their untimely deaths.

The town was like most others in that backwater of the Empire, in that a few of its families were slightly better off than the rest and could claim to be its intelligentsia. But a border town tends to develop its own way of life, its own rules, and its own special mentality, and frontier people are different from other people. There were no government offices in the town and no professional administrators; there was no military garrison and naturally enough very few inns or taverns. The Empire was represented by a small detachment of gendarmes and the highest official of the Austrian regime was the *gendarmerie* commandant, Kaidan, who shared the uneventful lives of the inhabitants and closed his eyes to the smuggling which is the habitual activity of any border town, and by which he too supplemented his meagre pay. The people of the town got along with him, liked him, possibly even respected him, but certainly did not fear him.

Later, after Poland had regained her independence, Kaidan came to be greatly feared. He lived up to his name, which in Polish means 'shackles', as a zealous and patriotic police officer in Lwow. The Polish novelist Stefan Zeromski has left a portrait of this brutal anti-Semitic torturer in his book *Przedwiosnie*. In Kaidan's eyes every Jew was a communist and vice versa, and his devotion to duty took the form of inventing new tortures, for which the Polish police were to become infamous. In the town Kaidan had had under his orders an official of the 'secret' police (known to everyone, of course) which later became part of the Polish police. This man retained some of the small-town attitudes and traditions, and although a staunch patriot and anti-communist would occasionally help his former neighbours—unlike Kaidan, who was especially hard on them —by warning them of an impending arrest.

In the days of the Empire, the boundary with Russia was a river on either bank of which was a small settlement. Thus the river separated two towns, two empires, two worlds, but at the same time served as a link between them. In the summer children from either bank would meet swimming in the river and in the winter skating on it. Adults also crossed it: in the daytime they travelled legitimately, presenting their passes to the frontier guards; at night as smugglers they waded across the shallower parts.

Not all the smugglers smuggled goods, however. There was one who smuggled people. He knew secret ways of getting fugitives from the Tsar's prisons into Austria. As he was also a porter and owned a horse, with which he met trains coming from Russia, he could provide transportation for his customers. The town looked upon him with awe for he was often gone at night, meeting his charges somewhere in Russia. He was credited with having smuggled famous revolutionaries across the border, but he himself was reticent about his activities— possibly because he was afraid of Kaidan, possibly because there was much less to what he did than public rumour supposed. It was also said that he never took any money for his services; this is improbable, as the escapes from Russia were usually quite well organized. The boys who grew up in the little town, however, were always to remember this man fondly as one who, in a small way, contributed to the downfall of the Romanovs.

There were a few shops in the town whose owners were naturally considered well-to-do, and there were also a few artisans. The majority of the people, however, led an insecure and ill-defined existence as middlemen between the merchants on either side of the border. Their livelihood depended not only on their connections but on the weather, as the bulk of trade was in grain. A bad harvest was a disaster for the merchants, but for the rest of the town it meant semi-starvation. In these circumstances and in the times of crisis before the beginning of the war, poverty, of course, was the rule. If there were several children in the family only the oldest boy could hope to continue his schooling and to better his lot by learning a profession. The others stayed behind and learned their father's trade. There were one or two unmarried girls in almost every family, for there were no husbands for these daughters of 'middlemen' unless they would consent to marry someone who earned his living 'with his hands'. This was rare indeed, and as there was no prospect of work for them, many girls remained at home as spinsters.

The Austrian middlemen themselves often tried to marry girls from the other side of the river. This, however, they could only do if there was a shortage of local men, or if the girl had no dowry, was one of several daughters, or was quite unattractive. Otherwise Russian families were most reluctant to marry their daughters to men from the other side of the river, one reason being that the Russians had for some reason never acknowledged the Habsburgs as emperors and persisted in looking on them as mere kings of Hungary whose subjects were definitely lower on the social scale. These *Kira*, or king's subjects, were viewed moreover as shifty, untrustworthy, and much less intelligent than Russians since they were on the whole poorer. A bride from Russia considered she had suffered social degradation when she followed a man across the river.

Still, such marriages did occasionally take place, and one of them was that of Ludwik's parents. His mother was Russian and although the town she came from differed very little from that of her husband she came to embody for her children that mysterious world across the river where there were pogroms and where students threw bombs at the Tsar. They feared this strange country but were at the same time attracted to it. Ludwik's mother spoke little, but often hummed to herself; and although his parents never seemed to quarrel Ludwik remembered no show of warmth or tenderness between them.

His father was a cultivated man and in his own way a philosopher. He talked to his children of the books he read, of countries he had never seen and of music he had no opportunity to listen to. He asked his daughter to bring her friends to the house, for he loved having young people about; the sight of a pretty young girl delighted him. But few girls ever came, and the family kept to itself, in a cramped gloomy house.

Ludwik, the youngest, was his mother's favourite and she often took him along when she visited her family on the other side of the river. These were beautiful days for the little boy and he could not understand why his mother always returned gloomier than she had set out. His aunt's home seemed so much nicer and more cheerful than his own. There were good things to eat there, wonderful cakes, and people laughed. They never returned empty-handed; clothes and food, meat in particular, could be bought much more cheaply there. The child thought it was the sight of the soldiers that scared and depressed his mother, as they scared him. The Russian guard at the bridge was a grim sight indeed in his long grey coat reaching down to his ankles and his long bayonet on the end of his rifle. But the soldier scarcely looked at her when she showed him her pass. And there seemed no reason to be afraid of the Austrian soldier on the other side: he did not look forbidding, his coat was blue and reached only to his knees, and he had no bayonet. Nor could she be afraid of having the meat found; that was securely hidden under her skirts. It was only later that Ludwik understood his mother's gloom after the visits: she was desperately ashamed of her poverty.

Ludwik and his elder brother were among the few boys from the town who had a chance to continue their education. Their father wanted them to have a better start in life than he had had and sacrificed everything he owned to give it to them. He also believed that the school in the near-by district town would not be good enough and he therefore arranged to send his sons to Lwow,[1] the provincial capital.

Children who went away to school normally boarded with families who earned their living in this way. Very often five or six children of about the same age lived together, sharing

---

[1] Then called Lemberg; for the sake of simplicity latter-day names are used here.

beds or makeshift accommodation on boards or on the floor. Their parents paid for their keep with small sums of money supplemented in the winter by potatoes, in the summer by chickens and eggs. Ludwik and his brother did not live together. The older boy had little time to look after Ludwik, taken up as he was not only with school work but with tutoring other boys. This was usual and at fourteen Ludwik also began giving lessons. He learned early in life to walk long distances to save the train fare, and wore out his soles going to the houses of lazier and wealthier classmates.

At one stage it looked as if the family's fortunes might improve and there was talk of moving to a better house. This one year of relative prosperity was also the last in the life of Ludwik's father. Tired out by years of struggle and poverty he died of cancer of the throat while still a young man. Whatever money he had saved was used up during his illness and after his death the family was worse off than before. Ludwik's brother found a job in Lwow, and seldom came home. His sister found work in their town, and from the age of fourteen Ludwik had to fend for himself.

He continued his tutoring work while going to school and during the summer would find a job with some prosperous family whose son had to be prepared for examinations. This meant going to the country which he loved; it meant good food and fresh air. But mostly it meant the country way of life, its folklore, and the sad Ukrainian songs which he grew to love. In the country, besides the familes he stayed with, he came to know the rural teachers, who were almost always radically inclined, and the hospitableness of a Ukrainian priest. His fondness for Ukrainians, among whom he later found a number of close friends, dates back to this period.

Ludwik was always nostalgic about these early days which in spite of the hardships were happy ones for him. His best friend in Lwow was a Ukrainian from his home town named Kalyniak, who was studying for the priesthood. Kalyniak was the son of a fairly prosperous farmer and did not have to do any tutoring. The family with which he lived in Lwow was large but there always seemed to be plenty of room in the house, and Ludwik looked forward to visiting them. The Sundays the boys did not spend with this family they strolled about the city, eating the good farm produce Kalyniak's family sent him, and would climb a fence to watch a football game. They joined with delight the students who threw dirt and emptied chamber-pots, usually under the impassive gaze of a policeman, on the statue of a former governor, a nobleman who as a faithful servant of the Dual Monarchy had opposed any Polish aspirations to independence.

Thanks to a friend who later became a concert violinist, Ludwik had the opportunity, rare for a poor boy, of attending many concerts. His friend was a student at the conservatory and could get him cheap tickets, and after school he would stand at the back of the hall and listen to music which he loved. Such memories gave him an affection for the city of Lwow in spite of the imprisonment he was later to suffer there. To him it always stood for friendship and music.

At holidays he went home where he spent whole days playing with his friends, usually along the river. Their play was interrupted, however, by trips to the railway station. Like all stations in small towns, this one played an important part in the lives of the townspeople, especially in the summer months. As the Russian railways had a wider gauge, travellers had to change trains at the border. Those going to the Austrian spas or farther west, to Italy or France, had to wait, often for hours, during which the girls of the town could look at the elegantly dressed Russian ladies; the boys might collect tips by carrying their expensive luggage. The older boys usually stayed away, as they resented and were humiliated by the wealth of the visitors, but the younger children never missed a train.

The trains returning from the west were, if anything, even more exciting. The Russian ladies had to abandon whatever flowers they carried with them as some Russian *ukaz* forbade their importation. The people of the town never knew why this was. Some believed it to be a sanitary measure, others thought that the Russian police were afraid that bombs might be hidden among them. The flowers were left at the station and the children collected them and brought them home. They were exotic and fragrant, quite unlike the flowers in their own gardens, and evoked distant lands. They also made the children think what a strange country, whose inhabitants were rich and could afford to travel yet where flowers were forbidden: an intimidating yet fascinating country.

As grown men, these revolutionaries who travelled throughout Europe and died in the Moscow purges were always to remember these flowers, argue about them and use them to justify their trips to the railway station; none of them could admit they had gone there to look at the wealthy, to enjoy life.

Among the boys in the town was Willy, later a Red Army officer, the first to hoist the Soviet flag on Mount Elbruz. An orphan, he never had the chance to finish school or to go to the capital, but from the age of thirteen helped to support his numerous half-brothers and half-sisters.

Another boy, Walter, who later used the name Krivitsky, lived with a brother and sister, both much older than he, and his widowed mother. The family did everything they could for him and he continued his schooling in the district town where he was well cared for by relatives. When the war came he was evacuated to Vienna with his family. A girl who was to have a great influence on all of them, Krusia, whose special favourite he was, used to say that Walter had been born with a silver spoon in his mouth, and that he was lucky and would go far— and indeed for a long time it appeared that way. His early years were free of care, his work was successful, he was never imprisoned and never arrested. But he too, like his comrades and so many others who shared his convictions, was to die a tragic death.

Two brothers, Berchtold, or Brun, and Misha Umansky, also lived in the town with their widowed mother. The mother was Austrian, hence Brun's German name; but the father had been Russian—hence Misha. Their mother would have little to do with the townspeople. The fact that she had originally come from Bohemia and spoke German gave her—or so she thought— a superior status. In spite of this she had remained in the town after her husband died. She received money from her brother in Pilsen and when the time came for the boys to go to school they were taken in by relatives in the district town. She read books and newspapers which her brother sent her, played the piano and taught the boys to play. Her one aim was to leave this backward area and go to live either in Bohemia or in Austria, but her plans were disrupted by the war. Forced to remain in the town under the Russian occupation, when the Austrians retook the place she did manage to get to Vienna, but died soon afterward, leaving the two boys to fend for themselves.

Fedia, later known as Fedin, was about five or six years older than the other boys and was looked upon as an authority on most things. His prestige was further enhanced by the fact that he was away at school in Vienna most of the year, and only returned to the town during the summer holidays. His conception of the world was quite different from that of the younger boys. To him, the small town in which he grew up was not so much on the boundary of the old Austria they all knew, as the gateway to a much more fascinating world, the Russian empire, where a relentless struggle was being waged against autocracy and for liberty. Russia was grim but not forbidding to Fedia, nor was it mysterious. It was to him the country where the coming world revolution would begin.

Unlike the other boys and young men of the town Fedia knew a great deal about Russia. He had friends there, students with whom he corresponded, and he knew the literature well, occasionally translating short stories from the Russian into German. Before the eager eyes of the adolescents he unfolded the epic of the Russian revolutionary struggle for freedom and as their mentor told them the books to read. All of them remembered, much later, how he had given them Stanislaw Brzozowski's *Flames* to read and the impression of these memoirs of a Polish member of the Russian revolutionary group *Zemlya y Volya* (Land and Freedom) had made on them. Fedia helped translate into German this book which became a bible to the generation born at the turn of the century in a Poland under triple occupation by Austria, Germany, and Russia. The story of these revolutionists—most of them hanged by the Tsars— became sacred, an example to be emulated. Fedia also told the boys of the working-class movements in other countries, of their painful birth and long struggles and of the creation of a Youth

International at the Socialist International congress at Stuttgart in 1907.

Fedia's life and background differed somewhat from the others. For one thing he was the only one who still had both his parents. His father, who was reasonably well off, had left Russia to escape military service and settled in Austria as close as possible to the Russian border in order to be near his relatives and business connections. Like all those from Russia he had nothing but contempt for his new country and for its mere 'king' whose relatively mild rule disqualified him in Russian eyes. Naturally enough, this contempt extended to the king's subjects, who were not to be trusted. As for the Russians, Fedia's father never succeeded in ridding himself of the fear they inspired in him and accordingly he respected them. Not all Russians, however: to him the huge, uncultivated Russian masses were 'Asians' and therefore contemptible. His wife he also considered an 'Asian', largely because of her high cheekbones and slanting eyes.

Fedia used to say of his father that he could conceive of only two kinds of people, the stupid Austrian *Kira* and the 'Asians'. In actual fact, he himself came close to being a perfect example of his own conception of an 'Asian'. He ruled the family with true Oriental despotism, and as Fedia was usually away his younger brother bore the brunt of this petty tyranny. Fedia's brother, so their father had decided, was to enter the family business and the rather cursory schooling he could get in the town was considered quite adequate. Fedia used to argue with his brother, urging him to run away from home, but according to Fedia the younger boy lacked the courage and the intelligence to take this step. The only one of his children whom the father loved was Fedia's sister Lia, a beautiful, exotic-looking girl whom Fedia also adored. She died later of Spanish 'flu and Fedia never got over this blow.

Fedia's father had reluctantly given him permission to study medicine in Vienna. He would have preferred a Russian university for his son but Fedia wanted to go to Vienna. Once there, he made friends among the socialists, joined the Socialist movement, and entered into contact with Russian émigrés in Switzerland. He was soon spending more time in parliament listening to the speeches of the Socialist members than in medical school. Occasionally he succeeded in persuading his father to send him to an Austrian health resort—he suffered from diabetes, which he considered a blessing as it enabled him to travel. But he also loved to come home in the holidays to see again his childhood friend and sweetheart, Krusia, and his younger friends who listened avidly to what he had to say.

Fedia was at home on 28 June 1914, when Archduke Franz Ferdinand was assassinated. This murder was to launch the First World War, and in Ludwik's mind it was for ever associated with Fedia's confident prediction that war would not come.

It was a hot day in June, Ludwik remembered, and they were playing football along the river. Fedia who had come to watch the game was telling them that there would be no war. He quoted from the speeches the Austrian Socialists had made in parliament against the war-mongering aristocrats, and assured the boys that the workers of the world would never kill their brothers in other countries but would rise up against their oppressors. 'We had stopped playing', Ludwik said, as he told me the story years later, 'and were hanging on every word he spoke, when suddenly we heard a drum beating. This was the way grave events were announced to the town. In a second we were all at the market-place, the whole town was there. The policeman, beating his drum, kept repeating: "The heir apparent, the Archduke Franz Ferdinand, has been assassinated at Sarajevo." '

The town was stunned although the victim was not particularly popular or even well known in the area. Nor was the murder of royalty an altogether unprecedented thing. But everyone dreaded the consequences, although no one really knew what these might be; in any case they feared change. A few of the Ukrainians (or Ruthenians, as they were known in Galicia) were rather pleased with the demise of the Archduke, not because they had anything against him but because his nephew Karl, next in the line of succession, was said to favour Ukrainians over Poles. Karl had spent some time in a Galician garrison town and was alleged to have considered the

Ukrainian regiments the *Kaiserjäger*[1] of the East. The Ukrainians hoped that the accession of Karl to the throne would give them more autonomy than they had had under the Polish aristocrats who served the Habsburgs as provincial governors.[2]

A small group of Ukrainians in Galicia known as 'Muscophiles', looked towards Russia rather than Austria to achieve their ultimate aims, among them a union of all Ukrainians, including those in the Great Ukraine, under the Tsar. The poorer masses of the Ukrainian peasantry in Galicia did not share the views of this group, nor did progressive elements in the Great Ukraine, who wished to develop their own language and culture, and bitterly resented being called 'Little Russians'. The 'Muscophiles' were usually prosperous professional people or landowners who liked to be considered Russian although they were not Orthodox in religion, and who spoke Russian in their homes. It is probable that some were agents of the Okhrana, the Tsarist political police. When war broke out these people escaped to safety in Russia. The great majority of Ukrainians in Galicia, who had not shared the views of this group, were promptly classified as Muscophiles by the Austrian authorities and many of them imprisoned and even executed, allegedly for treason.

In the summer of 1914, after the initial shock of the Archduke's assassination wore off, people again began to feel secure. After all, the old Emperor was still alive. Life in the little town began to change, however. This last outpost of the Empire, neglected for so long, began to interest the authorities in Vienna. New faces were seen in the streets, strangers from the capital. Passes to cross the bridge were no longer issued and smuggling began to die down. People said that there were Russian troop movements across the river and that arrests had been made, but in fact no one knew anything. Still nobody

---

[1] The *Kaiserjäger*, composed of German-speaking Austrians, were an élite corps of the Imperial Army rated as especially loyal to the crown.

[2] These governors were unpopular with all the younger patriotic groups. Polish students agitating for independence regularly defaced the monuments to former governors, as Ludwik and Kalyniak had helped do in Lwow; a Ukrainian student named Sichinsky (who later went to live in the United States) in 1908 asked for an audience with the then ruling governor, a Pole, and shot him dead.

really believed there would be war, Fedia least of all.[1] He was convinced that the working class would prevent a war and that strikes would paralyze the armies. Moreover he believed that the Great Powers would never start a war that would lead to their destruction through revolution.

People kept their illusions even when war finally did break out. The war was certain to be short, it would be over by Christmas, and afterwards things would be much as they had been, possibly even better.

On 31 July 1914, a fanatic shot the French Socialist leader Jean Jaurès in Paris and war did begin immediately afterwards. Reservists in the little town were called up, among them Ludwik's brother and Fedia. Orders were given to evacuate the town. Efforts were made to keep the evacuation orderly but there was not enough room on the trains and panic broke out. People took to the roads laden with bundles that were eventually thrown away. In the wake of the retreating Austrian troops the population made for the district town and found it empty. No orders had been given for its evacuation but its population had fled anyway, hampering the movements of the army on the crowded roads.

Those who could not get away either stayed in the district town or else returned to their homes and fearfully awaited the Russians. Those who had not lived in the border towns had never seen Russians, but what they had read about them was not reassuring. As far as they were concerned all Russians, or Muscovites, were barbarians, all the Russian troops were Cossacks with their *nagaikas* (whips) and long knives. The Jews expected pogroms. The one good thing was that there was no shortage of housing. People simply moved into empty houses and made themselves at home.

Finally, the invaders came: long lines of tired, dusty soldiers, officers, horses, wagons. People watched from behind their windows, looking for the dreaded Cossacks. But there were no Cossacks, just ordinary soldiers who requisitioned some

---

[1] Nor did Lenin. In a letter from Cracow, where he then lived, he wrote to Gorky in Capri; 'War could be very useful to the revolution . . . but it is rather doubtful that Franz Joseph or Nikolashka [Tsar Nikolai] would do us this favour . . . ' (*Sochineniia*, vol. 35, pp. 46–48).

quarters but left the townspeople completely alone. Gradually, people began to go out into the streets, even women who had firmly believed that the Cossacks would rape every one of them.

A few days after the arrival of the Russian troops a notice was posted in the town hall asking that two citizens of the town report to the military governor. This naturally caused great alarm and the two representatives chosen, a Ukrainian and a Jew, were by no means flattered by the honour their fellow-citizens had bestowed on them. They expected to be asked to make a large financial contribution (an impossibility, as all the more prosperous citizens had left taking their money with them) and probably to be sent to Siberia. They bade adieu to their families and reported to the governor. To everyone's surprise and pleasure they soon returned. The governor, it appeared, had asked that the local shops and cafés be re-opened and that a small band be provided for the café. Since the owners of the shops and the café had gone and there was no money to pay for having it done, the townspeople themselves cleaned and repaired the café, which soon reopened along with a barber's shop.

Young people volunteered to serve as waiters in the café and did not ask payment for their services, as everyone assumed the Russian customers would never pay. This again proved wrong. The Russians not only paid but left generous tips—and the Russian ruble was worth more than the Austrian crown. The café turned out to be such a successful venture that it was decided to organize the band the governor had asked for. Brun and Misha, the Umansky brothers, and Ludwik offered their services. They found a girl and formed a quartet. The boys brought food home from the café and Ludwik said that he had never known such opulence in the days before the war.

As winter closed in, the townspeople settled down to a peaceful existence. Life was easy and food plentiful, as the peasants who could not eat all their own produce sold it in the town at low prices. As far as the town was concerned Austria had ceased to exist; the front to the west had cut off all communication and nothing was heard from those who had left before the Russians arrived. The inhabitants got along very well with the invaders; no one was carted off to Siberia, the Russians paid for everything they bought and only asked for Russian songs to be played in cafés. Furthermore there was scarcely any language barrier, for Russian and Ukrainian are close enough for each to be understood by those who speak the other. Ludwik told me later of the change in his mother's attitude: 'My mother suddenly regained her speech; I had never heard her talk as much before. It was a very cold winter, people in fact claimed that they could not remember a colder one, but then again people said this every time and anyway war winters always seem to be colder. Nevertheless we were nice and warm in our kitchen.' A Russian officer was billeted in their house and his orderly would bring in wood from the yard and water from the frozen well, and would chat with Ludwik's mother in the kitchen. 'He spent most of his time talking to my mother about his village and his family,' Ludwik said, 'and my mother told him of my brother who was in the army. The orderly used to reply: "If it is God's will he will return, but if the Lord does not permit him to come back cities will not collapse nor will the skies cave in." At this Mother used to cry and so the winter went on and we lived far away from the war. But I knew that it was not over for us.'

Peace ended when the ice began to break up and with spring the Austrians attacked. The Russians retreated and the Imperial Army reoccupied the area. Some of the troops were German-speaking Austrians, and to them at least the townspeople could talk, but many were Hungarians whom they could not even understand. 'All food was requisitioned,' Ludwik said, 'and, contrary to the habit of the invaders, "our" army did not pay for it. Whenever they took a pig from a peasant they gave him a slip of paper in exchange on which some obscenity or other was scribbled. One of the most common "requisition slips" used to read: *"Ich hab das Schwein, du hast den Schein, lieb Vaterland magst ruhig sein"*[1].' The 'liberators' promptly drafted all the men between the ages of twenty and forty and all the peasants and their horses were forced to accompany the armies' supply columns.

There was much worse, however. A vicious hunt for 'Musco-

[1] Roughly translated: 'I've got the pig, you've got the slip, dear Fatherland, may you rest in peace.'

philes' began and hundreds of Ukrainian peasants and Jews
were shipped off to concentration camps in Lower Austria. A
Ukrainian priest and a schoolmaster were hanged and their
corpses left up for a few days as an example of what happened
to 'traitors'. There they were, with their tongues hanging out
and an inscription attached to their feet: '*Mit Gott, für Kaiser
und Vaterland*'. This pointless terror had one result: when the
Russians reoccupied the area in their next offensive the population kept away from them, fearing to be found out by the
'liberators' who might retake the town.

The Austrian reoccupation meant that news was again
available and travel possible. Ludwik went to Vienna. Fedia
was there recuperating from a leg wound, not very serious in
itself but because of his diabetes taking an extremely long time
to heal. Most of the other boys from the town were in Vienna,
and Ludwik met in Krusia's little room many young Austrian
socialists as well as the others who were later to become the
nucleus of the Soviet intelligence service.

Krusia, Fedia's sweetheart, had guided the little group and
kept it together in his absence. A pharmacist, she earned her
living in a chemical plant and in spite of her poor health—she
suffered from a heart ailment of which she died in 1928—was
extremely active. In her room members of the then illegal
Socialist Youth movement rubbed shoulders with soldiers on
furlough as well as deserters or draft evaders who occasionally
found refuge with her. She always offered her visitors food, an
additional attraction in a half-starved city, for her job as a
'heavy worker' in the plant entitled her to a larger food ration,
and she herself ate very little. When I met her some years later
I could not help laughing at the official classification of 'heavy
worker' being applied to this small, frail person who, although
several years older than I, looked like a child.

Krusia was soon to drop all political activity and connection
with the group. After the war she went back to Poland and
married a young man, a classmate of Fedia's, who was quite
conservative in his views. The last time I saw her was in Berlin
in 1923. She stayed in our flat on her way to take a cure at a spa.
Fedia, who was then also in Germany, very much wanted to

see her but she refused. 'No,' she said. 'Fedia belongs to my youth, to my dreams of a revolution. That is all gone now. It is no use trying to get back to things that are gone forever.' Fedia was very much hurt when I told him. 'Yes, it is all gone now,' he said. 'I could not marry Krusia as long as there was still hope, for then I did not belong to myself, I belonged only to the cause. Now, I could live for her.'

Krusia remained a treasured memory to all of Ludwik's friends, yet no one in Moscow ever heard of her. In later years, if we wanted to send a message we did not want understood by anyone outside the group we used to sign it with her name. Thus when Krivitsky broke with the Soviet regime and wrote to me he signed his letter 'Krusia'; the N.K.V.D. intercepted the letter, but did not connect it with him, for the name meant nothing to them.

I did not meet Ludwik's friends until later, but this is perhaps as good a place as any to say what I knew of them. The one I came to like best—although I may have respected the intellectual qualities of some of the others more—was Willy Stahl. He remained single all his life and this perhaps accounts for the fact that every one of us somehow felt he belonged to us. I recall once asking him why he did not marry. He answered in an offhand way that there were so many girls in the world he saw no reason to tie himself to one. Then becoming more serious he said that he had seen so many odd marriages in his own family that he had been cured of marriage for life. The marital record of his family would scarcely have been tolerated anywhere except in that rather strange town. His father had been fairly well off and hired a tutor for Willy and his sister. This tutor, a law student, was preparing for his examinations away from the university because he could not afford lodgings in a big town. He was a strange person, a dreamer, a poet, and of course a free-thinker. A romance soon developed between him and Willy's mother and when the father died the tutor married the mother. They had two children and when the mother in turn died the tutor married Willy's elder sister, by whom he also had a child. The ill-assorted family group lived more on miracles than on anything else, their main source of income being the small amounts Willy earned. The former law student had by then become a lawyer, but he had no clients and in any event thought poetry much more important than earning a living.

The family was broken up by the war. Willy himself went into the army and the rest scattered. After the war they were partially reunited and Willy again had to help them financially. The youngest of his half-brothers went to Berlin, where Willy put him through an engineering school. In the depressed days of the twenties the young man could not get a job in Germany, however. Eventually, with Brun's help, Willy brought him to the U.S.S.R. But to get work there he had to become a Soviet citizen, which was by no means easy. In Moscow in 1937, when I saw Willy for the last time, this half-brother was still without citizenship and unemployed. He and his young wife were sharing Willy's room. As long as he lived Willy never managed to free himself of his family.

When I first met him he was in his twenties. Athletically built, strong as a bear—which was one of his nicknames, along with the unflattering 'blockhead' earned him by his apparent *naïveté* and clumsiness—the balding Willy was always full of pranks and jokes. As a so-called 'technician' in the Polish party, he had his own ways of doing a job and these were not always completely successful. When taxed with failure he would advance some excuse an eight-year-old might have given, laughing his head off the while. On a dangerous assignment he was quite different. Perhaps he had a sixth sense that protected him, for he could always get out of the tightest spots and was never arrested.

Ludwik's other close friends the Umansky brothers, Brun and Misha, I found very different in looks and character. Both were dark-haired, but Misha was handsome in the manner of movie stars of the day, with black, sleek hair and rather languid eyes, while Brun was quite ugly. Misha was polite and reserved, spoke in a low, persuasive voice, and was by far the more cultivated, but was possibly not very bright; his brother (who later took the name Ilk) was clever, cynical, short-tempered, and given to foul language. They were the only ones of the original group to join the N.K.V.D. while still abroad. The others, following Fedia, went into the Comintern and eventually the Fourth Department of the Red Army.

Krivitsky was the youngest of the group—Krusia called him 'the little one'—and looked very frail and thin, obviously marked by the wartime famine years. He had a rather remarkable pale face whose bushy eyebrows gave him a stern look which contrasted sharply with his childish smile. With him when I first met him was a girl, Magda, whom he introduced as his wife. She was quite insignificant and shy but had her claim to nobility, for that time, being a true proletarian from a working-class suburb. Krivitsky seemed very proud of Magda and I think he was trying to prove he was a better socialist than the others for having married a proletarian. In any event the marriage did not last long. He also thought of himself as politically more mature than the others. This was true to some extent, for unlike his friends who had been either at the front or in a Russian-occupied backwater, he had spent the war years in cosmopolitan and sophisticated Vienna. He also felt a bit superior for having joined a socialist group before the rest of them. Knowing that Krusia was responsible for this, I was less impressed. To me they were all communists. I was attracted to Walter, but never liked the way he criticized his friends.

Fedia, of course, was the leading figure in the group. His diabetes may have saved his life, by keeping him in hospital while his wound healed instead of at the front, where he might very well have been killed; it had also introduced him to the Party. Once just before the war, when he was a medical student in Vienna, his parents had sent him money to take a cure. Fedia went to Karlsbad, wrote and post-dated a whole stack of postcards, and bribed a hotel porter to send these to his parents at regular intervals. He then went off to Capri where he met Maxim Gorky. The disease came in handy when he joined the revolution. In 1917 he deserted from the Austrian army, his only papers—so he said—a urinalysis made in a Russian field hospital. 'I was stopped by a Russian soldier one day', he told me, 'and asked for papers, so I gave him my analysis. The soldier looked at it and repeated to himself: "Negative, good." "No sugar, good." He then wanted to know what acetone was, of which I also had none according to the analysis. "Flour", I told him. The soldier seemed much impressed by a man who, according to an official document, had neither flour nor sugar and was negative. "What do you have?" he asked me. "Tobacco", I told him and gave him some. "That proves you are no smuggler", was the sentry's verdict and he let me go.'

One day one of our friends, Jacob Locker, had the bad grace to tell Fedia: 'Look, the last time you told that story it was different. Which is the true version?' Fedia looked at him gravely and gave his favourite reply—one I was to hear often in the future: 'The latest version. You must remember this, the latest version is always the true one.'[1]

Fedia used to tease me and the others. 'I bet you wouldn't trade your elegant nose for my Kalmuck one'—referring to his flat, almost Asian face—'and what is more, you wouldn't trade him'—pointing to Ludwik—'for me either.' Ludwik was by far the best-looking of the group, his bright blue eyes contrasting with his very dark hair. 'You are quite right,' Fedia continued, 'you are no Marmurek.' This was the first time I heard of this person who was, according to Fedia, the very incarnation of petty-bourgeois stupidity. I strongly suspected that Marmurek was a figment of Fedia's imagination, for after all none of the others from the town had ever met their alleged fellow-townsman. Fedia, however, swore the man had actually existed and was always producing new anecdotes about him. A shopkeeper and by local standards a well-off man, Marmurek, according to Fedia, fled the advancing Russians by scrambling aboard a train, carrying a live chicken and the top of an old samovar. He saved these possessions but in his panic left all his money and silver behind. This, Fedia said, was the way of the Marmureks of this world. Marmurek may never have existed, but Fedia's contempt for him was real. When I last saw Fedia, in Moscow at the height of Stalin's terror, even then he would not have traded places with Marmurek.

From Vienna Ludwik went to Germany, where he had friends in Leipzig, and where he wanted to get in touch with young

[1] In his years abroad Fedia carried an Austrian passport with the name Alfred Krauss, which for a long time I supposed to be his real name. Sometimes I would call him 'Mr. Krauss'. The last time I did so, in Moscow in 1937, he laughed and said Krauss was not his name either. One never knew whether to believe him or not.

German Socialists. One of the people he met in Germany, in a socialist students and actors' group, was Gertrude Schildbach, a lonely young woman whom he befriended at that time, and with whom he was to remain in touch and to help for nearly twenty years—until 1937.

Ludwik was the only one of the boys to return to the town during the war. He worked there on the railway. The place had been deserted, but with the outbreak of the Russian revolution it suddenly came to life. The trains from the west were filled with Russian prisoners of war being repatriated, and those from the east with Ukrainian troops being shifted from the Russian to the Italian front. Soldiers by the thousands filled the cattle cars and thousands died there of typhus. Sick and starved men remained for weeks among the corpses in the railway station.

Kalyniak's father told Ludwik that his son, Ludwik's friend, had been carried off by the Austrians along with other Ukrainians. He assumed that he had been drafted into the army and sent to the front. The father had not heard from him since and believed that he was dead. Every day he would go down to the station to look for him. Once he pointed to a dead soldier in Austrian uniform. 'This is my boy', he told Ludwik. 'Look at his hair, and he still has the wrist-watch I gave him.' Both looked at the soldier for a while and finally the father worked up the courage to turn the body over. 'It is not my son,' he said finally.

Young Kalyniak came back alive from the Italian front late in 1918, and a month later was again in uniform, this time with a Ukrainian regiment which had occupied Lwow while a committee of Poles and Ukrainians was sitting in Cracow, trying to work out temporary boundaries for the area until a plebiscite could be held. The occupation of Lwow touched off a Polish-Ukrainian civil war. When a hastily mustered Polish unit, consisting mostly of students, counterattacked the Ukrainians entrenched themselves in the citadel. Kalyniak was killed there, on the spot where he and Ludwik had played as schoolboys.

The Poles gathered reinforcements and retook Lwow. Its fall marked the end of large-scale fighting in the civil war, but skirmishes continued throughout Galicia for many months.

Murder, pillage, pogroms,[1] and typhus continued to rule the countryside, which was almost completely cut off from the rest of the world. During the fighting villages occasionally changed hands and those who could not get away in time were killed. Ludwik remembered how when his town, then held by Ukrainians, was surprised by a Polish unit, those Ukrainians who could not escape hid as best they could. One of them just managed to hide in a drain where he remained for days while children threw food to him. But one day the Poles heard about it and opened the sluice. When the Ukrainians retook the town some time later, they found him drowned in the sewer.

Ludwik's brother had returned from the Italian front at the end of the war to find the little town devastated and poorer than ever. There was nothing to do there and when the undeclared war between Russia and Poland broke out in April 1920, he joined the Polish army. The company he commanded was ambushed and wiped out by the Bolsheviks and he was awarded, posthumously, the highest Polish military decoration. A senior Polish officer made a special trip to the town to bring the decoration and details of her elder son's death to Ludwik's mother. At about the same time Ludwik threw in his lot with the Bolsheviks.

The brothers had never been very close. They were far apart in age, in temperament, and even in political ideals. Whereas Ludwik from his earliest youth had leaned towards socialism, his brother was always a staunch conservative. Ludwik never talked about his brother nor did I even see a picture of him, and I believe that Ludwik deliberately erased him from his memory. Fedia, who had been the brother's classmate and who described in minute detail the most obscure individuals in the town— when he did not invent them altogether—never once mentioned him. The brother, having died on the other side of the barricades, had simply ceased to exist as far as Ludwik and his friends were concerned.

---

[1] No sooner had Lwow fallen than a three-day pogrom broke out. The Jews were alleged to have supported the Ukrainians—although an Allied commission later found no evidence that they had. The Poles blamed the pogrom on 'criminal elements', but it took place after the fighting had ended and with Polish authorities, both military and civilian, in control.

He was so thoroughly forgotten that it was generally assumed no one in Moscow had ever heard of him. So it was a shock to us when Krivitsky was asked by the N.K.V.D. in Moscow in 1937 whether he knew Ludwik's brother had been killed in the Polish army fighting against the revolution—and was told that it was on this brother's orders and in the service of the Polish government that Ludwik had 'infiltrated' first the Polish Communist Party and then the Soviet intelligence service.

CHAPTER II

The Polish Party

As the victors of the First World War met at Versailles to discuss the shape of the new Eastern Europe, the old one was dis-
integrating. Dynasties disappeared, civil wars were raging, and
their echoes reached the conference table. New countries were
emerging and old ones were regaining their independence. One
of the latter was Poland, independent for the first time since the
third Partition of 1795. The character of the Polish nation re-
born after 1918 and the peculiarities of its Communist Party
have much to do with the fate of the protagonists of this book.

With the collapse of Austria–Hungary the old enmities
between ethnic minorities in Poland, reinforced by differences
in culture, language, and customs, came to the fore; in eastern
Galicia, as we have seen, the civil war between Ukrainians and
Poles ended in a Polish victory but incorporated into the country
a hostile population. In Galicia the Polish nation also acquired
a sizeable Jewish population, to whom independence was to
mean ferocious anti-Semitism and pogroms in areas where they
had been unknown for over a century. But the Poles were for
the most part overjoyed at achieving their century-old dream of
national independence and unity. Patriotic fervour reached its
peak in the formerly Russian areas which had lived under the
harsh rule of the Tsars. It was less intransigent in the Austrian
part, where the Habsburgs had granted a certain amount of
political autonomy, and in the German parts, where the political
intolerance of the Prussian rulers had been somewhat offset by
better living conditions. Despite these regional variations, the
Polish part of the population showed considerable cohesion,
great national pride, and enthusiastic willingness to build a new
state.

This, however, was not sufficient to create political stability in a country that had been so long divided. Political groups in the three parts of the country were marked by the traditions of the empires under which they arose, and even those movements which were truly national in character faced completely different problems in the different areas of the country. Moreover, by a peculiarity of the peace treaty the criminal and civil codes prevailing under Austrian, German, and Russian rule were to remain in force for ten years after independence before being replaced by unified legislation. This had its effect on political activity, which in practice was limited to those parties that were patriotic in character, that is those which did not question the nature or the extent of the new state. Parties representing minorities and contesting Polish rule in certain territories, and parties of the extreme left were from the beginning suppressed, often with considerable brutality. Such parties led an illegal existence and were often allied with each other by their opposition to the Polish state, although they differed widely in their aims or ideologies—as, for instance, the Polish Communists differed with certain liberal anti-Communist minority groups.

The Polish Communist Party itself was the product of a fusion of various left-wing Marxist groups which had existed in the three pre-war empires. The Communist Workers' Party of Poland (K.P.R.P.), which came into being officially in December 1918, was a fusion of two earlier political groups, the Social-Democratic Party of the Kingdom of Poland and Lithuania (S.D.K.P.iL.) and the left wing of the Polish Socialist Party (P.P.S.), generally called P.P.S.-Left, a group which had broken away from the main body of the Polish Socialist Party in 1906. The use of the term 'workers' in the new party's name emphasized the Rosa Luxemburg tradition in the S.D.K.P.iL. and at the same time ensured the adherence to the new movement of the P.P.S.-Left, which had a considerable influence with the urban proletariat.

The newly created Polish Communist Party was greatly influenced by its S.D.K.P.iL. heritage. The earlier party had been politically very close to the Bolshevik wing of the Russian Social-Democratic Party after its 1903 split into Bolsheviks and Mensheviks, and one section, led by Radek, favoured amalgamation with the Bolsheviks. But the more influential faction of Rosa Luxemburg opposed this on the grounds of the Bolshevik attitude towards the peasantry and the problem of nationalities, and most importantly on the role of the party and its relationship to the proletariat. To Rosa Luxemburg the party wa he political organization of the working class, not, as Lenin held, an instrument of the political leadership designed to seize power. She believed that the proletariat would develop spontaneously, and that at the historic moment, when the working class was ready to assume power, it would orient the party in the proper direction. The fact that there existed in Poland a genuine industrial proletariat, politically much more sophisticated and mature than the Russian workers whose roots were essentially in the villages, lent strength to these hopes.

The leaders of the Polish party were always closer to their members than the Russians were to theirs. The average Polish party member knew the men who made up his Central Committee, while for the Russian party member, isolated in an enormous country, the Central Committee was an almost mythical body of anonymous men whose very remoteness elicited esteem and respect. The Polish leaders were respected but never venerated. No one ever thought of Rosa Luxemburg and the men around her as infallible. What is known today as 'the cult of personality' was not practised by the Poles.[1] And though the Polish revolutionaries had shared Tsarist jails, exile, and occasionally the gallows with their Russian comrades, and the years of common conspiratorial activity had brought them so close together that to foreigners they often looked and acted the same, the Western influence was much more marked among the Poles than among the Russians. The belief of Western European socialists in political action and in a gradual evolution which would bring about socialism, was also held by

[1] Nor was it by the Russians in the pre-revolutionary period. In spite of his unquestioned authority within the party, Lenin's colleagues often disagreed with him and with each other, especially after the failure of the 1905 revolution. The 'party line' at that time was not considered infallible; disagreement could be expressed and frequently was. When disagreements arose Lenin himself often acted as arbiter. The party line remained relatively fluid, and dissidents were usually reinstated after the dispute was settled. It was only after the revolution and especially after Lenin's death that such disagreements or oscillations away from the basic line became known as 'deviations' and were considered a crime.

the Poles, whereas in Russia, once the Bolsheviks had seized power, the concern of the leaders was always with the tight discipline through which the party would maintain itself as a ruling elite.

The Communist Workers' Party of Poland was represented at the founding congress of the Third International in March 1919 by Julian Marchlewski (also known as Karski), a leading figure in the old S.D.K.P.iL. and a friend of Rosa Luxemburg. He was one of the signatories of the manifesto inviting all labour organizations to join the newly created international movement, and he also signed the similar document issued at the second congress in July 1920. A few months later, following its own second party conference, the Polish party formally adhered to the Third International, henceforth bearing the title 'Polish Section of the Communist International'. In doing so it accepted the 'Twenty-one Points'—that is, the conditions which all member parties had to subscribe to—presented to the second congress by Zinoviev.

Many of the left-wing revolutionary and labour groups which attended the congress and eventually signed the Twenty-one Points did so with grave misgivings. They had broken with the Second International, the Socialist one, over the issue of the war, which the major Socialist parties of Europe, contrary to their expressed policies and their long-standing tradition, had supported. These groups had not gone to Moscow with the idea of creating a new international body. But the dramatic atmosphere of the congress—the stage setting, the banners, the revolutionary anthems, and the fact that the majority of the delegates to this international congress were Russians, members of the first party to have made a successful revolution—won them over despite the poor impression created by Zinoviev, who glorified the Communist Party as 'the elite of humanity' which must be kept free from petty-bourgeois influences, and arrogantly maintained that the Russian Communist Party—by virtue of its achievements—was the most advanced and most far-sighted of all parties and would act as a teacher and 'elder brother' to the European proletariat. Though the member parties would supposedly all have equal rights under the new

International, Zinoviev's speech made it clear that the Russian party arrogated to itself alone the right to decide who could or could not join. In the end, however, all the groups but one, the German Spartacus League—the only sizeable body strongly under the Luxemburg influence— signed the manifesto.

Once they had returned home, away from the intoxicating atmosphere of the congress, most of the foreign groups realized that they had accepted the centralization of all Communist parties under a body invested with tremendous power and authority. But in spite of the resentment aroused by the Twenty-one Points, the Third International soon consisted of many parties, some of which were influential and powerful in their own countries. To a younger generation, sickened by the slaughter of war, disgusted by the treachery or weakness of the traditional socialist parties, the new grouping which appealed to social justice and condemned all wars proved enormously attractive. Membership in the foreign Communist parties grew rapidly and the Russian party, needing their support, moved cautiously in its process of controlling and subjugating them. It took years to get rid even of those elements of the foreign leadership which had opposed the Bolshevization of their parties from the very beginning.

The Polish party however was immediately affected. It had always shown considerable independence *vis-à-vis* the Russians and even manifested feelings of superiority. The Poles, with their older tradition, resented taking orders from a Moscow which—victorious revolution or not—they felt to be something of an upstart. A conversation was alleged to have taken place between Lenin and Marchlewski concerning the nature of the Polish revolution in which, when Lenin held up the Russian example, Marchlewski answered that it would be done differently in Poland—and better. Because of their historic association with the Poles, the Russians never permitted these differences to be brought into the open; even in the early post-revolutionary days before the Comintern became completely a Russian instrument, while it still refereed inter-party disputes, these were always treated as a family affair. But precisely because of this historic closeness, the Polish party found itself in a specially vulnerable situation.

Although the Polish party leadership was drawn from both the P.P.S. and S.D.K.P.iL., much was made by the Russians of 'Luxemburgist' tendencies in the party. It is true that the leaders were to a great extent under Luxemburg's influence, and remained so after her death in 1919; but it is doubtful whether the rank and file was deeply concerned with ideological questions. To the average party member Lenin and Rosa Luxemburg were forceful personalities who no doubt had their differences, but in his eyes the Russian revolution had solved these problems. Luxemburgism nonetheless became a vital issue to the Polish party, which during its short existence (1918–1938) saw repeated purges in the name of this 'heresy'. The original 'Luxemburgist' leadership was purged and replaced by a 'Leninist' group; during the terror of the 1930s this 'imported' leadership, which was genuinely opposed to Luxemburg's views, in turn perished—charged with Luxemburgism. Luxemburg and her tradition had been a source of pride to the Polish rank and file; after the Russian party took over this tradition became a capital offence. The 'Leninism' that was to replace it was only vaguely understood. By then Lenin himself was dead, and what had earlier seemed a conflict between two prominent leaders now became part of the oppositional struggle inside the Soviet Union.

The Polish party was soon completely confused and demoralized. When the original leaders, known as the 'Three W's'—from their initials—were charged with various deviations, the charges were couched in language that almost no one understood. The new 'Leninist' leadership, obeying directives from the Comintern, backed Marshal Pilsudski's *coup d'état* in May 1926. The results of the *coup* were disastrous for the party, which was promptly blamed for the 'May Day errors', although it had simply carried out Moscow's orders—with reluctance. As Moscow had to be exonerated, the new leadership took the blame, and this time the rank and file, who had no love for Pilsudski, joined in the condemnation and in desperation Moscow reinstated the old leadership.

To make matters worse the Poles had been drawn into the factional struggle within the Russian party, and had aligned themselves with the opposition. To the Soviets a German revolution was a paramount goal and in their view the Poles were to play the role of intermediary in bringing it about. But to become the 'midwife' of this revolution meant that the Polish party must sacrifice whatever independent goals it had. Moreover the German leadership knew perfectly well such a revolution could not possibly be 'imported': their only hope lay in independent action suited to German conditions. The attempts of these German 'Luxemburgists' to keep their party free of Soviet control made the Poles their natural allies.

The Polish party's stand on the German revolution was bad enough; but to the Russians the unforgivable sin was its stand in the matter of Trotsky. Not that the Polish leaders were his adherents; but they took a position that Stalin could not forgive. At the height of the oppositional struggle the Polish Central Committee sent a letter to the Comintern stating that, while they were inadequately informed of the details of the controversy, it was inconceivable that Trotsky, whose name in the eyes of the entire movement was synonymous with the October revolution and the creation of the Red Army, could ever be expelled from the party. While they did not take sides, the Poles expressed indignation at the treatment of Trotsky's followers and warned of the possible consequences to the rest of the movement. They thus committed a double offence in Stalin's eyes: they had backed—if only indirectly—his mortal enemy, and they had dared to appeal directly to the Comintern. He never forgave them. At the time he had not yet sufficient power to liquidate them physically, but his only comment, 'This should be firmly remembered', was ominous. Later he indeed remembered it and in 1937 and 1938 Polish Communists were liquidated on charges of Luxemburgism, Trotskyism, Bukharinism, treason, and espionage, in the Soviet Union and in Spain, in a wholesale massacre that affected virtually the entire party membership, from the top down through the rank and file.

Stalin's terror had begun to make itself felt much before that, however. Polish Communists on missions to the Soviet Union began to disappear in the early 1930s. In 1934 Jerzy Sochacki, a member of the Central Committee of the Polish party and one of its most popular leaders, as well as a gifted writer and propagandist, vanished on one of his trips to the Soviet Union. Soon it was announced from Moscow that Sochacki and a group of Polish officers who had served with him in Pilsudski's Legion during the war, and who had joined the party with him, had been executed as Polish spies. The news stunned the party, as Stalin had intended it to. Radek, on hearing it, said: 'If Sochacki was a spy, so am I.' (A few years later Radek too was to 'confess' to having been one.) Those Polish Communists who dared discuss the case among themselves believed that Sochacki had been the victim of machinations by the Polish police who, unable to get rid of him, had put 'proof' of his 'treason' in the hands of the Russian secret police. To the Polish police all Communists were 'traitors' and any means of getting rid of them justified.

This attitude was held by the Polish population in general, as well as the police, and went back to the pre-revolutionary period. Rosa Luxemburg and her followers had never, in contrast with the P.P.S., taken a stand for Polish independence. In Luxemburg's view a revolution in Russia and the collapse of the Tsarist empire would in itself ensure Poland's independence.[1] The profoundly patriotic Poles, the great majority of whom were anti-Russian as well, obviously resented this attitude. The elimination of the party's 'Luxemburgist' leadership did not help matters, for the new 'imported' leadership was 'Muscovite' to the Poles and, if anything, worse. The population at large considered the party to be against independence and pro-Russian, and membership dwindled.

The fact that the party contained both Ukrainians and Jews also weakened it internally and gave the state a further weapon against it. Government propaganda, taking full advantage of Polish anti-Semitism, seized on the presence of Jews in the membership—where they were a minority—to picture the party as a Jewish 'hireling of Moscow'. As for the Ukrainian Communists, it was convenient to confuse them with the right-wing Ukrainian para-military formations which engaged in terrorist activity such as the murder of Polish officials and

[1] Before Rosa Luxemburg, the Polish revolutionary Ludwik Waryński expressed this opinion by saying: 'I know a nation more unlucky than the Poles—the working class.'

arson in eastern Poland. That the two groups were of course enemies was a distinction conveniently forgotten.

The Jewish members of the party posed no particular threat to its internal cohesion, but the adherence of the Ukrainians in 1923, as the Communist Party of the Western Ukraine, created difficulties. The hostility between Poles and Ukrainians eventually affected even Communists, who began to suspect one another of nationalism. Worse, the Russians had reason to distrust the Western Ukrainians in the Polish party. They had a close relationship with the Ukrainians of the Great Ukraine, in the Soviet Union, and dreamed of a united Ukrainian Communist Party—which did not at all suit the Russians who were then engaged in a ruthless russification of the Ukraine and of its Communist Party. The Western Ukrainians could scarcely be accused of 'Luxemburgism', but were regarded as separatists, and when the Communist Party of the Soviet Ukraine was purged they shared the fate of their comrades. This, of course, further weakened the Polish party which had admitted them.

The Jewish and Ukrainian members were of only limited use to the party in any case. The Ukrainian peasantry was on the whole hostile to the Communists and the Ukrainians could hardly do recruiting and propaganda work among the Poles. The Jews, faced with rampant anti-Semitism in all classes of Polish society, were even more gravely handicapped. Many young Jewish intellectuals were attracted to a party which, whatever its other goals, also fought anti-Semitism. It represented a haven where they could, although in great danger, think freely and join a society which did not discriminate against them. But the effectiveness of these young men, often from good middle-class families, in dealing with the Jewish proletariat—which was in any event strongly attached to its traditional labour organizations—was limited. And in spite of the attempts of the Polish government to portray it otherwise, the majority of the party's members were Poles, who often jokingly said that they were the only true Communists, as they were not in need of a comradely haven but could, if they wished, be reintegrated into their own society.

The Polish party had all but disintegrated anyhow by the time it was dissolved in 1938; Stalin was to claim that this was due to police infiltration, but in fact it was due more than anything else to the pressures applied by the Russian party. The Polish police did, of course, attempt to infiltrate the party and with some success. It is also true that the party's national composition worked against it. Also it was severely hampered by the state's repression of its activities; its members were hunted by their own government and denied its protection. But the worst inroads on the party were made by confusion and demoralization, caused by changes in the party line and the leadership, and attended by a loss of mutual trust. The fear of stepping out of line, of being considered an oppositionist and of being denounced by one's comrades as a 'Luxemburgist' or a 'Trotskyist', took a much larger toll than police action ever did. Open discussion and a comradely atmosphere vanished, problems and grievances were no longer aired, and party life became completely sterile. The same phenomenon occurred in more powerful Western Communist parties which did not have to fear the intervention of a hostile state. There too, men of considerable intelligence and integrity imposed a mindless discipline on themselves, fearing that doubts and questions might harm the revolution and the U.S.S.R., and dreading to face a life without purpose and hope. In Poland, where party members were isolated from one another and forced to act illegally, the effects were multiplied.

The peculiar history of the Polish Communist Party, persecuted by its own government and destroyed in the end by its Russian comrades, not only created an almost mystical feeling of attachment among its handful of survivors, it also explains how some of its members, although dreaming only of building a socialist Poland, were inexorably drawn from their purely political aims into serving the cause of the Soviet Union because it was impossible to realize their own aspirations.

CHAPTER III

First Assignment: Lwow

In a rambling old building in Lwow, not far from the citadel and almost opposite a police station, was an orphanage run by Sophie Kowal. She came from a family of landowners, once well-to-do, but early in life she had lost her parents and her possessions, and had remained unmarried so as to bring up her two younger sisters. Sophie was very small, almost dwarflike, and had an angelic, childlike smile, She also had incredible energy and a limitless capacity for work, and ran the large orphanage by herself, being at the same time its manager, teacher, cook, and even medical staff.

Sophie was a member of the Communist Party and in 1919 and 1920 her orphanage was the party's secret headquarters. The cellar was filled with illegal literature and there was a constant stream of visitors. Incredibly enough, the police never raided the place, although there was nearly always someone in hiding in the building, which had exits on several different streets. Sophie never refused anyone shelter, and her guests included not only Communists but Ukrainian Socialists and even nationalists—she would take in almost anyone, provided he was a political enemy of the government and an outlaw. The guests shared what food there was, usually little, and slept on refectory tables in the dining-room. But only a few knew who among them was a Communist or what was hidden in the cellar.

On certain evenings, when emissaries from other party cells or from abroad were in Lwow on serious business, Sophie would see that no one else appeared. Otherwise the to and fro of visitors, students, friends of Sophie's sisters, acted as camouflage and also helped in recruiting, for it was easy during the long enjoyable evenings of discussion to study the participants and to find out who might be of assistance. Some of the 'sympathizers' turned out to be helpful indeed, providing cover addresses, temporary quarters, and other aid. Some eventually became Communists.

Of the friends from the little town only Ludwik and Willy had remained in Poland. The others were all in Vienna, where the clandestine literature for Poland was being printed. It was smuggled into the country with the help of Czech railwaymen; whenever a consignment arrived at the border Willy would go and collect it from the Czechs and carry the bags back to the orphanage cellar. This was risky enough, but distributing the leaflets was even more dangerous. The people who did this work could scarcely be blamed for getting rid of the incriminating literature as fast as they could, as things could go very badly for anyone caught with such leaflets.

The emissaries from abroad who came to the orphanage brought news from other parties, from Vienna and Berlin, and from the Soviet Union. The German comrades, many of whom were working directly for Soviet apparatuses on 'temporary' assignments which in some cases never ended, were often men who had distinguished themselves in one way or another in Germany during the revolutionary days of 1918. Their fame had preceded them and they were treated with great respect, but in fact, as soon became evident, they were not suited to their assignments, having had no experience of illegal party work and knowing nothing of Poland or of the Polish language. They brought sweeping general instructions which could not possibly be put into effect in the local situation, and while quick to criticize what to them was lack of enterprise or courage, they were actually of very little help.

One of the German comrades sent to Lwow at this time was Franz Fischer, who in 1930 was to be involved in the hapless Soviet dollar-counterfeiting affair. He was quite depressed when Ludwik explained to him what was going on, and he realized there was nothing much for him to do in Poland or to report back to Berlin. The charming and handsome Franz, who used to boast of his romantic exploits in Berlin, later became a close friend of ours, and we came to love his mother very much when we met her in Berlin. She had been a friend of Rosa Luxemburg's and an active socialist all her life. A hard-working and beautiful woman who adored Franz, she had lost her other son at Verdun and lived with her daughter, with whom her relations became strained when the daughter joined a group in opposition to the German Communist Party. All Frau Fischer's children were socialists, of course, and I remember her saying: 'Some people take their children to church to have them confirmed. I took mine into the socialist movement.'

During the summer of 1919 Fedia came to Poland from Vienna, to discuss preparations for the congress of the Youth International[1] with the Polish delegate, Stanislaw Huberman—brother of Bronislaw Huberman, the famous violinist. I do not know whether Fedia and Stakh Huber-Wrzos, as Huberman was called in the party, had ever met before, but they became close friends—a friendship that was to last until Stakh's death in 1937. During this trip Fedia went back to the town in Galicia to visit the grave of his sister Lia. Everyone was opposed to this on security grounds, but Fedia was determined to go.

Fedia's visit to Lwow had another result: Ludwik was to go to Vienna to participate in the congress, not as the party's delegate but with its approval. He was issued a 'mandate'—a letter from one party to another, identifying the bearer—which was written on linen and sewn into the lining of his clothes. Linen had to be used instead of paper, which might have made a noise if the clothes were subjected to a thorough search. The mandate was to remain one of Ludwik's most treasured possessions. It was in this yellowed piece of material, whose faded ink attested that 'Comrade Ludwik' had been a member of the Polish party since 1919, that he wrapped the insignia of his Order of the Red Banner when he sent it in 1937, with the

---

[1] The Socialist Youth International had been created by the Second (Socialist) International at its congress in Stuttgart in 1907, but it developed along lines independent of the main body of the Socialist parties. It was soon joined by other independent left-wing youth groups, and had the support of the more radical Social–Democratic leaders such as Lenin and Rosa Luxemburg. The Youth International took a resolutely anti-war stand in 1914 and broke completely with the Social–Democrats. It was thus one of the forerunners of the Communist parties in Europe. In 1919 the Youth International surrendered its hard-won independence and became part of the Third International. Many of the young revolutionaries who had belonged to it thus found their way—without realizing the long-term implications—into the service of the Comintern and ultimately of the Soviet Union.

letter printed on page 1, to the Central Committee of the Soviet Communist Party.

Soon after Ludwik's trip to Vienna in 1919 the Russo–Polish war began claiming all the attention and the efforts of the party workers in Lwow. Marshal Pilsudski had been under pressure both from the French government, which was anxious to build a *cordon sanitaire* against the rising threat of communism, and from his own advisers; although anti-Bolshevik, he knew a victory by the White Russian armies in the Civil War might well be a threat to Poland's independence, for the Whites envisaged Poland's role as that of 'the most favoured nation among the indivisible and undivided Great Russia'. In April 1920, Pilsudski reluctantly sent Polish troops into the Ukraine.

When the war began the activities of the Polish Communist Party changed radically. Propaganda directed at the Polish army and at the rest of the population was to be stepped up. Attempts were to be made to win over the railway workers and to induce them to sabotage troop transports. Intelligence on troop movements and defences was to be gathered and transmitted to the Red Army and subversive activities and sabotage were to be carried out behind the Polish lines. The party was also to co-operate with an 'international brigade', made up of German and Austro–Hungarian prisoners of war and refugees from the Soviet Bavarian republic, whose aim was to bring the revolution to Germany after the Red Army had defeated the Poles. The Russians had at first been reluctant to create this unit, but with the outbreak of the war and the collapse of the right-wing Kapp *putsch* in Germany, the Soviet government apparently changed its mind. Manned by experienced soldiers and led by former officers of the imperial German and Austrian armies, this international brigade might have made a valuable adjunct to the Communist forces. Its main concern was Germany and not Poland, however, and the brigade appears never to have had much opportunity to participate in the Polish hostilities. Most of its members eventually joined the Red Army or served in Soviet agencies abroad.

Willy and Ludwik continued their work throughout the military campaign, and Krivitsky came to Lwow from Vienna.

Now there was scope for the military expertise of some of the foreign comrades. Franz Fischer was again in Poland, and escaped to Germany after a particularly daring operation behind the Polish lines. The work the party was doing was of course extremely dangerous. Martial law had been proclaimed and anyone engaged in intelligence or sabotage, or even in handing out literature, ran the risk of being shot. In spite of this, the leaflets proved easier to distribute than in peacetime. Also their impact was very much greater, as a result of the incredible chaos then prevailing in Poland.

The initial Polish advance into Russia and the Ukraine had been halted by the Red Army and turned into a rout. With its army in headlong retreat the Polish government panicked and its various organizations and departments fled before the advancing Red Army. Those responsible for maintaining law and order were often too busy running away and the impact of defeat made the population more receptive to Communist propaganda than ever before. The membership of the illegal party grew; unexpected allies materialized, such as the Peasant Party leader Dąbal, who in parliament welcomed the advancing Red Army. The Poles were by then only too willing to believe in the myth of an army of barefoot peasants and workers sweeping all before it and bringing the revolution to the world.

It would certainly have been wiser for the Russians to have stopped at the border, but they too had their dreams. They hoped to aid the then tottering Hungarian Bolshevik uprising and they expected to be met by an uprising of the Polish peasants and workers.[1] Some of them even looked forward to 'watering their horses in the Rhine'. Then came the 'miracle on the Vistula'. Incredibly, the Poles stopped the Red Army outside Warsaw and drove it back eastward. Dąbal was arrested, with many others, and charged with treason. Later, in an exchange of prisoners, he was sent to the Soviet Union, where he was treated as a hero and given an important position in the

---

[1] Years later Lenin, as his widow reported, had the good grace to admit to Clara Zetkin that he had been wrong, and Radek right in his warnings against the revolutionary illusions of the Bolsheviks. 'Evidently,' Lenin said, 'he knew the West better than the rest of us did.'

Comintern which he held until the great purges, when he was executed as a Polish spy.

The period of the Russo–Polish war was the last time Ludwik worked strictly for the party, and even then party interests were subordinate to the cause of the Soviet Union. After the war he made another trip to Vienna on, as he thought, purely political business. Later on he went to Moscow, where I met him. When he returned to Poland the following year he had become a Soviet agent.

Ludwik was not aware of having taken an irrevocable step. The collapse of the Bavarian and Hungarian revolutions and the recent defeat by the Poles had left the Soviet Union more isolated and exposed than ever, and as a Communist Ludwik believed it his duty to contribute to its survival. If it were to perish he felt all hope for the triumph of socialism would come to an end.

The step he had taken involved considerable sacrifices, the first and most obvious that of cutting himself off from his party and his comrades. This was essential as a security measure, not so much to protect him as to protect the party. When he met his former comrades he had to remain aloof and uninterested. They not unnaturally assumed he had broken with the party and simply deserted the cause; or, if they did not consider him a traitor, they taxed him with cowardice. There was nothing he could do about their suspicions. It was only later, after he was arrested, that he found acceptance, for in jail he had no need to hide his political beliefs from the authorities, and as he was a political prisoner he could share in the discussions and hunger strikes of his comrades. At liberty, however, he was cut off from the party which to all Communists was a source of strength and guidance. What gave him courage to continue was the conviction that what he was doing was only temporary and that some day he would again work in the party—if not the Polish party, then some other—and be in contact with the workers and surrounded by friends. When some ten years later he was offered a chance to work for the Polish section of the Comintern, which theoretically at least meant party work, I reminded him of his wish to return to such work. But he merely said: 'Party work? What party work, what party for that matters?'

His shift from party work to intelligence had begun with his 1919 trip to Vienna, when he was introduced to Joseph Krasny-Rotstadt. Krasny, as he was known in the party, had been a close friend and follower of Rosa Luxemburg in the S.D.K.P.iL., but had sided with the Radek group on the issue of relations with the Bolsheviks. This was perhaps one of the reasons why he, a prominent leader in pre-war days, had not assumed an important position in the newly-created Polish Communist Party. The February 1917 revolution in Russia had brought him back from exile in Siberia. Together with his old friends Dzerzhinsky, later head of the Cheka, and Unshlikht, Krasny took part in the October revolution, and was eventually to be given major responsibilities in the Soviet party.

Now Krasny was working for the Comintern, directing propaganda in Poland, Hungary, and the Balkans. He supplied the young Communist parties with literature and leaflets, and also published theoretical journals such as *The Struggle*, which reproduced the speeches of Soviet leaders and Comintern resolutions; a weekly called *The Dawn*; and a monthly, *The Civil War*. He encouraged the young men around him to contribute to these journals, and Ludwik had a few articles published in *The Civil War* under his party name, Ludwig.

In Vienna, however, emphasis was put on other things as well. The setting up of information-gathering networks was something for which the idealistic young Communists had not been trained, and had never thought of engaging in. But the fact that the Soviet Union was in danger and that veteran revolutionaries like Krasny approved of such work and were directing it overcame any hesitations they might have had. While serving a long sentence in a particularly dreaded prison in Warsaw before the war, Dzerzhinsky had astonished the other political prisoners in his cell, as well as the guards, when he asked for water, soap, and brushes and proceeded to scrub the floors. He always volunteered to clean the filthy buckets which served as latrines and in general went out of his way to perform the most unpleasant tasks. Asked to explain, he answered: 'Some day there will be a really dirty job to be done and someone will have to do it; and it will be I.' Krasny, who told this story, had little trouble in convincing the young idealists that they too had to do dirty jobs.

When he came back to Lwow at the beginning of 1922 Ludwik was accompanied by Jacob Locker, whom he had met first in Vienna during the war. As a member of the Socialist Youth International, Locker had stayed out of the Austrian army on principle; the police were looking hard for draft evaders—as well as for members of the illegal youth organization—and Locker often found temporary refuge in Krusia's room, where he came to know the friends from the little town. When I met him he was already bald and portly, though quite young; with his heavy glasses his head looked like a billiard ball. Both Locker and his close friend Nebenfuehrer joined the Fourth Department and accepted dangerous assignments in Poland and Romania.[1]

The assignment Ludwik and Locker were to carry out in Lwow was not without its dangers. Ludwik was already known to the police in the town, and Locker was conspicuous—especially in a Poland suspicious of foreigners—through knowing neither the language nor the country. Krasny had sent them to Lwow to make contact with officers and non-commissioned men of the Polish army. They were to head a group of nine people. Three of these were party sympathizers who did not know the other members of the group or the work they were engaged in, and whose only function was to provide cover addresses; the others were party members temporarily detached from the Polish Communist Party. Contact with military personnel was, of course, nothing new for Communists. Only this time their task was not the traditional one of propaganda, but collecting information about weapons, troop movements, and the like: in other words, espionage pure and simple. Ludwik and Locker, of course, knew perfectly well that such work had little to do with the party. But neither gave much thought to the fact that their activities were quite out of line with the policy directives

[1] Ludwik and I saw Locker and Nebenfuehrer, with the latter's wife Erna, off and on for years. Locker eventually occupied a post high up in the internal organization of the Fourth, in Moscow. Loyal to his friends, he was also loyal to the Soviet Union, and would listen to our criticisms of the regime but never volunteered any.

of the Comintern. Nor did they realize that in all probability they were working directly for the Red Army.

In spite of its claims to the contrary, Poland was not pursuing a truly independent foreign policy but had aligned itself with the major European powers, all of whom were anti-Bolshevik. Political intelligence, therefore, had one been interested in obtaining it, would have been easier to find—and the information would have been far more trustworthy—on the banks of the Seine than on those of the Vistula. But it was military intelligence that was of primary interest to the Soviet Union, which feared another attack from Poland. An assessment of over-all Polish strength was needed, but also information on individual units, their deployment, and their national composition (Ukrainian units, considered of doubtful reliability, were never stationed near the Soviet borders, for instance), and on the condition of roads, bridges, railways, and the like.

It was not necessary to penetrate the higher echelons of the Polish army to acquire such information; it was available to quite low-ranking officers and even non-commissioned men. Nor was it very hard to get. The military were poorly paid and the country itself was miserably poor; in such circumstances a bribe of a few dollars represented a fortune. But the information had to be got rapidly, as the Polish police were very quick in making arrests.

This was not so much a mark of efficiency as lack of experience. Convinced that Poland was threatened from all sides and rife with subversion, the police in their nervousness displayed great assiduity. The need to justify a large budget may also have had much to do with their feverish activity. Later on they were to learn from the French the value of patient, long-drawn-out investigations and surveillance carried out in a professional manner, which could lead to the arrest of an entire network of agents and ensure relative security for some time to come. At this early stage, however, the Polish police contented themselves with arresting even the least important member of a network. Under torture the prisoner would reveal what he knew— usually very little— but by the time the police could act the rest of the network had vanished. Ludwik and Locker were not fortunate in this respect, however, and before they had been at work long they were both arrested.

I was in Lwow at this time, having come there to be with Ludwik, and I received the news of his arrest together with a bundle of his blood-stained clothes. I was interrogated by the police, and later on also by the magistrate who usually handled political cases. The latter, a pale-faced man in his thirties who was reputed to be severe but correct and fair, lived up to his reputation, and did not try to trap me with trick questions, but accepted my version of events. When he confronted me with Locker and we said we had never seen each other before, he accepted this too, although I am convinced he did not quite believe it. Like all the magistrates this man was hated by the political prisoners. Those who escaped wrote insulting letters, sent from abroad without any risk to the writer, to their magistrates: this for some reason was thought witty and courageous, and copies were circulated to entertain their comrades. I recall thinking at the time that this particular magistrate scarcely deserved the hatred directed against him for doing what was after all only his job. Other magistrates pestered the prisoners with petty restrictions, such as cancelling or shortening visits or forbidding them to receive letters or parcels, but this man never stooped to that.

His behaviour towards me was always cold, impersonal, and correct. He never smiled or said any more than was absolutely necessary. Once, however, he departed from this pattern. Ludwik had just been led back to his cell and I was preparing to leave when he motioned me to sit down. I noticed that he had sent his assistant away, and was apprehensive at the turn things might take. Looking at me he said: 'So you are his fiancée?' I knew he meant one of the *ad hoc* 'fiancées' whose job it was to keep in contact with any prisoner who did not have a wife, and who might be someone he had never known. Nevertheless I nodded. Then he asked: 'One of those or a real one?' I assured him that I was really Ludwik's fiancée. Still looking at his desk he said: 'I thought so. You don't look the type to be mixed up in such an affair. Do you understand what he is accused of? Do you realize that he will spend many years in prison? Are you going to wait for him?'—'Yes, I will,' I answered.—'Very well,' was his only comment. 'I have warned you.' He bent over his papers again. I was dismissed.

I was panic-stricken at the warning and afraid that he would be more severe than ever. I mentioned the incident to Ludwik's lawyer, a jolly elderly gentleman, who laughed. 'Don't worry, that's just his way of trying to make love to you.' I never believed it, then or later. It must have cost that stern, cold magistrate quite an effort to give me this personal warning.

The Polish jails at that time were crowded with Communists and with Ukrainian nationalists, whose terrorist campaign against Polish officials and the police continued unabated. One gray November morning I saw a small group in front of the prison watching two teenagers being pushed into a cart. These Ukrainian boys, mere children, were being taken to another prison to be executed for their part in the assassination of a Polish government official. I thought I could feel the eyes of one of them on me. They were enormous eyes in a livid, contorted, frightened child's face and for a long time I could not forget them.

One day soon after Ludwik's arrest I was leaving the prison, where I had gone to take him some food and books, when I was surprised to be tapped on the shoulder by a tall, dark man wearing foreign clothes. He said he was the emissary I had been told would be arriving from Vienna to arrange for Ludwik's defence. I was to meet him the next day at the lawyer's office, but supposing I would be worried, he had thought it a good idea to introduce himself now.

While grateful for his kind intentions, I was taken aback by what I thought this man's gross carelessness. To approach me in front of the prison under the sentries' noses, struck me as foolish and I told him so. He laughed and said that he was not worried: if there was one thing he knew, it was prisons and how to get out of them. One of his techniques, it seems, was to pretend to be a pious orthodox Jew so absorbed in prayer that he did not know what was going on and who moreover would not speak to infidels who asked him questions. He always wore the dress of an orthodox Jew and carried a prayer book. We had heard of him and of his technique and it really had suc-

ceeded on several occasions in Germany. I told him I doubted
whether this trick would impress the Polish police, who knew
a great deal more about orthodox Jews than the Germans, and
were unlikely to be taken in. He answered that it had worked
also in Budapest, where conditions were not unlike those in
Poland, and that he was not worried.

I saw him next day in the lawyer's office as agreed, and
after he left the lawyer told me he thought the visitor very odd
indeed. Contrary to the impression he had given me, he seemed
much afraid of being arrested by the Polish police. I was to see
this man again a year or so later in Berlin, where his behaviour
seemed stranger still, and he finally had a complete nervous
breakdown and was sent back to the Soviet Union. Later on we
were told that he had been confined to an insane asylum.

The Polish prison system was actually much more liberal
than that of many countries with a long tradition of civil
liberties but which make no distinction between political offenders and common criminals. In Poland political prisoners
were entitled to receive visitors, food parcels, and even books,
and were allowed to communicate with each other. After one
got past the initial beatings and torture[1] by the police, prison
life was not particularly dreaded, even if one's stay was prolonged. Sanitary conditions were appalling, of course, the cells
were overcrowded and vermin-ridden, but prisoners had an
opportunity for free political discussion—something which was
impossible outside, where contacts had to be brief and furtive
if one was to avoid arrest. In prison the Communists and the
Ukrainian nationalists, thoroughly hostile to each other when
at liberty, got along quite well, and friendships were formed
which lasted a long time. The months in prison gave time not
only for reading—the magistrates almost invariably allowed
the prisoners to have literature that was quite subversive—
but for psychological relaxation: the constant anxiety of waiting
for the almost inevitable arrest was over. The prisoner knew

---

[1] Torture was a standard method of police interrogation. This has been denied
officially, and the average Polish citizen obviously knew nothing of it, but I know
of many people who underwent it. Recently a distinguished Polish writer told me
that he had been deeply disturbed by false allegations of torture made by the
American writer Louis Fischer whom he considered otherwise trustworthy. He was
much chagrined when I could only confirm Fischer's statements.

that he was not forgotten by his comrades, from whom he received parcels and books. And on May Day he was allowed to hang red rags out of the window and to sing revolutionary songs.

The conditions I have described applied, of course, to prisoners awaiting sentence for political offences, as Ludwik was. Anyone condemned to a long imprisonment, especially for espionage or high treason, was sent to a fortress, which meant forced labour and often solitary confinement. Under these conditions prisoners often broke down, and suicides were frequent. On the whole, however, the Communists withstood imprisonment better than other offenders. Their dedication and the knowledge that their families were being taken care of helped them survive the hardships of fortress life.

The guards in the ordinary prisons were often quite lenient, some of them even permitting a prisoner they were escorting to shake hands with a visitor, when they knew very well that in this way a message was being passed him from outside. Occasionally a guard was bribed, but the prisoner and his friends seldom knew which one would be on duty at a given time. Some of the guards of course were not so gentle, but the prison authorities did not tolerate brutality and all a guard could do was to shove the prisoner or his visitors around a bit.

One guard who was famous with anyone who was ever a political prisoner in Poland at that time was Reway, a huge man with a drunkard's nose and a stentorian voice which he used to full advantage. When he roared, 'It is forbidden to approach the prisoners', he could be heard throughout the building, and so could his favourite form of address to a prisoner: 'Is this Reway speaking to you or a bull farting?' But everyone knew that when he escorted a prisoner he would pretend not to notice a handshake by which a message was passed; and it was an unwritten law that one never attempted to escape from Reway, or from any of the other decent guards, who would have been severely punished even though they had not assisted in the escape.

Escapes were quite frequent, none the less. They were made relatively easy by the long corridors which the prisoners had to traverse to be interrogated. Most of those who escaped were

Ukrainians, whose people were near by to help and hide them, but a few Communists also got away. The general practice was to hide a few days and then cross the mountains into Czecho-slovakia. Some even managed to get to the Free City of Danzig by train.

Some of the escapes were unplanned, such as one I witnessed. I had just passed through the prison door, after visiting Ludwik, and looked at the sentry outside, who nodded as usual. There seemed to me something odd about his gesture, but before I could decide what it was he pitched forward and rolled down the stairs, till he lay at the foot with blood streaming from his head. He had evidently had a heart attack, and was quite dead. At this instant a guard happened to be passing with a prisoner. He, like everyone else, turned to the stricken man and the prisoner ran away. By the time his escape was noticed and the alarm given he had vanished. I doubt that the police looked very hard for him—in some ways they must have looked on such escapes as good riddance.

When Ludwik and Locker were finally tried, after months in prison, their trial coincided with that of the members of the Central Committee of the Polish Communist Party, known as the St. George trial from the church where the men had been arrested with the help of an *agent provocateur*. The imprisonment of the entire Central Committee of course decapitated the party, but the public trial, which lasted several weeks, gave it much publicity and prestige. Contrary to what the public had been led to believe, the accused turned out to be not little Jewish boys and girls, but responsible political leaders. A few were Ukrainians, but most were Poles of all classes, including even a count. The trial gave the arrested leaders an oppor-tunity to engage in political debate with their accusers and they charged the state with being tyrannical and racist, with denying its citizens the most basic of liberties.

As there was no Communist press— at least no legal one— such trials in fact served as a forum. Anyone arrested for party activity immediately recanted his confession in court, accusing the police of having obtained it under duress (this was invariably true), denied that any 'bourgeois' court had the moral right to judge him, and generally made as much propaganda for the party as possible. As the trials usually got a fair amount of coverage in the press the accused were often defended by prominent non-Communist lawyers who could thus make a name for themselves.

At Ludwik's and Locker's trial, however, it was in everyone's interest—that of the state as well as that of the accused—to be as discreet as possible. This was also in the Soviet interest. The two were charged with being agents of 'a neighbouring state'—which did not have to mean the U.S.S.R., since Poland had other neighbours, with most of whom it was on bad terms. The accused denied any connection with the Communist Party and insisted they had acted from purely mercenary motives.

In some ways the fate of an arrested agent was easier than that of a man arrested for Communist activity. The latter was charged with high treason, the former with espionage. Since for a decade after independence the legal codes of the former ruling powers prevailed, as I have mentioned, in the different parts of Poland, a man arrested in Warsaw was tried under Tsarist law, one in Poznan under German law, and one in Lwow under Austrian law. The same offence might carry quite different penalties. In the former Austrian provinces a foreign agent would be sentenced to three to five years, while a man convicted of high treason would have to serve ten years, to which a one-year sentence for belonging to the illegal Communist Party was usually added for good measure.

The arrested agent could also look forward to possible exchange with some Polish agent in jail in Russia; if none were available, the Russians would not hesitate to arrest any Pole they could lay their hands on, on a trumped-up charge. Or a member of the Catholic clergy would serve just as well: the Soviets once arrested an archbishop for the sole purpose of trading him for some of their own people—a deal the deeply religious Poles had no choice but to accept.

Ludwik was given the maximum sentence for espionage, five years, but managed to escape eighteen months after his arrest. He got as far as Cracow, and was stopped there not by the police but by a railway strike. The strike was one of the most imposing the Polish working class ever engaged in and the first in which the army refused to fire on the strikers. Led by the Socialist trade unions, it soon spread to other industries. It was the last struggle of the Polish working class Ludwik was to witness, and one in which he could not take part, although his convictions and ideals had made him dedicate his life to precisely this kind of action. He crossed the border into Germany on foot, never to return to Poland.

CHAPTER IV

Berlin and Vienna

I

When Ludwik arrived in Germany he found his friends in feverish activity. The Comintern was preparing the 1923 rising, on instructions from Moscow, and though not all the men from the little town were in the same organization, in the atmosphere then prevailing no one seemed to care much about administrative matters: they were all working towards the same goal.

Fedia, who had just come back from the Soviet Union, was with the international liaison department, known as O.M.S. from its Russian initials, of the Comintern. The illegal work he was organizing was to be financed by the sale of jewels.[1] Another purely intelligence-gathering group had been organized within the German Communist Party by a man known as Felix Wolf; although nominally under the Comintern, this group was in fact directly responsible to the Fourth Department of the General Staff—that is, to Red Army intelligence. Finally, there was the foreign section of the N.K.V.D., also known by its Russian initials, I.N.O. The work was co-ordinated locally by a close friend of Fedia's, Mirov-Abramov, head of the O.M.S., who handled instructions and money[2] from Moscow. Mirov-Abramov's official position was that of press attaché at the Soviet Embassy, which meant he was under the N.K.V.D. as well, since that commissariat controlled the press. The Fourth Department, although nominally a section of the Army,

[1] Rumour had it that these were the Imperial crown jewels, which exiled grand dukes were later to recognize in shop windows. But in fact the Soviets never sold the crown jewels; those they did sell were much less valuable and in their agents' inexperienced hands brought in very little.

[2] When the time came to destroy him, Mirov-Abramov was accused of having used these funds to finance Trotskyite movements in Europe.

was also operating through the Embassy–O.M.S. network, so it is easy to see why jurisdictional conflicts eventually arose.

At the time Fedia's immediate superior in the Comintern was a Balt from an aristocratic family whom everyone called 'the Baron'. A man in his fifties, he had brought to Germany with him his young Russian wife, a peasant girl, who almost went crazy when she saw all the luxuries in the Berlin shops, and bought everything she could lay her hands on. She was especially wild about cosmetics, and was totally enchanted by face powder; she used to mutter the Russian word '*pudra*' to herself until inevitably she became known to everyone, including her husband, as 'Pudra'. 'Pudra', however, came to mean something else to all of us: the Russian *mujik* face to face with the West for the first time.

While Fedia had no use for the Baron's wife, he had a great deal of respect for him and for his abilities. The Baron had a long revolutionary career behind him, had spent years in Siberia, and had served with distinction during the Civil War. Fedia was furious at the time with Willy, who often played chess with the Baron but would never let him win. Willy was a first-rate player and either could not or would not lose a game. Fedia would shout at him: 'Brun is right, you are a blockhead! Can't you see how happy he would be if you just let him beat you once?' Willy, however, was obdurate and the Baron never won.

One day, while playing golf, the Baron died. After his death the whole group in the O.M.S. came under the supervision of the Fourth Department. The exceptions were Brun and Misha; through his job with Rosta, the official Soviet press agency and predecessor of Tass, Misha was already under N.K.V.D. jurisdiction and soon he and his brother joined its services.

Fedia resented the fact that two of 'his boys' should have taken this step. At the time there seemed to be no difference between the N.K.V.D. and the Fourth Department, but Fedia made a distinction. He felt that by joining the military intelligence section, the Fourth Department, of the Red Army he was not leaving the political movement for pure espionage, as every party, legal or illegal, belonging to the Comintern had a military section controlled by this department. Indeed, in those early days it was common practice for members of these sections to switch back and forth between the Red Army and the Comintern. The N.K.V.D., on the other hand, had scarcely any contact with the European parties and took its orders directly from Moscow. From the earliest days of the I.N.O. the N.K.V.D. made strenuous efforts to recruit personnel from the Fourth Department and the Comintern, but only succeeded when intrigues in those organizations became policy and their staffs were completely overhauled.

In 1923 Fedia still believed that not everything was lost in the Soviet Union. In spite of the oppositional struggles Lenin, though ill, was nominally at the helm and there still hope of his recovery. Nevertheless Fedia always frowned on Brun's working for the N.K.V.D. I remember an incident in a Berlin café when someone slipped an envelope into Brun's hands. 'That's a fine pack of lies you've got there, and you know it,' Fedia said to him. 'Better start growing a moustache, you can't be a good gendarme without a moustache; make it a fine, bushy one and wax it, the way the gendarmes did under the Tsar.'

The leaders of the Comintern were frequently in Berlin at that time and several meetings took place in the flat we rented from a young anarchist who had just lost his parents. Although he was vaguely aware of what was going on and had a considerable amount of sympathy for us, our landlord did not learn until much later that among our visitors had been Karl Radek and G. L. Piatakov.

One of our house guests was Larissa Reisner, who came with Radek and stayed with us rather than at a hotel, as she had a false German passport. She had stayed one night at a German hotel where the manager told her: 'Madame, if you want people to think you are German, do not smile like that. German women cannot smile that way, only Russian ones can.' This had not been intended to annoy her, but was simply the reaction of all men to her; the manager could no more help it than anyone else. When Fedia met her at our place he was, for once in his life, struck speechless. She was stunningly beautiful.

At the time Larissa was not in Moscow's good graces. Her father, a professor of law under the old regime, had rendered the illegal party many services and after the revolution worked closely with the party leaders and drafted the first Soviet constitution. But he also wrote many articles on the dangers of concentrating power in the hands of one party. Such writings scarcely made him popular and he was quietly dropped from his official position. In order to make this sudden eclipse more acceptable rumours were circulated to the effect that he had collaborated with the Okhrana.

Her father's eclipse would not, however, have affected Larissa who had made a brilliant record of her own during the Civil War. She had been called the 'meteor of the revolution' by Trotsky and had written articles and a book on the Civil War. She was the wife of Fedor Raskolnikov, whose record in the Civil War had also been spectacular. As an officer in the Tsarist navy he had organized the attack by the Kronstadt naval detachment on the Winter Palace in St. Petersburg. Raskolnikov had had sympathies with the opposition, but had renounced them and been reinstated in the good graces of the party: with other leading figures from the opposition, he was appointed an ambassador and thus removed from active political life in the Soviet Union.[1]

At the time when we met her Larissa was no longer living with Raskolnikov. They had separated in 1922, when they returned from Bokhara, where Raskolnikov had held a post. It was then that Larissa was reprimanded by the party for 'conduct unbecoming to a party member'. It was rumoured that in Bokhara she had had numerous love affairs with British officers, whom she used to visit in their quarters nude, covered only by a fur coat. Larissa told me that these rumours had been circulated by her husband, who was insanely jealous and terribly violent. She showed me a vicious scar on her back made by Raskolnikov's riding crop.

In spite of having been placed in a delicate position in the party, Larissa could still go abroad thanks to her relationship with Radek. From Berlin she went on to Hamburg; she later wrote a book about the uprising there, called *Hamburg aud den Barrikaden*. After the complete defeat of the German uprising she returned with Radek to the Soviet Union, where she died of

---

[1] His last diplomatic post was in Bulgaria; when he was recalled in 1938 he refused to return and died in Paris in 1939.

typhus in 1928, at the age of thirty-one. Those who saw Radek at the time of her death said that the blow to him was crushing. In January 1937, when he was one of the chief accused in the second Moscow trial, he must have blessed fate for Larissa's early death.

When another of those who were later defendants at the second Moscow trial, Piatakov, came to Berlin, an incident occurred that was indicative of the state of affairs at the time. Piatakov took Ludwik with him on a trip to Dresden, where he was to meet the leaders of the Left Socialist government of Saxony. They registered at the same hotel and only then found to their embarrassment that each carried a false passport alleging him to be an Austrian citizen called Reinhold Hauer. Although the passports listed them as both the same age, Piatakov was visibly much older. Nevertheless he convinced the reception clerk that Ludwik was a nephew of his with the same name and born in the same town. The art of forging passports was then still in its infancy, and in any event the Soviets were not much concerned, as they considered Germany their private preserve.

The work that Ludwik and his friends in the various agencies were doing at that time was of course primarily military. The efforts of the Comintern and the other agencies to round up arms for the Communist groups preparing the rising were difficult and dangerous. The men involved had to elude not only the German police, who were efficient and active, but representatives of Allied services enforcing the terms of the Treaty of Versailles, which limited German arms and therefore controlled all arms traffic, Communist or otherwise. Weapons and ammunition were actually fairly plentiful, as was natural in a country that had until recently had a large army, and in theory it was not hard to buy them. But the sellers often informed the police of the transaction and the buyers were arrested; at other times the heavy cases, once opened, turned out to be full of stones.

With the failure of the rising this kind of work came to an end. The collapse of the German attempt had long-lasting effects, both on policy and on the functioning of Soviet agencies abroad. It was clear there was to be no revolution in Europe, only abortive uprisings or doomed *putsches,* and policies adapted to 'revolutionary situations' gave way to those adapted to dealing with a 'temporary stabilization of capitalism'. Fedia deeply discouraged, returned to Moscow and made strenuous efforts to leave the intelligence services, though he was not to succeed in this until much later.

The German police, on the lookout for Communist activity, were hard on the Comintern networks, breaking them up and arresting the members; but they appeared to have almost no interest in the Soviet intelligence agencies, whose operations they knew were aimed not at Germany but at the Allied powers. It was necessary nonetheless for the Comintern to maintain its agents in Germany, since that country, with the Free City of Danzig, was a logical base for its work in Poland and its liaison with the Soviet Union. The N.K.V.D. and the Fourth Department, however, while they retained headquarters in Germany, began to transfer men to Austria where more urgent tasks awaited them.

The N.K.V.D. found in Vienna a convenient place from which to keep an eye on the remnants of the White armies settled in the Balkans and in Turkey. The Red Army's intelligence service, though not suspending operations in Germany, also expanded its activities in Austria, a better headquarters for operations in Eastern Europe. Very few of the Polish and German Communists who had worked for the Soviet agencies in Germany on what they believed to be a temporary basis went back to their own parties. Almost all of those who had worked in the military apparatus under the supervision of the Fourth Department wound up as members of it.

2

Ludwik, with Felix Gorski, a Pole who had come to Germany from Moscow, went with the Fourth to Vienna, where all the work centred in the Soviet Embassy. In later years such open contact with Soviet diplomatic officials would have been unthinkable, but at the time there had not yet been police raids on Soviet trade missions and similar bodies so no precautions seemed necessary.

The Soviet Embassy in Vienna was a world in itself or so it seemed to us. This was all the more so since it served not only as an office but as a residence for many staff members. No doubt embassies in other places and of other nations were staffed with a mixture of remarkable individuals and mediocrities, and no doubt all had their share of quarrels and intrigues; but the staff of the Soviet Embassy in Vienna at that time really seemed unique. Not only were many nationalities represented (by no means all Soviet officials were Russian) but many political groupings as well. In those days when the Soviet authorities wanted to get rid of an oppositionist—as in the case of Larissa's husband Raskolnikov—they did not execute him but appointed him to a foreign post.

Even the military staff in Vienna had its share of oppositionists, Russians, Ukrainians or russified foreigners. One of the military attachés, Inkov—that was not his real name— was a German, whom I mentioned earlier as having worked in the German party under the name of Felix Wolf. As Wolf, he had been assigned to carry out liaison between the party and the Comintern. He was totally opposed to the revolutionary policy in Germany and he soon made enemies both in the German party and the Comintern. As a result, he was branded an oppositionist and accused of having collaborated with the German Communist leader Paul Levi, who had by then resigned from the party. The latter charge was quite untrue, although Wolf was an old friend of Levi's. (He had also remained a close friend of Karl Radek in spite of his opposition to the revolution Radek was supposed to oversee.) Soon the intrigues made Wolf's work impossible and he left the Comintern for the Fourth Department. Having been arrested, and thus rendered useless in Germany as well as suspect through his opposition, he was appointed to Vienna.

The use of assorted cover names has led to much confusion, of which this is a good illustration. Whenever Wolf-Inkov worked in Germany for the Fourth, which he did occasionally after his arrest and exposure, he used the name Nikolai Rakov, which was merely a Russian version of his real German name Krebs. (As Krebs he had sided with the Bolsheviks in 1917, done effective propaganda work among German troops in the Ukraine, and returned to Germany in 1918 under the name Wolf.) In Vienna, of course, a German name would not do, so there he acquired yet another one, Inkov, an *ad hoc* invention based on nothing more than the Christian name of his wife Ina—a very pretty dark-haired, blue-eyed Russian girl, often called Inka.[1]

Our relations with the Inkovs were good in spite of the fact that he was not easy to get along with. He was moody and depressed and though he and his wife had a baby boy—like every son of a good Communist named Vladimir, in honour of Lenin—their domestic relations were poor. In 1927 he returned to the U.S.S.R. where the family separated. As he had always been on close personal terms with Radek, Inkov was automatically classified as a Left oppositionist. He was expelled from the party and arrested. After his release he hung around Moscow unable to get a job. We heard from him occasionally until 1934 when he disappeared and must have perished in the purges.

One of the most attractive and striking personalities at the Embassy was Juri Kotsiubinsky. The son of a writer, himself a gifted poet, People's Commissar in the Ukraine, and with Piatakov an organizer of the Civil War, he had been a party member since early youth and was rightly considered one of the old Bolsheviks. During the Civil War he had narrowly escaped execution by a White firing squad when at the last minute the position was taken by Red troops. But Civil War hero and old Bolshevik or not, he had also been one of the earliest oppositionists, belonging to the group of democratic centralists. Like many of his comrades, he was afterwards posted abroad, first to Vienna and then to Warsaw. As time went on, oppositionists were no longer treated so leniently. Kotsiubinsky was recalled, accused of belonging to the 'united opposition', expelled from the party in 1927 and shot without trial a few years later. His liquidation was probably due to his friendship with Piatakov who was a Trotskyite; he himself was not one, although he never hid his admiration for Trotsky and was out-

---

[1] Bessedovsky in his exposè of Soviet services (*Oui, j'accuse* [*aux services des Soviets*], Paris 1930) makes much of this name. The soft accent which he could not place and the definitely Slav name Inkov led him to assert that Inkov was a Bulgarian, and it was on this tenuous basis that he proceeded to develop a theory of the 'balkanization' of the Soviet Embassy in Vienna. That the 'Bulgarian' Inkov was actually a German named Krebs, who before the war had worked in Russia and Latvia—hence his accent—hardly bears out Bessedovsky's rather fanciful theory

spoken in his criticism of the dictatorial patterns then developing in the party.

Kotsiubinsky was quite out of the ordinary physically as well as in other ways. Tall and slim, he wore a high-necked Russian blouse and a beard. He had a good sense of humour, was well liked, and never took part in the petty intrigues that flourished in the Embassy. He spent more time with friends outside the Embassy than with his official colleagues and many non-Embassy people, including us, came to see him off when he left Vienna.

Another prominent Bolshevik at the Embassy was Alexander Shlikhter. During the Civil War he had been People's Commissar for Food and Agriculture and his name had appeared on many decrees alongside Lenin's. But though he had countersigned Lenin's decrees, Shlikhter never showed the ruthlessness towards the peasants that the party felt necessary and he too wound up in the diplomatic service. Although not belonging to any of the oppositions he was not in Moscow's good graces either and made no attempt to hide his disillusionment. He was very depressed and drank a good deal, and would tell stories of the revolution and of the old Bolshevik leaders in a hoarse voice. Ludwik admired him as an old Bolshevik and he in turn treated Ludwik as an affectionate father would. Although Shlikhter was not party to the intrigues, these invariably revolved around him. That Moscow learned of his drinking and of his alleged love affairs was in a way the doing of his Polish wife, Mania, who was wildly jealous and kept him under constant surveillance. To make matters worse she spread all sorts of rumours. It soon became impossible for him to function at all in such circumstances and at his own request he was relieved of his post.

There were any number of people in Vienna at that time who had left the Soviet Union and who displayed varying degrees of hostility to its government. Most of them had left for no better reason than that no one had prevented them from doing so. But once in Vienna, they were at loose ends. Some found work at the Soviet trade mission, even some Whites, whose hostility to the regime gradually lessened and who even showed a willingness to help with the work of the Fourth.

Among the old socialists and early friends of the Communists who had broken with the Bolsheviks was Angelica Balabanova, who had been secretary of the Third International. An old-style socialist and eternal rebel, she found that the revolution she had worked for was not what she had expected, and that she could not agree with the other leaders of the International. She expressed a desire to leave, and Lenin and his comrades were quite pleased to have her do so but they wanted to avoid an open break. An arrangement was accordingly worked out by which she was to go abroad—in fact the Soviets did everything they could to see to it that she did go—where she was to receive financial assistance. She lived in Vienna among her Italian friends and rationalized her acceptance of funds from the Soviet Embassy by the fact that the Ambassador, Joffe, was himself in opposition.

Nor had Lenin put any obstacles in the way of the Mensheviks' leaving Russia. He was genuinely concerned about their fate and would have liked to support them in some way too, especially their leader Martov, who though his political enemy had for years been one of his closest personal friends. The Mensheviks, however, were steadfast in their attitude. They had left the Soviet Union as political opponents of the Bolsheviks and this they remained. They never accepted any financial help from their old comrades and bitter enemies.

The intrigues at the Embassy seldom arose from political concerns but were almost always the result of petty jealousies and frictions among the wives. A preoccupation with rank is in any case not uncommon, but with these women who knew nothing of the West, or of diplomatic usage and whose main experience in life had been of privations during the war and Civil War, questions of precedence and the like were magnified. Some of the men had diplomatic status and their wives were proud of it, others did not and the wives resented it. The men were by and large unaffected by all this and relations between the N.K.V.D. and the military—who called each other 'neighbours'—were good.

The man in charge of Balkan labour relations at the Embassy was later the centre of a world-wide *cause célèbre*. His name was Luft and he had served as a trade union specialist in the Far East, and was to serve there again. He was then about thirty-five years old, not unattractive-looking but extremely tense, forever moving about and switching from one to another of his three languages apparently without noticing. Although not in the opposition, he often spoke too openly about the way the party was being run; moreover he was friendly with the prominent oppositionist Joffe.

Luft led a solitary life, associating with one no except his secretary, a young Latvian girl who did her best to keep his office in some sort of order. The poor girl was very lonely and lost among the crowd of overbearing and intriguing women in the Embassy. Luft was always very kind to her and she took his kindness for a manifestation of love. When she realized that he did not love her and had no intention of marrying her she was bitterly hurt and poured out her heart to me. Overcoming my reluctance I spoke to Luft on her behalf. He told me that he had only felt sorry for her loneliness and had devoted some of his free time to showing her the beauties of Vienna. He was not in love with her, he had no intention of tying himself to her, he was too devoted to his cause to burden himself with women, and furthermore, he said, he was not the marrying kind.

Fate, however, caught up with him. On one of his trips to Rome to confer with Balkan labour leaders, he met the secretary of the Soviet Embassy there and married her. They were an oddly assorted pair, he having come from a poor family in the Ukraine while she had been educated at the Smolny Institute in St. Petersburg, a finishing school for the daughters of the aristocracy. They had a child shortly afterwards and eventually left for the Far East.

In August 1931 it was announced that the secretary-general of the Pan-Pacific Trade Unions and his wife, both Swiss citizens, had been arrested in Shanghai. Their names were not given, and no one knew who they were. Shortly afterwards the Shanghai authorities, still without mentioning names, announced that evidence had been found making it clear that the 'Swiss labour leader' had been up to something very different from mere trade union activity. The International Red Help society and a 'Committee to save the labour leader' immediately began an intensive campaign, directed by Willy Muenzenberg, to get the couple released. Propaganda efforts were hampered, however, by the absence of any names to attach to the victims.

Moscow could not help, as it had no idea what name the couple had been using when arrested, although it knew well enough that they were its agents. Then the Chinese authorities announced that a Swiss citizen named Paul Ruegg had been sentenced to death and his wife to life imprisonment.

On 21 August Willy Muenzenberg produced an article in *Imprecor,* the Comintern journal, that set off the campaign. He had no idea who Paul Ruegg was, nor did it make matters any easier when the Shanghai police announced that Ruegg also used the name Noulens and claimed Belgian nationality, but his publicity was superbly effective. The world at large soon believed that the Rueggs, although they might have been Communists, had been engaged in straightforward labour union work and were being unjustly accused for no other reason than their allegiance to trade unionism. In order to get rid of trade unionists, so the argument went, the Chinese had framed the two Swiss as Soviet spies. The campaign was so skilfully mounted and aroused so much moral indignation that the Chinese finally gave in and released the Rueggs.

The identity of the couple remained unknown. Inquiries in Switzerland were inconclusive; there had been a Paul Ruegg in the town the arrested man's passport alleged he had come from, but this man had vanished long ago and there was no way of proving he was the man in a Chinese jail. Some time before their release we found out that the 'Swiss' Paul Ruegg was our Vienna associate Luft. I believe the only other person who knew this and survived the purges was Gerhard Eisler. Willy Muenzenberg never learned the real names of the subjects of his brilliant campaign, which gained an enormous moral victory for the Communist Party and gave much confidence to party members everywhere.[1]

While in jail the Lufts had known nothing of what was happening in the outside world or of the frenzied campaign on their behalf. When he came out Luft learned that the Left opposition had been defeated and that Trotsky had gone into exile. We heard from friends that on his release Luft expressed the desire to return to the U.S.S.R. but said that he would like to talk to

[1] An echo of this may be found in Richard Sorge's statements of much later to the Japanese police.

Trotsky first. We were not too surprised; it was just the kind of thing Luft could be expected to say. He did not see Trotsky but returned to the Soviet Union. No doubt he was dealt with immediately, for no one ever heard of him again.

Among those at the Embassy in Vienna when we were there was Ivan Zaporozhets, the N.K.V.D. representative, a good-natured giant who was not particularly intelligent. He got on with his job, and outside working hours devoted himself to his wife and children, ignoring all the petty intrigues and plots around him. These he left to his wife Rosa, a Ukrainian Jewish girl who, having known nothing but pogroms, suddenly found herself married to a high-ranking diplomat. Zaporozhets' main job consisted in keeping an eye on the remnants of the armies of General Wrangel which had retreated into Turkey after the Civil War and had mostly settled in the Balkans. He was also responsible for watching over the Balkan émigré organizations in Vienna. The White armies, though defeated and demoralized, might still represent a threat to the Soviet Union, but this could only happen with the connivance of their host governments. Zaporozhets' assignment, therefore, consisted in infiltrating not only the White remnants but the agencies of the Balkan governments, which, if possible, were to be influenced.

Zaporozhets did his work well and did not bother with his secondary assignment of supervising the Embassy staff. Though we never knew him very well, we knew that he was loyal and he eventually turned out to be helpful. His name was widely mentioned during the purge trials of the thirties.[1]

The military attaché at the Embassy who represented the Fourth Department was also concerned with the Balkans, but primarily with the Communist or pro-Communist para-military

[1] When Kirov was murdered in Leningrad in 1934, Zaporozhets, then deputy chief of the N.K.V.D. in Leningrad, and his chief Medved were arrested and both sentenced to three years' imprisonment for negligence. They apparently did not even serve out these relatively light sentences, for Krivitsky tells in his *I Was Stalin's Agent* (New York and London 1939) of having met Medved, completely free, two years later. At the third Moscow trial, however, Yagoda when questioned by Vyshinsky about his 'accomplice Zaporozhets' in the murder of Kirov, answered the accusation—as he did so many others—with 'It did not happen quite that way, but it does not matter'. The mere mention of Zaporozhets' name in this connection leaves no doubt as to his fate.

formations there. To a certain extent therefore both the
N.K.V.D. and the Fourth used the same approaches and net-
works and were interested in the same political groups, primarily
Balkan refugee organizations in Vienna.

One aim of Soviet policy at the time was to further interest
in a Balkan federation and it hoped to do this through the
various Communist parties of the area. Unfortunately most of
these parties consisted of a variety of left-wing groups that were
often at odds with one another. This was particularly true of the
Bulgarian party, which was numerically one of the most important but whose various elements were not under the control
of the central committee. A primary task was to re-establish
control over these scattered and independent factions, and
Ludwik, Gorski, and their colleagues made as many contacts as
possible with the Bulgarian Communists, dissident or otherwise.

After the failure of a Communist rising in 1923, the Bulgarian
party had transferred its Central Committee to Vienna, where
it succeeded in imposing dictatorial rule. Members both abroad
and in Bulgaria were expelled from the party on the slightest
pretext, because they were suspected of past, present, or poten-
tial dissidence or simply for petty personal reasons. The con-
sequence for those cut off from party contacts and funds was
often literally starvation.

A good friend of ours, Dr. Alexander Lykov, had such an
experience. He was an attractive and cultivated man who had
been a socialist before the war. While studying in Geneva
he had met many of the Bolshevik leaders. After the revolution he became a Communist, returned to Bulgaria, was
arrested several times, miraculously escaped death after the
failure of the rising, and came to Vienna. There a personal
enemy accused him of dissidence and he was expelled from the
party. This was a major blow to him, as he could no longer
carry on any political activity and could scarcely return to his
own country. Ludwik and his superiors in the Fourth, who
valued Lykov highly, did their best to persuade the Bulgarians
to reinstate him, but to no avail. Ludwik even appealed directly
to the Comintern, on one of his trips to Moscow, but they were
unwilling to intervene in the internal affairs of the Bulgarian
party. Soon after, Lykov left Vienna for Berlin, where he went

into business and gave up all political activity. We remained friends and saw him whenever we happened to be in Berlin. When the Nazis came to power he went to Scandinavia and that was the last I heard of him during Ludwik's lifetime. Later on I was told that he returned to Bulgaria after the war, along with other Bulgarian Communists who had survived the purges in Russia.

A number of Bulgarians did survive the terror, perhaps because of Dimitrov's protection, although I believe political considerations also played their part. Probably because of a long pro-Russian tradition, the Bulgarian government accepted the convenient fiction that the Comintern was a body over which the Soviet Union had no control, and was thus able to lock up its own Communists without taking an anti-Soviet position. This may have been instrumental in saving some of the Bulgarian Communists who fled to Moscow to escape the police of their own country. Many of them, who possibly had a good deal to account for to some of their comrades, were later on executed, as was Traicho Kostov, by their own people.

The complexities of Balkan politics and internal strife made Ludwik's work difficult. The Communists were blamed by the Bulgarian government for the blowing up of the cathedral in Sofia in April 1925, during a funeral service for General Georgiev, who had been killed by left-wing terrorists, and this led to a wave of terror. Arrests, torture, murders in prison as well as official executions disorganized the party. The Comintern had not—certain sources to the contrary notwithstanding—ordered the attack on the cathedral; it had little to gain and much to lose from such an act. The Bulgarian Communists were blamed for not being able to control their movement. The party itself blamed dissident elements outside the party, and some of its own more militant elements in turn accused the party of conniving with the government. There followed a wholesale settling of scores—many of them personal—in the Bulgarian party in Vienna.

Scarcely a month later the Macedonian revolutionary leader Todor Panitsa was shot and killed during a performance of *Peer Gynt* at the Vienna Burg Theater, by a young woman who had been a guest of the Panitsa family. Panitsa was not a Communist, nor was his associate Vlahov, but their interest in a Balkan federation movement coincided with that of the Soviets. Panitsa was obviously the victim of a plot by Macedonian former colleagues who considered him a traitor to their cause and had made use of a foolish and hysterical woman. Although we had few connections with Panitsa, we did have a link with Vlahov, and it was through him that I met one of the lawyers who had acted for the Panitsa family, the well-known Viennese Socialist Dr. Emil Maurer, when shortly afterwards we needed a lawyer ourselves.

A few days after the Panitsa affair, I was expecting Ludwik home for lunch with me and Dr. Lykov. When he had not come by three o'clock Dr. Lykov left. A few minutes later the doorbell rang, and two plainclothes policemen informed me that Ludwik had been arrested and that they had come to search the apartment. They either would not or could not tell me why he had been arrested and said I must go to the police to find out. As it was a Saturday afternoon, there was nothing I could do until Monday. I got in touch with Zaporozhets and he arranged for Vlahov, whom I had not met, to introduce me to Dr. Maurer.

Maurer's reaction, the first time he saw me, was characteristic. He threw up his hands and groaned: 'Oh, not the Balkans again . . . ' When he saw me come in with Vlahov, he took it for granted that it was some Balkan affair. For all I knew it might have had something to do with the Balkans; I had not the faintest idea of what it was all about. Maurer was too discreet to ask where I had met Vlahov, but was somewhat reassured when he discovered that at least I did not come from the Balkans. He immediately went with me to the police and told me that Ludwik would be out in no time. In fact he was not released for two months and we never did find out why he had been arrested.

During those two months I got to know Dr. Maurer quite well. He was extremely popular in Vienna, for he handled not only big political cases but those of any poor devil who could not afford a lawyer's fee. He was a self-made man who started out as a baker and became one of Vienna's best known lawyers, a Socialist leader and one of the organizers of the *Schutzbund,* the armed Socialist militia which in 1934 was to fight heroically against the fascist *Heimwehr*. His office was full of photographs of himself marching in demonstrations with Karl Kautsky and other great men of the socialist movement. He told me his greatest joy was to parade through the streets with the *Schutzbund*, a red sash round his prominent paunch, and that his only regret was that the first of May came only once a year. The last time I saw him was after the bitter street fighting of 1934, in which the Socialist militia was smashed and Starhemberg's fascist troops destroyed the city's magnificent working-class housing estates of which Maurer had been so proud. He was a broken man by then, and when the Nazis threatened in their turn, he emigrated to England. He came back to a ruined Vienna after the war.

In the political work Ludwik and Gorski were doing in Vienna, they had to gather their own information and use their own judgment in dealing with extremely complex problems such as the political and national rivalries among the Balkan countries, their main interest. It was a difficult assignment for young men with little or no previous experience in the field.

In theory their work was performed under the guidance of the local military attaché. In practice the military attachés—especially those who succeeded Inkov—not only knew a great deal less about the Balkans than Ludwik or Gorski but knew virtually nothing about Europe. These men all had considerable military experience from the war or the Civil War, but they were useless as far as political intelligence work was concerned. Many of them were completely unable to evaluate or understand the reports the men submitted and a surprising number showed signs of mental instability. Most had brought with them an extraordinary contempt for the capitalist world which they had never seen before and which they did not understand. This manifested itself in forms of exhibitionism which were worse than anything that took place in the Embassy. Sooner or later this was reported back to Moscow and transfers followed.

Since Moscow had no experienced men available to do its intelligence work or to train the young men starting out in it, a network had to be built out of nothing, and men like Ludwik, Gorski, or Krivitsky had to acquire for themselves the skills necessary to compete with the well-established and trained intelligence services of the other European states. There were no 'schools for agents', as certain romantically inclined writers would have one believe; the men were chosen for these assignments, as our friend Richard Sorge, who worked for the Fourth in the Far East, said later, 'for their integrity, talent, and devotion'.

In order to learn something about the Balkans Ludwik sought out men with first-hand knowledge—newspapermen first and through them former officers and civil servants who had worked in those countries. One of his Austrian contacts was a former officer of the Imperial General staff who had served in the Balkans and was now retired and only too glad to supplement his meagre income by supplying written reports on the area.

Ludwik's first meeting with this man was amusing. He went to the small Austrian town where the officer lived and made himself known; they went to a café for their discussion. Once they had sat down, Ludwik noticed that the other man kept staring at him and shaking his head. He finally asked the reason for this, but was answered by a question: 'Excuse me, do they have many more like you?' Ludwik was baffled and the old officer, visibly embarrassed, continued: 'I am very much impressed by you. Frankly, I expected someone with dirty fingernails!'

The officer was familiar with the minorities in the Empire and also knew quite well what a Russian might look like; a Communist, however, was a new experience for him and nothing in his background had prepared him for this. What might a Bolshevik look like? Perhaps like a bandit, but not necessarily so; most probably like a tramp. Ludwik became quite friendly with this old gentleman, who not only supplied valuable analyses of the situation in the Balkans but told him many instructive anecdotes about the old Dual Monarchy.[1] As for the officer, he found out that there were Bolsheviks who had clean fingernails.

There was no shortage of intelligence to be had, but what was

[1] Among these was the story, then little known, of Colonel Alfred Redl, who before the war was found to have committed a breach of honour in supplying the Russians with military information. The Austrian army, in accordance with its time-honoured custom, placed a loaded pistol at Redl's disposal and the colonel duly shot himself—thus making it impossible to find out with whom he had been working, what his channels had been, and most important of all, how much and what kind of information he had actually handed over.

sadly lacking was the skill and experience to evaluate it. Vienna was literally flooded with documents, most, if not all, forgeries, either by White Russian émigré organizations or the Polish counter-intelligence. False or genuine, these documents had to be acquired—and paid for, photographed, and eventually sent to Moscow. One document sent back purported to be a secret agreement between the Polish and French general staffs out-lining their future military collaboration against the Soviet Union. It was only in Moscow that this 'treaty' was recognized as an outrageous forgery. The document, allegedly composed by the French general staff, was couched in the most incredible French, with syntax and spelling no Frenchman could have perpetrated. Unfortunately, no one working for the Fourth De-partment at the Embassy in Vienna had known any French.

Moscow was lenient in such matters. It knew that its young, untrained agents could not help being taken in and probably it also considered that this was the only way they could learn their jobs. The men in the field took it badly, however. It raised the old question of whether they were serving the revolutionary cause by defending the Soviet Union or whether they were not in fact—though unwittingly—harming it by sending back mis-information, and by doing a job for which they had no ability and especially no liking. It also demoralized the men and they began to wonder what point there was in pitting themselves against the intelligence services of the capitalist nations. Many began to look on their jobs as futile or, like Fedia, to sneer at reports as 'a pack of lies'. It took years of hard work and successes such as Krivitsky's helping to break the Japanese code[1] or Ludwik's placing an agent high in the British services, before this inferiority complex was overcome. Such major achieve-ments, of course, were rare. The run-of-the-mill activity re-mained strenuous, and the hazardous work was often marked by failure. With the years, however, there developed a feeling of professional skill and confidence, and failures were accepted as *risques du métier*.

---

[1] Though Krivitsky in his ghost-written book (op. cit.) readily took credit for operations he had nothing to do with, unaccountably he mentions only casually his greatest *coup*: the securing of copies of correspondence in Germany in 1936 which, when decoded, revealed the secret pact the Nazis had made with Japan.

CHAPTER V

Prague and Amsterdam

In 1927 Ludwik made a trip to Moscow to see some of his Fourth Department colleagues and also to receive the Order of the Red Banner—then the highest Soviet decoration—which he had been awarded 'for services to the Revolution'. The decree awarding him the decoration was published early in 1928.

His arrest by the Austrian police, though unexplained, had made Ludwik a liability in Vienna, and on his return from this trip to Moscow he was transferred to Prague. Much to my regret we stayed there, I believe, scarcely a year. Prague was exhilarating after the hectic atmosphere of Vienna. Not only was the town very beautiful, but life seemed much easier there. Everything was plentiful and much cheaper than in Austria— in fact the Austrians used to come regularly to Czechoslovakia to buy shoes and clothing, which cost less and were of much better quality.

The people we met in Prague were different from those in Vienna. There were fewer refugees from the Balkans and so less intrigue, and those who had fled to Prague from the U.S.S.R. were mostly artists, intellectuals, and university professors. These people were not opposed to socialism as such, but had left the Soviet Union in order to be free, as they found they were in Czechoslovakia, to pursue their intellectual work. This feeling of freedom somehow communicated itself to us.

From the point of view of Ludwik's work the situation in Prague looked promising. Along with the decoration he had been given much greater initiative and freedom than he had had at the Embassy in Vienna. Of course he had much more responsibility as well, and this meant more frequent absences from home on trips to Berlin or Moscow. His assignment in Prague was to organize a network to operate in Poland.

Czechoslovakia was not on good terms with its neighbour and was not disposed to interfere with Soviet intelligence operations directed at Poland so long as they did not endanger Czech security. Furthermore, the Czechoslovak Communist Party, although rent by internal struggles, was large, powerful, and well-connected, and useful contacts could easily be established through its membership.

Ludwik, however, had hardly begun to organize operations from Prague when the Fourth Department decided to give him a much more important assignment; he was to direct operations aimed at obtaining information in Great Britain. The headquarters were not to be in England but in the Netherlands.

Ludwik, who had been in Holland before, had chosen it as the most suitable base for political work directed against Britain. The Fourth Department usually preferred its agent—or 'resident', as he was called—to live in the country his work was aimed at. This was justified and indeed essential in the case of Poland, for instance, where the resident's work was mainly gathering military information, but it was not necessarily true elsewhere. As Britain was not, like Poland, an immediate neighbour of the Soviet Union and as no directly military espionage operations were contemplated, there was little reason to have a resident in England. The Netherlands were much more easily accessible from the rest of Europe, and seemed much safer to the Soviets.

Britain was greatly respected and envied in those days, especially for its intelligence service; and as one of the foremost capitalist powers, it was considered the most dangerous enemy of the Soviet Union. Several inimical acts, such as the British Government's having chosen in 1924 to treat the 'Zinoviev letter', possibly a forgery of Polish–White Russian origin, as genuine, or the raids on the Soviet trade mission in London, where no incriminating documents were stored or found, had done more to stimulate the then flagging morale of Soviet agents than any Communist propaganda could have done. The Soviets were of course aware that some of these acts were motivated by internal political considerations, but in carrying them out the British reinforced the zeal of many an agent. They also unwittingly helped to bring about the reorganization of the

Soviet services. Unlike their British counterparts the Soviets found they could not carry on effective intelligence work through military attachés, and were forced to build up elaborate covers; this contributed to the gradual separation between legal and illegal apparatuses, and to an increase in efficiency and security.

The high repute of the British intelligence service and the fact that members of the 'best families' in Britain did not hesitate to serve in it out of pure patriotism also had a tonic effect on Soviet agents. What a British patriot could do for his country—so went the reasoning—a Communist could do for the Soviet Union, only better. Soviet agents were convinced that their historic role gave them an innate advantage in dealing with world politics, that—in Bukharin's words—'We Communists can hear the grass grow under our feet'.

British intelligence agents did not reciprocate the high opinion the Soviets had of them. They appeared to consider the Soviets mere rabble. This attitude was shared by British diplomats, who, when they met men like Chicherin or Rakovsky—men certainly their equals if not their superiors intellectually and culturally—at international conferences, grudgingly regarded them as exceptions. This feeling of contempt for the Soviets had prevailed throughout Europe since the war ended. Thus German officers, defeated and humiliated by the Allies, still preferred to deal with their former enemies, whom they considered their social equals, rather than with a Radek or a Krestinsky, representatives of their temporary ally.

Our stay in Holland in 1928 and part of 1929 was the most pleasant of our life abroad. Everything in the country seemed to lend itself to relaxation. After our years in war-torn and in-flation-ridden central Europe, this peaceful little country which had not known war, civil war, or famine was enchanting to us. Amsterdam with its canals and patrician houses, the nearby sea and miles of flowerbeds surrounding the city, was beautiful, and the weeks we spent strolling about looking for a place to live have ever since evoked the most pleasant of memories. We knew, of course, that our stay would only be temporary and that problems would soon arise again, but all this seemed in a distant future. The fact that we had no direct communication with 'home' was an additional blessing, although we knew very well that, should the need arise, it would be possible for 'home' to get in touch with us in a matter of hours.

Ludwik had made friends in Holland on earlier trips and also took up the contacts made by his predecessor, Max Friedman, whom we came to know very well. Max, who later took the name Maximov[1] when he lived in the U.S.S.R., was a tall, handsome man who had started out as an art student, professional training that stood him in good stead as a cover. He had travelled widely, and not only knew his way round Western Europe—and, what is more, round those strata of society to which many others did not have access—but spoke several languages fluently. In the early 1920s he had visited the Soviet Union and, liking it there, had decided to remain. Through his relation Unshlikht he was given an assignment in the Fourth Department and was sent to the Netherlands.

The striking thing about Max was that—unlike the others in the Fourth—he was not a Communist. Not only was he not a member of the party—though he never gave up trying to be admitted—he had neither the psychological make-up nor the mental attitudes of a true Communist. He sympathized with communism, of course, he was devoted to it and to his friends, and certainly acted out of pure idealism; but he was never a true Communist.[2] Even his wife, Anna Riazonova, who could with justification be called a 'hard-core Communist', never succeeded in making one of Max.

Max's cosmopolitan background gave him easy entrée to intellectual and artistic circles, and one of his major tasks in Holland was to attract left-wing and liberal intellectuals to the Soviet cause; the U.S.S.R. enjoyed the prestige of having such people as sympathizers. Max's acquaintance with prominent Socialists such as the poetess Henriette Roland-Holst, an old friend of Rosa Luxemburg's, and others, was very useful, as was his friendship with the well-known Dutch sculptor Hildo

[1] Krivitsky (op. cit., pp. 269ff.) refers to this man as 'Maximov-Unschlicht', presumably because Max was distantly related to the Polish Communist leader, later Soviet Vice-Commissar of War.

[2] Krivitsky's assertion that Max was a 'rock-ribbed Stalinist' is quite erroneous and incomprehensible.

Crop. Crop liked many things about the U.S.S.R., though he deplored the 'socialist realism' of its architecture and sculpture; he nonetheless remained a good friend of Max's.

As well as the 'sympathizers' Max had collected, Ludwik intended to find out what use could be made of the Dutch Communist Party. Even when he had orders to the contrary, an agent kept up contacts with the local party, which at times proved invaluable. This was the case in the Netherlands. The Dutch party, which was completely legal, was very useful, probably because Moscow paid little attention to it. This does not mean that what happened in the Soviet party did not matter to the Dutch Communists. On the contrary, there were serious opposition movements in Holland and after Trotsky was expelled quite a few members resigned from the Dutch party. They did not necessarily share Trotsky's views, but to them—as to Communists everywhere—Trotsky was a symbol and they could not conceive of a Communist movement without him.

On the other hand, many Dutch Communists, though hurt by Trotsky's expulsion, remained in the party, where they could discuss the case without being expelled, and although Moscow considered the Dutch oppositionists, and the party itself for that matter, as not worth bothering about, both groups remained devoted to the Soviet Union. To them the Russian revolution had been a tremendous experience, more so than to other Communists, perhaps because of their peaceful and orderly lives. Many of them had gone to the Soviet Union after the October revolution, others had gone to help the Communists in Hungary, and no matter how shaken by the opposition struggles, they never held us responsible for what was happening in the Soviet party. They could always be appealed to, and they never refused their assistance. In countries with much larger Communist parties which were very much under Moscow's influence, practical matters, such as cover addresses, were always a problem; in Holland addresses and passports could be found without trouble.

The Dutch Communists were as different from other Communists as the Dutch were from other nations. The Dutch party was living proof that a Communist party can be part of a nation. Communists proclaim themselves to be above bourgeois society and bourgeois society in turn considers Communists not as part of itself but as a fringe growth. But the Dutch Communists were, if anything, even more Dutch than the Dutch bourgeoisie.

To us the attachment of the Dutch Communists to their royal house was a source of amazement and delight. The marital life of the Queen and the pranks of the Prince Consort interested them very much. One of our friends even pretended when the Prince died that a clause in his will forced the Queen to wear white mourning clothes for a whole year, thus making her look even stouter than she was as a revenge for her past stinginess to him. The travels of Princess Juliana, affectionately known as Juliantje, to European courts in search of a husband were watched with concern. They were especially interested when on one of her visits to England some of her jewels were stolen during a religious service and, as none of the exalted persons present could possibly have been guilty, the two men who came under suspicion were Russians, Litvinov and a former archduke.

Later on, when the Princess had married, I asked the friend who told us these stories whether it was really true that a collection was being made in the party for a gift to the royal baby she was expecting. 'Why not?' he answered: 'She is a really nice girl and associated with Communists and Socialists at the University. Let us hope it is a boy, a little prince of our own.'

We soon adjusted to this unexpected behaviour on the part of Communists. Never before had we had so many friends among Communists and oppositionists alike and never had so many people known us where we lived. In other European countries our address had been known only to a few people designated by Moscow, but in Holland this was impossible. In the summer, when we took our three-year-old son to the seaside, our friends visited us with their families, and we in turn went to see them. We often visited Max's friend, the sculptor Hildo Crop, at his home on the Amstel. We also knew Professor Carvalho, a fine scholar, Richard Manuel, H. C. Pieck, and others with whom we formed lasting friendships, some of which I have kept up in spite of wars and concentration camps.

One of our closest friends was Henricus (Henryk) Sneevliet,

a member of parliament and leader of the railway workers' union. A friend and disciple of Rosa Luxemburg, before the First World War he had gone out to Dutch Indonesia, leaving his wife and twin sons behind, to organize native labour. After the mutiny of the Dutch warship, *The Seven Provinces,* he was arrested and expelled from Indonesia. He returned to Holland, and during the war remained in close touch with the leaders of the Second International. He took part in the organization of the Kienthal and Zimmerwald congresses in Switzerland. After the October revolution he went to the Soviet Union where, under the pseudonym Maring, he represented the left wing of the Javanese Socialist Party at the second congress of the Third International, which this party joined in 1920.

Shortly afterwards Sneevliet attended the first congress of the Chinese Communist Party in Shanghai. A young Ukrainian woman called Sima, who accompanied him on this trip, later became his second wife. When Joffe (later Ambassador in Vienna) arrived in China as the first representative of the Russian party Sneevliet joined forces with him and stayed in China for two years. It was largely thanks to his work that Sun Yat-sen accepted the Communists into the Kuomintang. But Sneevliet was already beginning to resent Soviet interference in trade union matters, in which—in spite of his friendship and admiration for Joffe—he felt himself better qualified than the Russians.

Speaking of his first disagreements with the Russians, Sneevliet said that they knew nothing about either colonial peoples or trade unions but were always trying to outwit him, adding: 'It did not work, for I am a Catholic.' This was not a profession of faith but a reference to the prevailing opinion that Dutch Catholics had an inherent shrewdness, acquired from their long struggle against Protestant domination.

Sneevliet's original misgivings were soon reinforced by a much more serious ideological quarrel. A group of Bolsheviks led by Shliapnikov, the so-called Workers' Opposition, challenged the party leadership on the trade union question. They demanded that the trade unions be made independent of the party and also protested against the stifling of democracy within the party itself. After a protracted debate which brought them no satisfaction, this group appealed, over the heads of the Russian Central Committee, to the Comintern.

The Communist parties of the West had followed the trade union debate with great interest and the Workers' Opposition had the sympathy of many party members. The group's direct appeal to the Comintern, at that time not yet completely subservient to the Russian party, appeared in the eyes of Western Communists to be fully justified. They were therefore surprised when the body examining their appeal, an international commission led by the experienced Clara Zetkin, rejected it on the grounds that no unfairness had been shown by the Russian party to the Workers' Opposition group. The other opposition groups, afraid of endangering party unity by washing their dirty linen in public, supported the Russian Central Committee. All stood by the party and, as Trotsky said on another occasion, 'at attention before the party'.

The rank and file of the Russian party was generally unaware of the nature and even of the existence of these opposition struggles. The cloudy phraseology of leadership and opposition alike eluded the understanding of the party masses. Thus when in 1927 Trotsky brought his differences with the party into the open by going 'into the streets' with an attempted demonstration on the anniversary of the revolution, he found the masses astonished at the existence of these divergences and quite incapable of grasping their import. These same masses, it is true, were shocked at Trotsky's expulsion and unable to visualize a party without him, but by then it was much too late. In the Netherlands and Germany, however, the Workers' Opposition created a deeper impression and led to many resignations. When Sneevliet returned home from the Far East he resigned from the party and founded a publication called *Tribune,* after which his group was contemptuously referred to by Moscow as 'Tribunists'.

Earlier, at the second congress of the International, Sneevliet had met M. N. Roy, the representative of the Indian movement. Like most other delegates Sneevliet was fascinated by the young Indian. The two men had much in common as both represented colonial peoples; but Sneevliet, although he had been expelled from Indonesia, was a citizen of a free and democratic country, while Roy was a colonial subject. Sneevliet could adhere freely to the programme of the Third International and its policy of promoting revolution among oppressed peoples, but by the same token he had no hesitation in breaking with it once he became convinced that the Soviet state no longer subscribed to these aims. He rapidly came to the belief that the Soviet Union would not, as a state, continue to antagonize colonial powers with which it wished to have normal diplomatic relations.

In his many discussions with Ludwik, Sneevliet used his own experience to demonstrate the impossibility of serving both a particular state and the international workers' movement. Ludwik agreed with him that the only way truly to serve the working class movement would be to cease working exclusively for the Soviet Union. The Comintern having become an instrument of the Soviet state, one had the alternative of breaking completely with the U.S.S.R., or of continuing to serve that state, as Ludwik was ready to do. Sneevliet, with reservations, accepted this.

M. N. Roy, on the other hand, whose goal was India's independence, was enthusiastic in his espousal of the International. While Sneevliet had realized rapidly that the Comintern could not fulfil its programme, Roy saw in it a means of realizing his goal. Sneevliet left the Comintern and the party; Roy remained and became deeply embroiled in the internal affairs of the Russian party, siding with the leadership or the opposition according to the amount of support he received for his own cause : Indian independence. He left the Comintern only when he became convinced that Russia had abandoned all intention of promoting a world revolution and was concentrating on 'building socialism in one country'.

In spite of their political differences Sneevliet remained in close contact with the Indians. Many of them had been educated in England and had connections there which were, of course, very useful to Ludwik. Ludwik had known Sneevliet since the mid-1920s, and it was only natural that he should call on him for assistance when he came to Holland. Sneevliet considered Ludwik's assignment part of the defence of the U.S.S.R., and worth supporting. His extensive contacts, both in his own country and among the labour unions in Britain, were extremely valuable to Ludwik.

The picture of Soviet espionage operations given by writers without first-hand experience is of a fairly rigid pattern laid down by order from Moscow, operating through networks organized along much the same lines in each country and closely supervised by the centre. This is more or less accurate—though considerably over-simplified—for the period which followed the great purges of the 1930s, but it is completely untrue of the earlier years. Far from following a fixed pattern, the methods of organization then differed from country to country and depended on local circumstances, often on luck, and, perhaps most important, on the personality of the resident—a man who was willing to spy for the Soviet Union out of ideological commitment.

Many of the time-honoured methods were still being used even in the post-war period, for example by the Canadian spy ring which was uncovered by the defection of the Soviet code clerk Gouzenko, but the men applying them were completely different. Marked by the Soviet terror, they appear from the Royal Commission report on this episode to be of much lower calibre; they are afraid of responsibilities, asking permission before carrying out even the most trifling acts and in doing so grossly violating elementary security precautions; they are over-anxious to achieve results, in order to protect themselves against criticism 'from home'; and the techniques they use are clumsy, such as forcing someone to accept a small sum and asking for a receipt, in the apparent belief that once a man has accepted money from them he will for ever be 'theirs'.

In the Canadian network there were no Poles, Latvians, or Germans (the nationalities most commonly found in the Soviet intelligence service of the twenties), only Russians. And those Russians appear to have been selected, not on ideological grounds, but primarily because they had roots in the Soviet Union and families who remained there. They were totally lacking in knowledge of the West: its languages, its culture; they do not even seem to have known anyone there. This background ensured their complete loyalty to Moscow, but deprived them of any initiative. The extent to which they were merely cogs in a machine is evident from their often not even knowing where they were being sent: Gouzenko was under the impression that he was going to the Far East, and was surprised to find himself in Canada. The most striking difference, however, is the manner in which these men broke with their apparatus. Gouzenko, having decided to defect, took all the documents he felt might be of importance and handed them over to the Canadian police. As his recruitment had not been ideological, neither was his break—in sharp contrast with the men who broke earlier, in a different manner, and died for their convictions.

Men like Richard Sorge or Ludwik did not believe in the tactics Gouzenko followed, nor did they ever attempt to use coercion. If for some reason a good source of information dried up, or a collaborator refused to work, Ludwik used to quote an old saying, 'The Lord giveth, the Lord taketh away, there is no use crying over spilt milk.' The men of the Fourth Department, 'recruited' as Sorge said 'on an ideological basis', and known to be thus motivated, had a great deal of freedom of action. Much was left to the judgement of the resident, although he obviously consulted periodically with his superiors.

Moscow, seeing Holland as an important outpost for political activity against Britain, attached considerable importance to Ludwik's assignment. He was to stay for several years and, in order to give himself a semblance of legality, was to open a business, in other words a cover firm. Ludwik thought cover firms more of a liability than an asset and knew that sooner or later they caused trouble, occasionally even leading to the detection of an agent, but Moscow believed the step to be essential. No one knew how efficient the police or counter-espionage agencies were likely to be in Holland. Anyone coming from Moscow, or who had worked in Poland, naturally enough expected police everywhere; although in a free, democratic country the police might not be as brutal as in Poland, they would certainly, it was thought, be more efficient. As it turned out, the Dutch police were so used to having foreigners in their country that they paid us no attention whatever and all the steps Ludwik took to make himself respectable were a complete waste of time.

One possible cover was a small art gallery in Amsterdam which had served as such in the days of Max Friedman. Ludwik, however, felt that a gallery would be too conspicuous and decided instead to open a small business by which he could, if need arose, prove his *bona fides*. Although he did not like business and did not really understand it, he opened a wholesale stationery firm, deliberately keeping it small so that he could better control it. A young former Communist who had joined Sneevliet's group, Jef Swart, himself in business, was entrusted with the running of the firm. The only other employee was a friend of Swart's, Pisaro, also a former Communist, who knew nothing of the firm's purpose and who believed Jef's story of a small inheritance which had enabled him to go into business for himself. The manager of the business had to be a Dutchman, but Ludwik could, if necessary, prove that he was the owner.

The business in fact made sufficient profits to finance Ludwik's stay in Holland and to pay for Jef's trips abroad. Predictably enough, it also got us into trouble, although not in the way we expected. Jef got involved in a love affair and, to make matters, worse, with Sneevliet's wife Sima. She left Sneevliet for Jef, taking along their small daughter. Sneevliet was deeply shaken by this and, although he knew we had had nothing to do with the matter, it affected our relationship and we saw less and less of him. Jef did not wish to remain in Amsterdam; the business began to suffer and had to be liquidated. Jef eventually went to the Soviet Union and we never heard from him again. Pisaro was to disappear into Auschwitz during the Nazi occupation of Holland.

Ludwik naturally did not advertise his friendship with Sneevliet in Moscow. Almost certainly, however, this link with a known oppositionist was no secret to the Soviets, who preferred not to make an issue of it any more than they did over his contacts with other members of the opposition. Ludwik did not let them know of his dealings with Jef Swart, but this was different, as Swart had been an insignificant party member, and as a businessman, he was very useful. His unfortunate love

affair, however, not only ruined the business but led indirectly to Ludwik's asking to be relieved of his assignment in
Holland.

More directly responsible were the contacts Ludwik had
made with the Irish. Although fascinated by the Soviet operation and willing to collaborate with anyone against the
British, the Irish turned out to be of little use and in fact were
the unwitting cause of trouble. As they were convinced that
their own problems were the world's most important—this
was even true of the Irish Communist Party, which was as
nationalist as the other parties, and from 1925 onwards
practically ceased to exist—Ludwik never took these Irish
contacts seriously. Unfortunately Scotland Yard did. It had the
Irishmen shadowed and when they met Ludwik in Holland
he and they were sketched and these quite accurate sketches
were reproduced in the British press.

The publication of Ludwik's picture in the British papers
and the failure of the firm in Amsterdam were not however
the only reasons pointing to a move. Ludwik had begun to
feel uneasy among his friends in Holland, who, although
disillusioned with the Soviet party, were, as he put it, 'untouched' by events in the Soviet Union and on the whole
quite unaffected by the upheavals in the party. This was
understandable, as they had no intimate ties, as he had, with
the Soviet Union; but it affected his view of Holland as a base
of operations. He therefore went to Berlin, where he met one of
his superiors and asked for permission to return to the Soviet
Union.

A visit to Moscow was the usual procedure whenever a
change of residence was contemplated, as a new assignment
was always preceded by consultations and discussions. It did not
mean that one was returning to the Soviet Union for good. In
the normal course of events, however, a suggestion for a move
originated in Moscow and not with the resident, and in this
sense Ludwik's action was an unusual one. In spite of the fact
that a transfer had not been suggested by Moscow, his request
was met halfway and it was agreed that he should return to
Moscow pending a new assignment. On his return from
Berlin he began to make preparations for handing his post over

to a successor so that he would not have to return to Holland from Moscow on his way to take up a new assignment.

The trip to Moscow was delayed for a considerable length of time, partly because Ludwik needed time to wind up his affairs in Holland but mainly because—as he had learned in Berlin—events in the Soviet party were having serious repercussions in the Fourth Department. Ludwik had few illusions as to what he would find in the U.S.S.R. and none about the future of a revolutionary movement. The forcible 'Bolshevization' of the European Communist parties, the constant changes of leadership imposed on them by Moscow, and the theory of 'social-fascism' then being propounded by the Comintern, had affected him deeply. Stalin's slogan of 'socialism in one country' showed clearly that henceforth every other interest was to be subordinated to those of the Soviet Union. Ludwik remained willing and ready to defend those interests through his work, but he could not accept the deliberate abandonment of the international revolution. He believed that in spite of the 'Bolshevization', or perhaps even because of it, there remained much useful work to be done in the parties of Europe.

Had he been free, Ludwik would never have returned to the Soviet Union. But in his position, and believing as he did in the necessity of defending the Soviet Union, he asked for reassignment without knowing whether this would mean another post abroad directly concerned with that defence or an assignment in the U.S.S.R. where he would be involved in the 'building of socialism'. When he did finally leave Holland, he did not know whether he was going to Moscow for a short time or for ever. We decided that until this question had been resolved I would move to Berlin with our child, where Ludwik could get in touch with me more easily than in Holland.

CHAPTER VI

Moscow, 1929-1932

I

It was some time before Ludwik could let me know what our future was to be, and when he finally asked me to join him in Moscow he told me to bring along two folding cots and some warm clothing; this was a clear indication that we would spend the winter there. It was not until the autumn of 1929 that I was ready to leave, as I had to wait for a passport. I sent my heavy luggage ahead, as I would have my hands full travelling with our small son.

In those days trains leaving Berlin for Moscow were fairly full. German engineers, unable to find work at home, often went to the Soviet Union to work either for German firms or on their own. In our compartment was an engineer who had been to the U.S.S.R. several times on behalf of his firm. He was therefore able to tell two other Germans in the compartment about working and living conditions in the Soviet Union. One of these men, also an engineer, was quite bitter at having to go to Russia. He kept saying he would never have gone to help the Bolsheviks build up their industry or ever have agreed to live among barbarians, had he been able to find a job elsewhere. The man who had been to the U.S.S.R. tried to reassure him, saying the Russians were not barbarians, but that it was really foolish of him to have come, given his opinions. He added that he knew very well the Russians would not have called in foreign specialists unless they needed them, and that after all they were paying good salaries, working conditions were decent for foreigners, and he could not help but sympathize with the Russians' tremendous efforts to industrialize their country.

After a while the other two men left the compartment. The German engineer asked me very politely what I was going to do in the Soviet Union. I told him I was joining my husband who represented a Dutch firm there. I was afraid he might ask me about my husband's alleged company, but he asked me instead whether I had ever been to the U.S.S.R. before. When I told him that I had not he began to tell me how beautiful the old town of Moscow was and that the experience of being in the U.S.S.R. made it well worth putting up with some inconveniences. He also told me that he would be staying at the Grand Hotel, and that, if I would permit it, on his return to Germany he would be delighted to send me packages from abroad which he said were highly appreciated in Moscow. While he obviously had no interest in my husband's firm, he was beginning to show altogether too much interest in me and I began to wonder how I might get rid of him.

As we neared the border I became quite anxious, since I knew my luggage would probably not be examined and that this could not fail to arouse his suspicions. I did not succeed in getting separated from him at the customs and in fact wound up standing next to him. Fortunately he was so busy opening and repacking his suitcases that he failed to notice mine had not been opened. When we got back to our compartment he asked me: 'They are pretty thorough, aren't they? How did you fare?'—'Not too badly,' I said.

Now that we were in Soviet territory the time was rapidly approaching when our day coach would be converted to a sleeping car. I noticed that the next compartment was occupied by a single woman, and when the engineer had gone out for a short time I asked the conductor, in Russian, whether it would not be better if my child and I were to share a compartment with a woman rather than with a strange man. The conductor, a cheerful young man, laughed: 'Why, citizen, we are in the Soviet Union now. Don't tell me you are afraid of some dirty bourgeois who is out of a job in his own country and looking for one in ours?' So I had to stay in my compartment. Luckily the engineer went quietly to sleep.

Nevertheless, the encounter ended embarrassingly. At the station in Moscow early next morning I was met by Felix Gorski, and at the very last minute, by Willy. The latter, now an engineer officer, had just come off duty and was dressed in his

Red Army officer's uniform. As was his custom, he embraced me and tossed me in the air. Felix berated him: 'You idiot, don't you know any better than to come to meet her in uniform? Don't you know that this train is full of foreigners who might recognize her when she goes back abroad? And don't you know that as far as foreigners are concerned all uniforms are G.P.U. uniforms?' One of the foreigners who saw us was, of course, the German engineer. We were to pass frequently in the street and at the Grand Hotel, where I too stayed, but we merely nodded politely to each other. I can imagine what he thought of a Dutch housewife who had never been to the Soviet Union before, but who was met at the station by Red Army officers. I suppose he was very glad he had not made any nasty comments about the Soviet Union to me.

Willy was not in the least bit abashed by Felix's dressing down, but immediately picked up my son who, once out of the station, asked him: 'Why do they have horse-drawn sledges in Paris?'—'Paris?' said Willy. 'But you are not in Paris, you are in Moscow!'—'Oh,' said the boy, 'that is even nicer. But then why did Mother tell me we were going to Paris?'

The entrance to the Grand Hotel was guarded by two huge, moth-eaten stuffed bears, the delight of my son, who always patted them on the head when he walked by. The room Ludwik had taken for us there was small, just big enough for two cots and a tiny table. But we were warm and had our meals at the hotel, a big advantage, for though Moscow was still the best-supplied city in the Soviet Union, the whole country had plunged from the relative affluence of the N.E.P. to the near-famine of the Five-Year Plans. In the weeks we spent in the hotel, before our luggage arrived and before the place we were to live in was ready, our little room was always crowded, for all our friends in Moscow were waiting for something, as we were. The hotel staff regarded us as foreigners and treated us accordingly. Whenever someone came to see us one of the staff would knock at the door on the pretext of checking the plumbing or the electricity in order to get a good look at our visitor. The performance was of course quite pointless, for the hotel manager knew who we were but could not let his zealous underlings know.

Ludwik told me that we were to be in Moscow for quite a while. He took me to the former residential section on the Smolensk Boulevard to show me where we were going to live, a one-room barracks with a huge Russian stove built on to a larger house which before the revolution had been occupied by one family. The house, where staff officers of the Red Army now lived, was in bad repair and very crowded. About fift— people lived there—a dozen families, most with children and sometimes domestic help living with them, and almost always some relative from the country staying more or less per- manently. Our room was linked to the main house by a very draughty gangway which led to a huge kitchen, which we shared with seven other families. It was furnished with seven identical little kitchen tables, a petrol cooker—a so-called Primus, a sink, and a kitchen range which was lit on family washdays, fortunately frequent, and thus gave an additional place to put a pot on. On the door to the bathroom was a roster listing the order in which families were allowed to use the bath, once every ten days. Beyond this were the rooms of the other families, a toilet whose door never closed properly, and at the end of the corridor the telephone. There was also an upper storey, which had been the servant's quarters in the old days, and where five other families now lived

Our barracks room was quite large but it had a low ceiling and only two windows of which only one pane could be opened. It was flimsily built of some cheap, thin material which was certainly not warm enough for winter. Even less inviting was that draughty gangway to the kitchen and to the toilet. Still, it was the best one could get in those days and it even had the advantage of affording some privacy, whereas the families in the main house lived side by side and were constantly in each other's way. Ludwik managed to get some wood to make a partition behind which our child slept and he also obtained a requisition for a table and four stools. Somebody gave us a rather nice-looking small cupboard and an iron bedstead and another friend got us a bed for the child. With these possessions, plus the two cots that were coming from Berlin, we had the essentials for our new home.

When the room was finished, and our belongings had

arrived so that we could move in, we settled down to share the life of our neighbours. In the evening, when the meals were being prepared, there was a great deal of traffic in the kitchen with all the children running around. The women would cook while the men bathed the children on their bath days. Before and after their baths the children had to be wrapped up in blankets and carried through the icy corridor. Under the staircase to the upper floor was the 'red corner' where the children were supposed to play, but they preferred to run up and down the rickety stairs shouting and yelling. The noise was such that one of our neighbours wore earmuffs in summer and winter in order to be able to read. It is true that he and his wife had no children; those of us who had them were more indulgent.

The street entrance to the house was permanently boarded up and everybody used a back entrance that took them past our windows on their way to the kitchen or to their rooms. In summer the children were outdoors all day and in the evening the adults played volley-ball in the yard outside, so that we had to keep our windows—which could otherwise have been opened in the summer—permanently shut against the clouds of dust.

The passage to the kitchen was always dark, for the electric bulb which was supposed to stay lit all night to keep thieves away was regularly stolen. To prevent this a metal grille was placed round it; next morning both grille and bulb were gone. After that we gave up and bumped into each other in the darkness. Bulbs were very scarce, and the few that were produced were for export. We were supposed to be able to get them at our co-operative but they almost never had any and the hunt for them was continual. Occasionally Willy would bring one which I kept in reserve. Tactfully, I never asked him where he got them. One day when I was meeting him at the entrance to the Military Academy where he taught engineering, there was the sound of glass smashing in the hall. Willy had dropped a light bulb. The other officers walking by only smiled. It was quite obvious now where he got the bulbs, but no one except me seemed in the least surprised: they all did the same thing. Willy laughed. 'Don't worry, I'll get you another one!'

Around six o'clock in the evening the communal kitchen in our house was jammed with people and all the Primus stoves were hissing loudly. We all ate the same thing, usually frozen fish from the Arctic and macaroni which looked like grey cardboard. The men would join their wives in the kitchen and all the children were running about. One of the men, a Caucasian, was fond of telling jokes about Stalin. 'Do you know what Stalin dreamed last night?' he would ask. 'Stalin saw Lenin in his dream and said to him: "Look, comrade Lenin, all the masses are with me."—"No," Lenin answered, "they are with me!" ' Nobody laughed at that joke; the allusion to the masses who were either silent or dead was all too clear. In those years Stalin had no popular support and the 'masses' had no love for him, but on the other hand people were not yet afraid and did not hesitate to tell such jokes.

From time to time the house 'commandant', one of our neighbours, would call a 'house meeting' to discuss certain problems. He would announce, for instance, that he had obtained trucks for the delivery of firewood but that the men of the house would have to fell the trees themselves on their next free day. This free day, called '*sobotnik*', was the sixth day following five days of work. It was supposed to be a day of rest, but in fact every Soviet citizen was called upon to contribute his sixth day 'voluntarily' to the speedier fulfilment of the current Five-Year Plan. In order to ensure uninterrupted work-schedules the free days were staggered; since not all the men in the house were off on the same day, the collection of the firewood was a long drawn-out affair.

Much-needed repairs to the house could seldom be made because of the difficulty of getting materials, but they were discussed at many meetings which took up the best part of an evening after a day's work. At one such meeting I learned that our house was 'classified' as an historic monument and that although the Red Army had the use of it, it belonged to the Commissariat of Arts which had to approve any work done on it. I asked why such a seemingly insignificant building was classified. Because, our chairman answered, it was three hundred years old; it was known to be that old because Napoleon had slept in it. Intrigued, I asked whether anything was known about the house before Napoleon. The chairman, sensing that something was not quite right about his dates, closed the discussion by saying firmly: 'It is an historic monument and Napoleon did sleep here.' Historic or not, the house went on decaying and the commission that was to come and indicate which parts of it could be touched never came.

We had our own 'improvement' programme, part of a campaign launched by the city of Moscow to improve sanitary conditions in living quarters. The Fourth Department had appointed its medical officer and one other person, myself, as the 'sanitary cell' for our house. It became my job to survey the sanitary conditions of the house and of two nearby shacks which belonged to it.

I knew very well that in our crowded quarters no improvement was really possible. In the one sink in the kitchen in the early hours of the morning the men would wash with one hand, clutching the soap with the other lest it disappear forever; later in the day the grandmothers or the domestic help would rinse their chamberpots there. I knew I would never have the nerve to stop them doing this. The doctor insisted that the door of the lavatory be kept closed and that no soiled newspaper scraps be seen outside it. The question of toilet-paper did not come up when the house was inspected: there was none. Though I really tried to build a 'sanitary cell' for the house and the shacks, I failed completely; the medical officer got tired of the whole venture, and things went on as before.

I must admit that until I went to inspect them I had never ventured into the miserable two-room shacks that adjoined the house. They were falling apart, and since like our own barracks room they were not 'classified', they could at least in principle have been repaired; but because no military personnel lived in them, nothing was ever done about them. It was one of my duties to see that the people in the shacks lived up to the standard of 'useful citizens', but I knew that one of them, Anushka, a woman in her fifties who came to help with laundry in the house, could never be made into a good Soviet citizen. She used to tell us whenever she had the opportunity that the Bolsheviks were the Antichrist and that the Lord would punish them in due course. She spent a lot of time with us and we were good friends, but whenever I went to visit her 'in the line of duty' she became angry and would say: 'Did you come to see how many icons I have? Better have a look at how I have to keep moving my bed around to find a dry spot in the room. Tell them there is no roof left on this shack.' I did not have to go inside to see this, it was quite visible from the outside. I promised her that I would report it.

In the other room lived a young woman with a twelve-year-old daughter. The little girl hung around the house; she was neglected, and I do not think she ever went to school. Her mother, a party member, was a street-car conductor and the little girl said that sometimes at night 'uncles' came to sleep at the house and would bring something to eat. The child was our special concern, and it was decided that I should speak to her mother. When I finally got hold of her and told her I would like to discuss the future of her daughter she said: 'Look, comrade, I know very well what you are going to tell me, but how do you expect me to live on my salary when a kilogram of bread costs three rubles? These men bring me food so the child doesn't have to go hungry!'

While I was a member of the 'sanitary cell', I visited certain medical services in the city in the company of a doctor who sympathized with my efforts. In this way I came to know a few hospitals and medical stations for children and to find out for myself how hard the medical staff worked and how bad the shortage of equipment and medicines was. One day I visited a birth control station, a small establishment where pregnancies could be interrupted at the request of the mother. There were twenty such stations in Moscow, known as '*abortaria*', for the convenience of factories in the district. The specialized agencies sent women patients to the appropriate hospitals; the Fourth Department, for instance, normally referred cases to the military hospital. But since there were long waiting lists at the hospitals women were also admitted to the municipal establishments, often in quite advanced stages of pregnancy.

The physician at the station I visited happened to be a military doctor whom we knew slightly. He was glad to show us round and told us: 'These happen to be civilian women, but

I apply military methods. You will see, they work quite well.'
He was responsible for three rooms with nine beds each and he
performed about eighteen operations between eight o'clock in
the morning and noon. He had acquired such skill that each
operation, quite properly performed, took no more than three
or four minutes. He took us into one of the rooms where he
examined the records of ten patients and spoke a few words to
each. To one woman in her forties he said: 'Well, you are
getting to be quite an old acquaintance. The last time you were
here, a few months ago, your insides were already paper-thin.
How many more times do you think this can go on?' He
brushed aside her story of a drunken husband who did not
care what happened to her, and went on to the next case, a
sobbing young wife, hardly twenty years old. 'Hey,' he said to
her, 'what are you doing here? Why don't you have the baby?'
She told him that she and her husband only had a corner of a
room to themselves. How could they possibly have a baby in the
circumstances? He sympathized with her. 'Stop crying. You
will be the first one I operate on. But think it over. You may
never conceive again and if you don't hold still I might harm
you.'—'Please, doctor,' she sobbed, 'could I have a drop of
anaesthetic?'—'Anaesthetic? I wish I had some for more serious
cases. And I wish you women would learn how to take care of
yourselves.' She was the first to be called, but she screamed so
before he even touched her that he sent her back and she had
to go through the agony of waiting. In the end, when he had
her brought in again, she only whimpered. These were his
'military methods', but he had done the job safely and at
terrific speed. He examined each woman quickly before leaving,
saying an encouraging word to each and admonishing them
not to come back. I thanked him for letting me watch. A few
years later Soviet women, who had had the right to decide for
themselves whether they wanted a child or not, 'voted enthusiastically' at mass meetings to give up this right when the
new constitution abrogated the law.

In a cellar in the courtyard of our house, used for storing
wood, lived two men, one on either side of the woodpile. One
was a 'former', a doctor in his forties who had somehow found

refuge there. No one ever bothered about him and I have no idea how he managed to subsist. I often saw him in the yard and once, when my boy had badly swollen glands, he told me what I should do; and I was very grateful, since the Fourth Department doctor was unable to come for some days. The next time the man spoke to me was to ask whether he could use the house telephone in what he said was an emergency. I was very much embarrassed, for I knew that because of his political status he could not even enter the house, much less use the telephone, an official line directly connected with the Fourth Department's switchboard. When I did not answer he smiled and said: 'It is all right, I only thought that in an emergency I could have used the phone just once.' I never mentioned the incident to anyone, but after that he and I avoided speaking to each other and only nodded when we met.

The other inhabitant of the woodpile was the so-called building 'superintendent', Diadia (or Uncle) Vasia, a peasant in his fifties who was loved by everybody but especially by the children. He was familiar with everyone's problems and in the winter he used to carry the firewood and do odd jobs around the house. He never hesitated to repair a short circuit although he did not know the first thing about electricity and his repairs never, of course, did much good. Sometimes when he knew I was alone he would come to our room and shyly ask me to play a record on our gramophone for him. He would listen to old Russian songs with tears in his eyes. Diadia Vasia did not mind the Bolsheviks at all; he never complained and in his own way I suppose he was happy.

Our gramophone, which we liked very much, soon proved to be a burden. We did not mind so much when our neighbours came to listen to records or even to borrow the machine for a party, but we soon found out that one of the neighbours, a certain Z., used it as a pretext for coming round whenever we had visitors so he could see who they were. We had many visitors from abroad at the time, some from the Comintern, some from our own department, mainly Poles, Germans, and Yugoslavs, and were usually speaking German. Z. pretended he knew German (being Jewish he did in fact know Yiddish), and would come in every evening, lean against the door and say : 'Comrades, can one have the *patifon* [gramophone]? Once Willy, who was often with us in the evening and who had got as tired as we had of this performance, removed part of the machine and when Z. asked his usual question Willy answered in exactly the same tone: 'No, comrade, one cannot have the *patifon*, the *patifon* is *kaput*.' This rapidly became a routine, and Z. was not even embarrassed. He laughed and would stay for a few minutes and then leave after having looked at everybody. Five minutes after he left, Willy would replace the missing part and put on a record. Z. had seen what he wanted, and was supposed to see, and thus the little game went on. It made me uncomfortable, for Ludwik never asked him to sit down and chat as he did all the other neighbours who dropped in.

Three of the men in the house were registered in language courses at the office, and another of my 'social duties' was helping them two evenings a week with their homework. I was happy that Z., whom none of us trusted, had not registered for the German course, since he maintained he could speak it as well as I could. Actually, none of the men was enthusiastic about doing homework, and I was not at all enthusiastic about having them there smoking in our one room where my child was sleeping. Ludwik would stay away on these evenings and little by little so did my 'students'. To account for his lack of zeal one of the men, the house commandant, said that he did not see any point in being taught by me since I did not know the subject anyway. A second was franker and told me that he had only registered for the course because he had to, and that he was not going to waste his spare evenings on it. Once again I had failed in my 'duties' and was about to report my failure when the first man came in to apologize. He had found out from his teacher that I did indeed know the language and was quite competent to teach it. He also said it was his fault that the group had fallen apart because he, as house commandant, should have kept it together. He was quite drunk and wept: 'What does a foreign language matter to me? I don't even know my own as I should. My trouble is I get drunk, and they will throw me out of the party for it some day.'

When I told Ludwik about my failure, he said not to worry

about it. 'God only knows what will happen to this country,' he said. 'The one who told you he only registered for the course because he had to has his troubles too. He is in charge of a warehouse from which a lot of proletarian property has disappeared. He looks suspect, and they will throw him out of the party soon. He is no Communist, and should something happen in Moscow one day, God forbid, he will be the first one to slit our throats.' There was a good deal of unrest at the time and in fact the man did not look very reassuring. He never spoke to anybody. His wife, a true Muscovite, was a very intelligent and delightful woman and their little girl used to play with my boy. I saw this man again in the terror of 1937, but did not dare ask what had happened to our neighbours, nor did he ask me to visit them.

Another of our neighbours, a woman whom I liked very much, was a schoolteacher. In the evening she often came to fetch her boy who was a playmate of my son's. Once I noticed that her coat was torn and her face streaked with dirt. 'Look,' she said. 'That's what it's like teaching school these days. Before they go home my students throw their galoshes at me and tear my coat off. No use complaining to the principal. That would only provoke a student meeting and I would be accused of being a class enemy!'

One day the boys in the house had a fight and I heard her son calling mine '*kipitalist*' (capitalist). 'What does that mean?' I asked the five-year-old Lerotchka. 'I don't know,' he told me, 'but it is a very dirty word.'—'Look here, Lerotchka,' I said, 'my boy is no *kipitalist*; if he were, you would not be playing with him.'—'That's right,' was the considered reply, and the boys were friends again.

On another occasion my son came back from the 'red corner' and told me he was very much ashamed because all the children except himself knew who 'Karamass' was. 'A great general,' he added. I was at a complete loss and thought that this might possibly be some Civil War hero. That evening when Ludwik came home I asked him. He laughed. 'Why, it's Karl Marx!' Next day I asked my boy: 'Tell me, is "Karamass" an uncle with a big beard?' — 'That's right! And he was a very great general!'

After we got the partition in our room built I started to look for domestic help. This was a serious step to take, for anyone who lived on the premises for a year was by law entitled to a 'corner' of one's room. That was how some of our neighbours had been stuck with strangers sharing their rooms. Still, I was by then working, and with my irregular hours I had to have somebody to look after the child. Lisa, the girl I found, was a peasant from a nearby village, a friend of Fedia's help. She liked our child and seemed quite willing to help; but she was enrolled in an evening school, a 'technicum' at which in two years an illiterate peasant could become a qualified engineer. This meant, of course, that she would never be there in the evening if I wanted to go out, but I had a moral responsibility for her education and could not very well ask her to stay away from classes.

Lisa was quite bright and in a few days she knew her way round the city much better than I did. She was especially quick to learn about the many ration cards that piled up at the end of the month. Usually the merchandise the cards called for was not available, but the coupons might entitle one to something else altogether several months later. In the meantime one had not only the unused ration cards but quite a bit of money, as there was nothing one could buy with it. Lisa loved the co-operative and invariably knew what was being 'given' there. Sometimes one could hardly believe what she said, but she was always right, as for instance when she told me that for the children's November butter ration one could be 'given' summer shoes. This was in February: as a general rule summer shoes were 'given' in mid-winter, while in August one got earmuffs.

Our German friends used to call the co-operative 'Rollenhagen' after a famous Berlin delicatessen. In our Rollenhagen two barrels stood side by side, one containing herring, the other liquid black soap, and no one ever objected that both were served with the same shovel. One was lucky to get anything at all. Sometimes there were cereals, of which I would get several rations, as some of our unmarried friends did not use theirs. Lisa would trade these to a cousin in her village for milk for our child. I knew that this was illegal, but I preferred to know as little as possible of Lisa's transactions. There were also good days on which our co-operative would sell goods that had been rejected for export. Beautiful apples from the Crimea, already slightly decaying, were held back for sale at holidays such as the anniversary of the revolution or the so-called 'Lenin days' in January. On such days there were even extra rations of flour, and once we got half a goose.

Lisa was an expert on other co-operatives in town that were better supplied than ours and she did not seem to mind standing in line for hours to get a kilogram of something. I too sometimes also found it hard to resist joining a queue. One day, without knowing what was being 'given', I lined up and when I finally reached the table I saw that it was salt, a very important item that could be bartered for food from peasants. I was told I could have some only if I had my own bag or a newspaper. I had none. From then on I always carried one, but this did not necessarily mean that one was equipped, for it might be vinegar that was being 'given' and then a paper bag would not be much good. Another time I lined up in front of a department store which announced that galoshes were being 'given' for some old ration coupons which luckily I had with me. The line was not very long and I soon got my galoshes. I looked at them. They were of different sizes. When I pointed this out to the clerk he looked at me and answered: 'But they are a pair, citizen, aren't they?' I took them home with me. They were not too bad, only one size apart.

There were long queues everywhere in Moscow. Our foreign friends used to say that one did not need to know any Russian except 'Who is last? I am next'. Nevertheless I still wonder how that undisciplined Russian crowd ever got itself organized enough to cope with the trams. If one managed to squeeze on, one was no longer pushed by people but stood in a tight line never moving at all. Somewhere in the distance the woman conductor, leaning against the driver's back, could be heard repeating: 'Get your tickets, citizens!' Then the money would be handed from one passenger to another up to the conductor and the ticket and the change would come back the same way. One had to fight just as hard to get out as to get on. When my son had to be taken to the dentist, Ludwik would come home from work to take him. As the bearer of a high decoration he could get on with the child at the front of the tram after producing the booklet showing the award.

It was the only such use Ludwik ever made of his decoration. He hated to wear his uniform, and was in fact the only one in our communal house in civilian clothes. Once on a holiday when there was an official reception at the Red Army house he did put on his uniform, with the insignia of the Order of the Red Banner in his buttonhole, and that was how our neighbours learned of his rank and the decoration. 'We never even knew he was a *krasnoarmieieta* [decorated Red Army man],' one woman said. 'Why, if my man had this decoration, you can bet he would wear it every day.' But Ludwik seldom went to parades or official functions; he much preferred to stay at home and read.

Bright as she was, Lisa was not a satisfactory help. She was always off on some errand of her own and I could never get her to spend an evening at home even when she was not in school. One day I saw a sweater of mine and a bar of chocolate a friend had brought from abroad in her open trunk. When I asked why she took things that did not belong to her she answered: 'Those are mine. I got them from a friend and I will go to the District Committee and tell them that Communist Party members accuse working-class people of stealing.' I said, 'Let's go', and we did. She was told to give the things back to me and never to do it again, but after that our relations were definitely cool and I told her I was looking for someone else.

One day her father came to see her. He was a vigorous peasant, still quite young. He was looking for some kind of job in the city, for he had been 'de-kulakized'. He cried when he told me this and showed me a thick silver watch with an engraved dedication from Kalinin. 'Look,' he said. 'I was chairman of the village soviet and I got this watch for good conduct during the Civil War. I am no kulak.' Lisa hardly looked at him and did not even ask for news of her family. Nor did she walk with him to the door when he left. When I asked her why, she simply said: 'I don't want to have anything to do with a kulak.'

Everyone in Moscow had not gone over to the new ways, however. One day I met in the kitchen an old Siberian woman who had come to visit her daughter, ten days and nights on the train. She found everything in Moscow delightful, the people, the shops, and most of all the winter climate which she thought very mild. She was telling Anushka, who was busy with the laundry, all about life in Siberia and the role the priest played in it. She was a Catholic, of Polish descent, but did not mind the Bolsheviks as long as they left the church and the priest alone. Suddenly the house was shaken by an explosion. The nearby church of Christ Saviour was being demolished to make room for the Palace of Soviets which was to have an oversized statue of Lenin in front of it. The two women crossed themselves and Anushka said, for everyone to hear: 'Oh! The Bolsheviks, the Antichrist, they are tearing down the Lord Saviour's home! They are going to sell the golden cupolas to the Americans so they can squeeze us still more. But they will pay for it. They will pay for it with their blood one day, and that day is not far away!'

Holidays were busy times in the kitchen, when women who were normally not on speaking terms would consult one another about baking and cooking. Towards the end of the winter, when their nerves were on edge, quarrels would flare up among them for no apparent reason. At the bottom of it was a fierce competition for the two or three places in rest homes in the Caucasus or the Crimea that had been allotted our house. The women suspected each other of using influence to get these places, and those who did get a holiday had to put up with the hostility of the others for a long time to come.

Although on friendly terms with our neighbours, we were not particularly intimate with them. We had our own friends and whenever we had enough food to share with them we would throw a small party, which helped keep up our morale. These were usually joint affairs with the Gorskis, Felix and Justina, given either at our place or at theirs. They shared a good, comfortable apartment with Ring, a member of the Polish politburo who was then on a mission abroad, in a pre-war building on Stoleshnikov Street in the centre of town. Since they had been in Moscow longer than we, they had better furniture. They too had a little boy and a reliable girl who looked after him.

The food at these parties was always the same: bad herring,

a sausage universally called 'Budenny's First Cavalry' because everybody suspected it to be horse meat, salted smoked fish called *vobla*, which made one's gums bleed, something called a 'vinaigrette' consisting of red beets and potato salad with sunflower oil, a red wine called Kagor and a quite good mineral water called Narsan. There was always plenty of sugar and bread as well as vodka and tea, and if anyone had a dollar bill he could buy real red caviar at the shops reserved for those with foreign currency. These was always a samovar in the middle of the table, never used but put there in imitation of the famous Filipov family. This typical happy Soviet family appeared regularly in Willy Muenzenberg's magazines abroad, in faked photographs showing adults and children of all ages, all very well dressed, enjoying a good meal at a table ornamented with a gleaming samovar. The pictures also showed a piano and little side tables covered with embroidered tablecloths. While none of us ever reached the degree of affluence of the mythical Fillipovs, we were still very much better off than the average Soviet citizen, than Anushka or the woman tram conductor in the shack adjoining our house. The Filipovs became a standing joke among those in Moscow who saw the propaganda material intended for the West, and whenever a hostess succeeded in producing some better fare, such as a decent smoked fish from the foreign exchange stores, she would invariably be cheered as 'Madame Filipov'.

Parties at Anna Mikhailovna Messing's were a treat compared with ours, for she was a member of the N.K.V.D. cooperative which was much better supplied than ours, and she often had foreign currency with which to buy fruit and smoked fish. She even had coffee which she got from the Unshlikhts who then lived in the Kremlin. But we had a good time at our small parties and get-togethers because we were among friends, while at her place there were frequently very high officials.

Our friends often came to our room for tea after dinner. One night in our third winter in Moscow, two Yugoslav friends came to say good-bye before leaving for jobs in the distant provinces.[1] A high-ranking Soviet officer who had been visiting other

---

[1] The Yugoslav party was then undergoing a major purge, and Yugoslavs were often sent into virtual exile on obscure assignments in remote places.

friends stopped by for a chat. He was a friendly, red-headed, rather portly man whom we liked but who was about the last person we would have wished to see that night with the two gloomy and depressed Yugoslavs. The colonel, a Russian, was on good terms with General Tairov, whom Stalin had recently appointed to keep an eye on the officers, including even Voroshilov. He had already had a few drinks but accepted another. Our Yugoslav friends, realizing that everyone was ill at ease, left. But before the red-headed colonel could go another unexpected visitor arrived, a Ukrainian from Kiev on business in Moscow. He had some tea and marvelled at the bread. It was heavy and moist but it was bread, and where he came from, the granary of the Soviet Union, there was none to be had. He began to tell us about the Ukraine, the famine in the cities, the bloated corpses in the streets, the hordes of abandoned children hanging around the railway stations, the ghostly villages where people were dying of starvation and typhus.

Listening to this terrible tale, we completely forgot our red-headed friend. He sat throughout the recital, his head bent, then suddenly started to sob. Between sobs he said: 'He, he is doing this, he, that'—followed a string of obscenities—'he is ruining the country, he is destroying the party.' Then he got up, opened the one movable pane of our window, stuck his head out and was sick. Ludwik had to drag him back inside for fear his ears or nose would freeze. When he got back to the table I offered him a slice of lemon, a rare treat, as I thought it might help him against the sickness. 'No, thank you,' he said. 'I will take it along and suck it later.' He shook hands with the Ukrainian, and Ludwik took him home. When Ludwik came back the Ukrainian was still there. I was worried that he had told his story in front of the colonel. 'It doesn't matter,' Ludwik said. 'He will forget it. He is the son of a peasant himself.' And in fact the colonel did forget, or pretended to, for when we saw him next, with Richard Sorge, he was as jolly and friendly as if nothing had happened.

2

Richard Sorge was one of the people who often came to our room, either alone or with Fedia or Alex Borovich, Sorge's immediate superior in the Fourth Department. We had known one another since 1939, when Sorge worked with Ludwik and Fedia in the military committee of the German party and in the French-occupied Ruhr. Sorge was known to his friends as Ika, from the initials of the International Communist Youth movement whose German representative he had been. After it became obvious in the 1920s that the German revolution was not just around the corner, and Fedia and Ludwik and others had gone to the Fourth Department, Ika joined the O.M.S.

I used to see him often in Berlin, sometimes with Ludwik and Fedia, but quite frequently alone. Once he took me to see his mother, and he told me that he had brothers and I believe he also mentioned a sister. He was always very friendly and attentive to me and I liked him very much. The fact that he was a few years older than the rest of us lent him an air of authority. Like Fedia he had gone through the war, but whereas Fedia had been drafted into the Austro-Hungarian army and later deserted to the Russians Ika had volunteered for service in the Imperial German Army—though he never mentioned this—and had been twice badly wounded and decorated for bravery. Some people wondered how he could have volunteered to fight against Russia when his mother was Russian, but he had after all been brought up in Germany and was a German. And Ika would have been quite incapable of staying out of a fight others had joined. Fedia used to say to him: 'Ika is all of a piece. Once he sees his way clear he goes ahead. For him there is only black or white, there are no shades in between.'

Fedia and Ika were very close, though they were as different mentally and physically as two men could possibly be. Fedia was tense, frail, almost bald, while Ika, tall, well-built, with a full head of hair, gave an impression of strength. His features, although sallow, were attractive, with a strong, prominent forehead which made his eyes seem very deep set. His very straight nose seemed to spring from his eyes and made his face look hard, compensating for his rather full-lipped, soft mouth. He was always elegant and impressive-looking and he wore sports clothes very well.

Accounts of Sorge's later activities in the Far East picture this 'formidable' secret agent as a hard drinker and a woman chaser, with a wife in Russia, another one, 'a schoolteacher', in the United States, and some twenty women around him in Japan. I do not know how many women he knew in Japan, or anything about a Russian wife, unless that was a girl in Moscow who attached herself to him and whom he suspected of having been sent by the N.K.V.D. to watch him. But the 'schoolteacher' in the United States was his real wife, Christiane, a distinguished-looking, reddish-blonde German girl whom Sorge met when they were both at university. It was said that he persuaded her to leave her professor husband and run away with him. We met Christiane for the first time in Germany in 1928, but never saw her with him. He rarely mentioned her, and she did not accompany him on his trips. For a time, while he was in the Far East, Christiane lived in England, and once visited us in Holland. When the war broke out she moved to the United States where she did teach.

After long service with the Comintern Sorge joined the Fourth at about the time most of his friends were leaving or had already left it. I believe Ossip Piatnitsky, then secretary of the Comintern executive committee, would have preferred to keep Sorge for the Comintern, which he no doubt hoped might still play a role in the world revolutionary movement. Piatnitsky was successful in keeping some of his best men by sending them abroad, but he also knew that Sorge was being wasted in the O.M.S., and that the Fourth Department was very short of capable men.

While his friends in the Fourth by now seriously doubted the usefulness of their espionage activities, Sorge was convinced that serving the U.S.S.R. as a spy constituted a service to the revolution. He knew well enough what was happening in the Soviet Union, and for that matter in the Fourth Department. Nor did Ludwik and Fedia bother to hide their opinion of Stalin from him. Ika himself spoke little and usually sat through these conversations, his face hard and unsmiling. But we knew that he was one of us and that we could say anything in front of him with complete faith and safety.

When he left the Comintern for the Fourth he was a German

citizen with a valid passport and was an established journalist. He could have refused the transfer, something which none of his friends was in a position to do. Yet he accepted his new assignment without hesitation, as was his way in everything he did. 'I transferred my allegiance from the international movement to the Soviet Union', as he later testified, in a statement that reveals much of his attitude and beliefs.

Some sources have maintained that when he joined the Fourth Department, Sorge 'put up several conditions', among them that he was not to have any contacts with the local Communist party and was to have no Russians or Germans on his staff. This is clearly nonsense. Contacts with local Communist parties were prohibited not by the agent's or resident's wishes, but by the Fourth Department itself. This ban, which went into effect in the late 1920s after several serious incidents in Germany and in England, was meant to protect the intelligence apparatuses from detection by police working through the parties. While I do not remember this particular point being discussed by Fedia and Ludwik with Sorge in my presence, I am certain he received these standing instructions when he took up his new work. They would probably have been given him even before he joined the service by Piatnitsky, who knew Sorge, coming as he did from a legal party, would have been used to frequent contacts with the local parties, and that the ban would be all the harder for him to observe after his years in the Comintern. Sorge submitted to the instructions and 'did not ask any questions'. But the ban could not be enforced, and as he himself later testified, 'many things were left to the judgement of the resident'. As for the other alleged 'condition', one has only to look at Sorge's staff: his first and closest collaborator, Klausen, was a German, whose wife was a White Russian, and Japanese police records refer to several obviously Russian first names.

Sorge's mission in the Far East has been called 'a faultless operation'.[1] But he certainly made mistakes which others would not have made. Ika could not be bothered with the little details that were essential to such work and to safety. His joining the Nazi Party in his own country, where he had a well-documented

[1] By Major–General Charles A. Willoughby in *Shanghai Conspiracy* (New York 1952).

police record, was hazardous, to say the least, even if, as some people think, he had protection from high up in the party itself. And his staying in the very lion's den, in Berlin, while his application for membership was being processed, was indeed flirting with death. Such actions were typical of Ika and of his superb self-assurance.

Recklessness and strong will, together with a certain political naïveté, characterized his whole career. The purges in the Soviet Union seem not to have shaken his faith either in Stalin or the Russian party. After Ludwik saw Ika for what was to be the last time, in Moscow in 1935,[1] I asked him what Ika's reaction had been to Kirov's murder and to the arrest of Zinoviev, Ika's mentor in the Comintern. Ludwik said Ika was well aware of the turn things were taking but that nothing could make him abandon his own way of serving the Soviet Union.

To the end Sorge seems to have believed that Stalin, whom he had warned of the German attack, would not let him perish in a Japanese jail. I remembered Fedia's words, 'Ika is attracted by Stalin's power and he is the kind that submits to power', when I read in the *New York Times* in 1943 a small news item to the effect that a certain Dr. Richard Sorge had been hanged in Japan.

Fedia, who had recruited all his friends to the Communist cause and into the various services, had been the first to be expelled from the party. Upon his return to Moscow after the German revolution failed, the Fourth Department had sent him to Rome. Krivitsky, then in the Netherlands, was assigned to work under him. Fedia had long since ceased to believe in *ab oriente lux*. On the contrary, he felt that the only hope for a socialist revolutionary movement lay in the European Communist parties remaining independent of the Soviet Union. But he still felt the U.S.S.R. itself was worth working for, and had

---

[1] Major-General Willoughby insists that Sorge went to Moscow in 1935 to attend the Seventh World Conference of the Comintern, held there that summer. But Sorge in his own statement says quite clearly that he was in the United States at the time of the conference, and indeed it would have been unthinkable for a member of the Fourth at that time to attend such a congress. Ludwik did not attend it either, being by then quite disillusioned with the Soviet Union and the Third International.

asked for a foreign assignment, partly because he preferred working abroad, but mainly because he was convinced that he would
be more useful there.

It was quite easy to do espionage work against Great Britain
from Italy. In 1926 the Soviet Union and Mussolini's Italy were
on excellent terms. The Soviet agents frequented the Soviet
Embassy quite openly, and Fedia told us that Mussolini himself
had issued orders to the O.V.R.A. not to disturb the Soviet
operations as long as the espionage was directed against the
British. In exchange the Soviets shared some of their information with the Italians. But Fedia was disgusted with such
work.

He did not relish the thought of returning to the Soviet
Union where he would in effect have been an émigré from
Europe. He had seen for himself how Krasny had been shelved
there and how other foreign Communists were faring. A bril-
liantly intelligent man, he knew it would be the end of all his
hopes and aspirations. What he wanted was to remain abroad,
where he had many friends, but not in intelligence work: he
wanted to become active again in the movement.

He did not bother to hide his opinions and, according to
Krivitsky, did not do much on his Italian assignment. It was not
long before he received a summons to return to Moscow. At first
he refused to go. But unfortunately his friends, who could not in
those early years conceive of breaking with the Soviet Union,
persuaded him to return. Had Fedia been allowed to remain
abroad, things might have turned out differently for all of us.
In those days there was relatively little danger in doing so,
although the disappearance of Yaroslavsky, who fled from his
post as military attaché in Vienna, was a preliminary warning
of the fate of a deserter.

When Fedia finally agreed to go back he said it was mainly
for the sake of a girl he had left in Moscow, and that he would
return to Europe soon, somehow or other. He must have believed that there was at least some chance of this, for on his way
to Moscow he met the girl's brothers in Warsaw. As she was
ancien régime, the daughter of a Tsarist admiral, it is highly
probable that her brothers were hostile to the Soviet Union. I
believe that Fedia may have arranged this meeting in order to

facilitate his eventual return to Europe, although he probably suspected that he would be under Soviet surveillance.

He was never to leave the Soviet Union again. On his arrival he was expelled from the party. He finally found a job on the government newspaper *Izvestiia* and on the *Deutsche Zentrale Zeitung*, a daily paper published for the Volga Germans. The N.K.V.D. was always keen to recruit former members of the Fourth Department for the press, and one of Fedia's duties was to keep the N.K.V.D. supplied with information on the state of public opinion in the country.

Fedia remained on close personal terms with Mirov-Abramov and his former associates in the Comintern and the Fourth Department right through the years of the terror. He did so because he had become convinced that it no longer mattered what he did. It was not a feeling of freedom but rather the pervasiveness of the terror that enabled him to discard that hateful Soviet 'watchfulness'.

In 1929 he was reinstated in the party, through Ludwik's personal intervention. On that day he came to see us in our barracks room in Moscow and pointed to Ludwik's lapel where there should have been, but was not, the insignia of the Order of the Red Banner. 'On the strength of that little red thing you could get me back into the party,' he said. 'But it won't be long before that same little red thing will get you into trouble, and, what is more, you will be in trouble before me.'

I remember looking at him wide-eyed and saying: 'Fedia, you are crazy.'

'Perhaps I am,' he answered. 'But there are only two things in store for the likes of us. Either the enemy will hang us or our own people will shoot us.'

I had first heard of Fedia's marriage from Ika, when he arrived in Vienna in 1927 from the Soviet Union. When he told me the girl was a 'former' I said to Ika: 'I hope that won't be held against him.' He looked at me gravely and answered: 'You are quite wrong; I hope they will hold it against him. After all, if they don't object to that, where does it leave us?' When we saw Ika in Moscow he was still very upset about the marriage. He was the only one of us who knew the girl; when we asked him what she was like he only shrugged his shoulders. Although by then they had a child, Fedia never asked us to his place to meet his wife, or brought her to ours. I did not meet her until 1937.

Curiously enough, another of the friends from the little town was also eventually to marry outside our circle. Brun, whom Fedia had advised to grow whiskers like a gendarme, had been sent by the N.K.V.D. in 1923 to the French-occupied Ruhr, where he worked closely with Krivitsky, who was in the Fourth. While there, Brun met and married his first wife: a local girl, Lene Lorenz, a Communist who was soon also working for the N.K.V.D., without being aware of it. They had a little girl. In 1925 Brun was sent to Hungary where he was arrested and tortured. However, he was released after serving a short sentence, and rejoined Lene and their daughter in the Soviet Union.

In 1927 he was sent to Berlin, where he was under the orders of Slutsky, later head of I.N.O. The two men simply could not get along. Slutsky held a much higher rank and was a much more important person at home, but abroad it was Brun who knew the country, spoke the language, and had the contacts. Brun, though not allowed to use the German party in his work, did succeed in mobilizing many fellow-travellers whom he was fond of calling 'the periphery of the apparatus'. Moscow no longer considered such persons reliable owing to the existence of oppositional elements, and Slutsky looked on most of Brun's recruits as useless, undisciplined, expensive, and dangerous to the apparatus. But in addition to their disagreements over tactics, their personalities clashed, Slutsky being a likeable and mild-mannered man, whom the cynical Brun insulted in the presence of others and then bragged about having done so. When Slutsky went home for a year and a half, Brun—who then had papers in the name of Steiger—took charge. He soon had a lot of people gravitating around him and spent a good deal of money. Some of his ideas were sound: he organized a press clipping service which kept him and his people well informed at very little cost—an idea any Russian resident would have thought of as 'useless spending'.

While in Berlin, Brun divorced Lene and married the youngest and prettiest daughter of a White émigré family. Alexandra, usually called Shura, was a Ukrainian of German descent whose family name was Plessner. She had three sisters. The oldest, Nina, worked for the Soviet trade mission in Berlin and was married to our friend Pavlo Ladan, the Ukrainian Communist. A second sister, Vera, would have nothing whatever to do with Brun, and neither did their brother, who was a Nazi and was killed in the German army during the war. When Brun returned to Moscow in 1929 he and Shura took with them the third sister, Lyda, who later committed suicide.

Lene, Brun's ex-wife, took advantage of his return complete with émigré family to cause as much trouble as possible. But he was nonetheless given a high position in the counter-espionage services of the G.P.U., a large and comfortable apartment, and did not leave the Soviet Union again, except for one short trip to Germany and the Netherlands, when he had visited us.

While we were in Moscow we saw the break-up of the marriages of some of our other friends. Alex Borovich, a good friend who later went out to the Far East, was losing his pretty wife Anya to the young and athletic Volodia Fisher, later Soviet consul in Denmark. And the Gorskis were separating: Justina had decided to leave Felix for Milan Gorkić, secretary of the Jugoslav party, then in Moscow awaiting an assignment abroad. Felix took this rather hard, and it obviously affected our little gatherings.

Justina had been secretary to Bortnovsky, chief of one of the sections of the Fourth Department, and followed him when he moved over to the Polish section of the Comintern. Gorkić, a young blond giant, had risen with astonishing rapidity in the Comintern. Capable and very ambitious, he was heartily disliked by his compatriots who had been pushed out and were now on their way to exile or prison for their sympathies with the Left opposition. Gorkić himself was not interested in the Left or any other opposition. Although rightly considered a protégé of Bukharin, he understood how to adapt himself to the new leadership when Bukharin was replaced by Molotov. He remained on friendly terms with his former wife Betty Glan, and was very much attached to their little daughter. When Gorkić finally obtained his foreign assignment Betty gave a very lively farewell party for him.

Betty was director of the Dynamo sports field of the Moscow Park of Culture and Rest. Her nickname 'Dynamo Betty' suited her perfectly. A pretty, plump young woman, she was vivacious and energetic and was extremely popular with everyone. Her position as cultural director brought her into contact with foreign delegations and the high Soviet officials who were their hosts. Nothing seemed to depress her, neither her divorce from Gorkić nor the horrible conditions in Moscow. One would have thought her the last person ever to get into trouble, and we were greatly surprised to read in *Le Temps* in Paris during the wave of arrests in the summer of 1937 that Betty had been arrested on charges of spying for the British.

Whatever the reason for it, her arrest certainly boded no good for Gorkić. By that time he and Justina were living in Paris where he was recruiting for the Spanish Republicans. From Moscow they had gone to Berlin, then to Prague and Vienna after the Nazis came to power. After the *Anschluss* they moved from Vienna to Paris, where I saw them occasionally. In 1938 the Soviet press reported that 'the Bukharinist traitor' Milan Gorkić had been executed as 'an enemy of the people'.

Gorkić was luckier, at least in his early career, than some of the other foreign Communists cooling their heels in the Hotel Lux during our years in Moscow. Our room was always full of comrades from abroad, some waiting to be reassigned, others on their way to jobs amounting to exile deep in the Soviet Union.

Otto Braun, a German Communist who had made a spectacular escape from a German prison, came to see us once or twice. He brought with him a handsome dark-haired young woman, Olga Benario, the wife of a South American Communist. Quite a few people claimed to have had a hand in Otto Braun's escape, but it was Olga, posing as his fiancée, who had engineered it. Braun eventually went to the Far East and Olga, a German Jewess, returned to Germany where she died a few years later in a Nazi gas-chamber.

Another Moscow friend whose marriage was going to pieces just then was Max Maximov-Friedman, whose place Ludwik had taken in Holland. Max had never given up trying to be admitted to the party, and in 1932 actually got as far as becoming a candidate, that is for a preliminary stage of probation. At that time he asked Ludwik to sponsor him for full membership, and Ludwik refused. This did not impair relations between them. I asked Ludwik why he had gone to so much trouble to get Fedia reinstated—which was much more difficult—and would not recommend Max. His answer was simple: 'Look, Max is no Communist and never will make one, that's all.'

Shortly after this Anna Mikhailovna Messing gave a little party in Max's honour, both to celebrate his candidacy and to wish him farewell on a new assignment in Germany.[1] Her husband, one of the top officials of the G.P.U., was there, as well as the Unshlikhts and others from the Polish party, some holding high positions in Soviet party and government agencies, others already in disgrace. Brotnovsky, Max's former chief, made a little congratulatory speech wishing Max a speedy admission to the party. Sophia Unshlikht, an old-time party member, but in opposition, protested. 'I wish Max the best of luck, but he is not a Communist and never will make one.' Ludwik looked at me and winked.

Max, good-natured and easy-going, was not a political person at all, and never understood the political developments around him. Unlike his friends who were party members, he was completely surprised by the events of 1937 and much more shocked. His main concern was that nothing should happen to his friends. Max never hated Stalin—unlike Willy, for example, an extraordinarily kind and good person who hated him ferociously. One had to be a Communist to hate Stalin. Max respected him and feared him even before the terror began.

One evening in 1932 Max came to our room greatly excited. Crossing Red Square on his way to work he had suddenly found himself face to face with Stalin and Voroshilov. Max's hands were in his pockets. His instinct, when confronted with authority, was of course to get them out of his pockets as quickly

---

[1] It was to prove a tricky and dangerous assignment, made more so, after the Nazis came to power, by Max's having acquired a German girl friend. As he was Jewish, this laid him open to a charge of *Rassenschande* ('defiling the race'). But Max was lucky as always and carried out his task unscathed.

as possible so as to show proper respect; but he was afraid
Stalin and his guards might see a sudden gesture of this kind as
that of a man drawing a weapon. He therefore stood paralyzed,
his hands half out of his trouser pockets. Stalin saw his embarrassment and the look of consternation on his face and understood. Walking by him he nodded and said, 'Good morning,
comrade'. Max was thrilled. Not only had he seen Stalin and
Voroshilov, but Stalin had actually spoken to him. Ludwik had
to quiet him. Pushing him into a chair he said: 'Sit down, calm
yourself. There will be lots more nice things like that from him.'

Ludwik was not the kind to be impressed by a 'good morning'
from Stalin. He had little use for Stalin even in 1932, and
none whatever for Marshal Voroshilov whom he despised. Once
when the Marshal paid a visit to our co-operative the clerk,
confused and surprised by the army chief's appearance, gave
me half a pound of butter more than my child's ration card
entitled me to. I remember showing Ludwik this incredible
windfall and saying: 'It's thanks to Voroshilov.'—'Yes,' he
said, 'and it's the best thing he ever did in his life.'

3

Most of the privileges Ludwik's decoration entitled him to were
meaningless under Soviet conditions, or at any rate in our
particular case. He was entitled to live rent-free, but rents were
ludicrously small and the Red Army paid ours. Free education
for one's children was again meaningless, as all schooling in
those days was free. The right I have already mentioned, of
getting on at the front of a tram, Ludwik did not care to use
unless he was taking our boy to a doctor or a dentist. The award
also brought a substantial pension—Ludwik's by now must
amount to a handsome sum. But most important was a twice-
yearly trip anywhere in the Soviet Union with a stay at a rest
home of one's choice. Unfortunately, this privilege did not ex-
tend to the decorated man's family and Ludwik therefore
availed himself of it only once a year. At the time of his regular
vacation he went each year to a different place in the Crimea or
the Caucasus to stay for four weeks.

By the time his annual vacation fell due in 1932 he had become deeply depressed by the state of the country and conditions

in the Fourth Department, and seized the chance to get away from Moscow to think quietly over what plans he could make for the future. Before leaving he managed to arrange a holiday for me and the child in a rest home not far from the Baltic, through an old friend in Leningrad, Doctor K. K. was of Greek descent and came from southern Russia. He had been a medical officer during the First World War, joined the Bolsheviks during the Civil War, and was assigned to the Red Army general staff. In 1923 he was relieved of his medical duties and sent by the Fourth Department to Germany, where he met Ludwik and most of his Polish friends. They became so close that Doctor K. was known as 'the Polish Greek'. In 1929 he was made director of the Military Medical Academy in Leningrad. The academy owned an estate in the village of Rozliv on the Finnish border, and it was to the rest home Doctor K. had built there, for the academy staff as well as for officers and some workers from Leningrad, that we went.

The rest home was on a lake across from the border and nearby was a hut, often visited by tourists who were rowed to it in little boats, where Lenin had hidden in 1917. The village of Rozliv itself, situated among lovely woods and surrounded by lakes, was uninhabited except for the rest home and a small colony of men and women with an incurable skin disease which badly disfigured them. The colony, hidden in the woods, had existed since long before the revolution. The people, who earned their living by handicrafts, had intermarried and had children some of whom showed signs of the disease while others seemed quite healthy. The political changes in the country had not affected them at all. They kept to themselves and when we met in the forest they would nod in friendly fashion and go on. Doctor K. visited them occasionally and brought them food; he and the other doctors assured us that there was no risk of contagion.

The rest home consisted of a large, new central building containing the offices, the dispensary and a communal dining room as well as a reception room and several guest rooms. The old villas surrounding it, where Doctor K. put up doctors from Leningrad with their families, as well as some personal friends, before the revolution had belonged to rich St. Petersburg families. Although in some need of repair, they were miraculously well furnished and quite comfortable. They even had heavy black curtains to keep out the bright daylight of the Far Northern white nights. The whole area had escaped the ravages of the Civil War and only time had brought about some deterioration.

We had our meals in common in the main building, and went there once or twice a day to fetch the post, or sometimes to see a film or to read the wall newspaper. This last was supposed to inform one of events of interest but was in fact a gossip sheet in which the factory girls on holiday told of their friends' love affairs. When the need arose we went to the dispensary, which was very well supplied by Soviet standards. The rest of the time we stayed in our villas enjoying each other's company.

The Leningrad doctors who were staying there were cultivated men somewhat older than I who had done their medical training before the revolution and had often studied abroad. The other guests seemed mostly to be Poles, for Doctor K. had his Polish friends to stay whenever he had a chance, and used to say jokingly: 'I am very happy to be almost a Pole, though those Poles for whom I provide a vacation are not the most reputable of company!' And indeed they were not. Sophia Unshlikht had by then been removed from her position as one of the leaders of the Polish party and was on the verge of being expelled as a Trotskyite; her sister Stephanie, although not in the opposition, was the wife of the literary critic Brun-Spisovich, who was in bad odour for having published in a West European bourgeois magazine an article which likened the Communist Party to a monastic order. There was even a genuine Trotskyite who had been expelled from the party and lost his post as a chemist as a result; Doctor K. was trying to find him another. There were also some Poles not in trouble, at least yet, among them the family of Lenski, a member of the Polish politburo, and of Kokhanski, a ranking Red Army officer attached to the Leningrad military district.

Doctor K., a very pleasant and handsome man, visited the villas of the Poles as often as he could. Whenever he came we all knew that within minutes his extremely jealous wife would stick her head in the door and say: 'Valentin Alexandrovich, you are wanted at the office!' She never actually set foot in the villas, and whenever we met her with her mother in the woods they would barely nod to us.

Those were restful days. There was no foraging for food and the company was very different from that of our neighbours in Moscow. We went for long walks along the Finnish border and chatted with the Soviet border guards, while our children had a fine time playing on the lake shore.

Every five days an old friend of mine from the orphanage days in Lwow, Galina Klinger, came to spend her day off with me. She was a highly qualified chemist and a medical doctor as well, who had come from Poland to head an experimental laboratory in a large chemical plant in Leningrad. Her position was important enough and she was sufficiently trusted to be allowed to go abroad to attend international congresses in her field, and in the past we had seen her either in Russia or in Europe almost every year.

Galina, who was quite a few years older than I, had never married but had devoted her life to her younger sister Maria, a polio victim whom she brought up after their parents died in an epidemic during the war. In the early 1920s Maria became a Communist, was soon arrested in Poland and, after serving a few years, was released. She then married a young Ukrainian, the son of a well-known professor, Hniatuk, whose family were liberals, deeply opposed to any extremism in politics. Young Hniatuk was not a Communist but was interested in the Soviet experience. He was glad to leave Poland behind, and followed his wife to the U.S.S.R. where they lived on the Dnieper in the heart of the Ukraine. Galina followed in turn, but as she could not find a position in the Ukraine had gone to live in Leningrad, hoping either to join them later or to persuade them to move to Leningrad.

On one of her visits she seemed perturbed and told me she had been approached by the secretary of the party cell in her plant, who explained that despite the esteem in which she was held, not being a party member she could not remain head of the laboratory. In order to maintain her in her position he was ready to sponsor her application for membership in the party. Galina unhesitatingly refused. I knew that such offers were extremely rare and was worried that a refusal might jeopardize more than her job. 'Why did you do that?' I asked. Galina answered very simply: 'Because I am not a Communist, I am a socialist. That is what I told the secretary of the party cell.'

Galina was aware of the consequences that would follow. A new director was appointed to oversee her work. He was not a professional, but he was a party member. Galina carried on with her job which involved the supervision of about forty people, mostly women. She soon became aware that her group was sabotaging the work. The tasks she assigned were not carried out as they had always been; in the morning her instruments and equipment were not cleaned and prepared for her as in the past. At length she called a meeting of her staff and asked them what they thought they were doing. At first there was no answer to her question. She appealed to their professional pride and reminded them how well the team had worked only a few days before; still no response. When finally she asked in despair why they would not work she got an answer. 'Why, did you say, Galina Germanova?' said one of the girls. 'Under you we will work as well as we ever did, but not under the new man!' 'I don't understand you,' Galina said. 'After all, he is one of you, he is a Russian and I am not, he is a party member and I am not, and many of you are party members. Why won't you work for him?'—'Galina Germanova, we don't care what he is. You are a lady, and a learned one, and he is a *muzhik*. Until you are restored to your former position we won't work!'

A few days later Galina resigned and went to work on Doctor K's. recommendation as a doctor in a laboratory of the Military Hospital.

Leningrad, where we often went to see friends, was no less hungry than Moscow, in fact there was even less to eat, but life was somehow much more bearable. The city was not as crowded and the people were different; even in rush hours one could get on the trams.

Occasionally I took my son into Leningrad to show him a sight I hoped he would not forget. Once I took him through the Tsar's summer palace, Tsarskoie Selo (then called Detskoie Selo), including the children's rooms where the Tsarevich's toys were on display. My boy was allowed to sit in a beautiful miniature automobile, in working order, and even to drive it a little. He was terribly impressed. He knew vaguely that the Tsar had been killed but it had never occurred to him that children could also be killed. 'Was the little boy shot too?' he inquired. I told him that the Tsarevich had been and rather hoped he would let it go at that. I could see, however, that he was perturbed and after a silence he said in a not very convinced tone: 'Perhaps it is just as well. If he had grown up he might have wanted to become a Tsar also.' He still remembers this incident, but has no recollection of the beautiful palaces and monuments such as Peterhof which I took him to see.

The weeks of rest, the calm surroundings, the beautiful city of Leningrad, so different and so far away from Moscow, had a great effect on me. When Doctor K. suggested getting me a teaching post in the Academy and said that he would be able to do the same for Ludwik, provided he got out of the Fourth, I was more than ready to try to persuade Ludwik to do so. Doctor K. thought it highly advisable for Ludwik to leave Moscow as well.

When the vacation was over and we were back in our barracks room in Moscow, back with the problems we had escaped for a few weeks, I told Ludwik of Doctor K.'s offer and how much it appealed to me. He too was tempted and would have welcomed the change. Unfortunately, the decision was not up to him. In the Crimea he had spent lonely hours watching the dolphins play in the waves and thinking what to do, but he had found no solution. He had missed us and was glad to be back with us, but was even more depressed about the future. His sadness affected my own enthusiasm for Leningrad, and once back in the tight grip of Moscow life the weeks went by with Leningrad being mentioned less and less frequently, until our plans were eventually forgotten altogether.

By 1932 the situation in the country had become worse and worse. Everyone knew about the desperate peasant uprisings, about the Young Communist Brigades sent into the countryside to help with the 'grain collection campaign', many of whom never came back. The mood in the party was dangerous. Programmes calling for the removal of Stalin were circulating in the party cells and there was a feeling of tense expectation. Some people began to hope for a miracle, but Stalin's grip on the party apparatus was much stronger than anyone had realized. The Left oppositionists, including those who had capitulated earlier, began to be arrested. Then it was the turn of the Right opposition. Even those who had never been in any opposition were being arrested. It became obvious that Stalin was removing not only those who were against him or had once been against him, but those who might some day oppose him. The hope that he would realize where his excesses were leading and call a halt to them dwindled steadily. The arrests were not confined to well-known personalities. Even ordinary party members who had had contacts with the leaders in the line of duty, were being arrested. The purge was coming closer to us.

The Fourth Department was of course affected. There were several arrests, followed by changes in key personnel. The position of Berzin, who had headed the Department since the 1920s, was none too secure and he could not do much to protect his men. Still, he did his best to keep his staff together, hoping that some day the storm would blow itself out. He had already transferred Ludwik from the operational division to a post in the department's archives, where there was little for him to do, in order to get him out of the public eye. Having told him to stay quietly in this job so as not to attract attention, one day Berzin told Ludwik he ought to consider an offer from Bortnovsky to join the Comintern.

Ludwik did not want to move to the Comintern. He knew it would mean involvement in the inner party struggles that were then tearing the international Communist movement apart. Ludwik was not a Trotskyite, on many points he disagreed with Trotsky, but like all old party members he could not conceive of a Communist movement without Trotsky. He was attached to him as an individual and as a symbol and since the vicious anti-Trotsky campaign, which had continued after his expulsion from the party and the country, Ludwik could no longer feel at home either in the Soviet Union or in the party. This campaign, which was of course echoed by all the parties abroad, would have made it impossible for him to work anywhere for the Comintern. When Ludwik left Holland for Moscow in 1929, there had still been some hope that the situation might change. But by the summer of 1932 there was no hope left, and Ludwik and Fedia agreed that they were living in full counter-revolution.

I must admit that I hoped Ludwik would accept the offer to join the Comintern and that we would go abroad. I had but one desire and that was to be as far away as possible from the Soviet Union. Although no one ever admitted it, this desire was deep in everybody's heart. I did not really grasp how untenable Ludwik's position would be in the Comintern, or if I did, I relegated this thought to the future and saw only a chance to get out. I reminded Ludwik that he had always considered his work in the Fourth Department as temporary. and had hoped some day to return to party work. This was the moment I have mentioned, when he looked at me sadly and said: 'What party work? What party? There are no parties any more, there is not even a Comintern. They are only instruments of that grave-digger of the revolution.' This was Trotsky's term for Stalin, and Ludwik liked to use his language.

'By removing all those who could have saved the revolution he has removed the foundation from under his own feet,' he went on. 'He has destroyed the Communist parties of the world, those parties that could still have saved the revolution in Russia. Instead of aiding these parties all the Comintern does is to incite internal party struggles which lead to constant changes of leadership at Stalin's whim. This will go on until every party is led by a blockhead like Thaelmann. Do you think Ika would have left the Comintern for the Fourth, after he had been in it so many years and knew it so well, if he had thought there was still room in it for people like himself, and that there was still useful work to be done there?'

'I know this,' I said. 'But wouldn't it be better for you to go abroad?'

'Yes, it would, but not tied to a party line.'

In the Fourth Department changes had been going on for about two years. Key positions had been assumed by Stalin's countrymen, protégés of General Tairov, himself a Georgian. S. Firin, the Fourth's deputy chief, had left for the N.K.V.D., where he took over an important post in the construction department. Felix Gorski had joined I.N.O., the foreign section of the N.K.V.D., and both Firin and Gorski urged Ludwik to follow their example while the opportunity existed. Ludwik was very reluctant to do so, although he knew that the objectives and the work of I.N.O. abroad differed very little, if at all, from those of the Fourth. The N.K.V.D. had a bad reputation, and he was not tempted by I.N.O., an organization held in contempt in the Fourth.

I.N.O., very short of able people, were jealous of the Fourth and never let a chance go by to undermine its prestige. They were also very keen on recruiting people away from the military and watched with great interest all the internal difficulties of their rival. They were of course greatly interested in a man like Ludwik, with his long experience, his prestige in the service, and his high decoration. As long ago as 1928, when they met in Berlin, Slutsky, now the chief of I.N.O., had urged Ludwik to join his unit. He could not understand Ludwik's hesitation and it was on his urging that Firin and Gorski both tried to recruit Ludwik. While Slutsky may not have understood Ludwik's attitude, Gorski, an old and good friend, understood it very well. He knew perfectly well that Ludwik wanted to leave the Soviet Union—although Ludwik of course never said so—and also that joining the N.K.V.D. offered the only possibility for a foreign assignment. Whenever Gorski came to visit us he spoke to Ludwik of joining I.N.O., knowing that eventually he would have no choice.

Firin was not a particularly close friend and did not visit us as frequently. Still, it was not unusual for him to drop in and whenever he did he also attempted to persuade Ludwik to make the move. He was much more direct than Felix. According to him, the Fourth Department was bound to go under in the coming upheaval and the only agency which had a chance of survival was the N.K.V.D.

Also frequent, much less natural, and most disagreeable to Ludwik, were the visits of Valentin Markin, whom Ludwik had met in Germany and did not like, much less consider a friend. Markin, who was known as Oscar, had been sent to Germany in the 1920s by the Fourth Department. He was a few years younger than Ludwik, under whose supervision he had been put. He was very bright, learned German very rapidly, and soon knew his way round, giving every promise of becoming an excellent worker. Unfortunately, he almost immediately began drinking heavily and as he picked quarrels in bars he could by his carelessness have exposed the entire apparatus. As if this were not bad enough, he took to intriguing against his fellow workers, sending home all kinds of derogatory reports about them. This behaviour was not appreciated in the Fourth, which prided itself on selecting its people carefully, and on trusting them. Markin was soon recalled; but back home he intrigued all the more. If something was not to his liking he did not hesitate to appeal, over the heads of his superiors, straight to the party authorities. Berzin was eager to get rid of Markin and when the N.K.V.D. offered him a job, saw to it that there were no obstacles. The I.N.O. was glad to have anyone who had been in the Fourth, and Markin was precisely the man they needed for their own intrigues.

This was the man who now took to visiting us to urge Ludwik to join I.N.O. Ludwik distrusted Markin and made it obvious that he did not enjoy his visits, but this did not discourage him. If anyone could have reinforced Ludwik's reluctance to make the transfer it was Markin, and Ludwik only got in touch with Slutsky after Markin had left for abroad. Markin understood what this meant and, as he told Ludwik when they saw each other in Paris, never forgave him for it.

Markin went to the United States where, one day in 1934, he was found in a New York bar with a fractured skull. He died a few days later in hospital. The cause of death was never established, though most of those who knew him believed he had been hit on the head with a bottle during a drunken brawl. Some people suspected the N.K.V.D., but this seems improbable, for the N.K.V.D. had not yet begun to kill its own people abroad, and even if it had, would hardly have been so careless as to leave a man dying who might after all regain consciousness and start talking, rather than killing him outright. Moreover, anyone as useful as Markin would certainly not have been killed. His death followed the particularly ill-advised Soviet attempt to flood the world markets with counterfeit dollars. The

Fourth Department had wanted no part of this affair but it was forced on them by Stalin who apparently believed in the usefulness of such operations. The numerous arrests which followed in the United States and in Europe gravely compromised the Fourth and Berzin himself, largely because Alfred Tilden, a Latvian like Berzin and a protégé of his, had been implicated in the scheme. Markin rendered the N.K.V.D. an invaluable service by bringing this whole matter to the attention of the highest party echelons, naturally enough placing the blame not on Stalin but on the Fourth. The N.K.V.D. was given the assignment of cleaning up the mess, and the man chosen for the job had been Markin himself.

Shortly after Markin's death I met Justina and Gorkić in Vienna and told them about it. Before I could go into the circumstances of his death Justina asked: 'Did he die, or did he get died?' (a pun in Russian). I told them the details and they agreed that the N.K.V.D. could not possibly have done such a clumsy job.[1] Gorkić's last comment was: 'Well, whoever did it, he's no loss!' He was, however, a loss to his mother, a schoolteacher in Moscow, whose only son he was, and possibly also to his wife, a nice Armenian girl who worked in the Soviet trade mission in Berlin, and to their little polio-stricken boy.

One of the victims of the counterfeiting fiasco had been Franz Fischer. I had seen Franz with Alfred Tilden in Berlin some time before the operation was exposed and was greatly surprised at the screaming headlines and at seeing his name in all the papers with notices of a reward for his arrest.[2] After months of hiding from the police in Europe he succeeded in reaching Moscow. We saw him there once and it was hard to recognize the handsome, dashing young man we had known, who had been famous for the boldness of his operations when he was a member of the revolutionary committee in Germany in 1923.

[1] In his book Krivitsky says that Slutsky told him some years later that Markin had been a Trotskyite; from this Krivitsky deduces that he was killed on the orders of the N.K.V.D. But Slutsky was the kind of man who might tell one story one day and another the next.
[2] Actually, Fischer had not been directly involved but acted as a go-between for Alfred Tilden and one of the banks. He had done so because as a German citizen he had a genuine passport.

(Once, wearing the uniform of an army officer and leading a few alleged soldiers, he had turned up in a government office and in the arrogant tones of a Prussian officer directed the staff to hand over to him all the most confidential files. The *coup* was carried out in a few minutes and by the time someone sought to check and to call the police he and his squad had vanished.)

No sooner had Franz got to Moscow than he was sent off to a distant outpost in the Arctic North, so that no one who might have seen his picture in the European papers would recognize him in Moscow and thus implicate the Soviet government. Possibly he was forgotten there in the Far North and may even have survived the purges.

Most of the men Ludwik knew in the N.K.V.D. had served in the Fourth before joining I.N.O.; the fact that he knew almost no long-time N.K.V.D. men except Slutsky contributed to his hesitation. Oddly enough it was Fedia, who had always frowned on the N.K.V.D., who helped him make up his mind. Fedia said: 'What difference does it make? If they were to send me abroad I would join them too. Unfortunately, they won't. With my long experience in the Fourth I am too useful to them here in the press. Do you think you can afford to play the prima donna? I wouldn't, if I were you. You have no choice, but you do have a chance to go abroad and that is the most important thing.'

While Ludwik was hesitating, things were getting worse. We learned that Stalin's young wife Nadejda Alliluieva had committed suicide after a quarrel with him. We began to hear of arrests in the Ukraine and of some inexplicable ones in the Fourth, the latter blamed, rightly or not, on N.K.V.D. intrigues. One day one of our neighbours was arrested. We did not know the family very well as they had no children, and children were one of the main links in the house. Ludwik told me that the arrest had all the earmarks of a frame-up and that it might be cleared up. The man was charged with espionage for Poland, which was odd as the man and his wife were both Russians. He did however work for Colonel Swierchiewski, a russified Pole whom we also knew, and for a while it looked as though Swierchiewski might be in trouble as well.[1]

Of these mysterious affairs the one that affected us most involved Pavlo Ladan, whom we had known since 1922. One evening in 1932 Ladan was coming to have dinner with us; he was going abroad and had promised to leave his alarm clock with us. (It was customary to leave such valuable and unobtainable possessions with one's friends when one went abroad.) I prepared dinner and we waited for Pavlo. The food got cold, and he did not appear. I was annoyed and said that after all he could have called us to let us know he couldn't come. Ludwik, who was also a bit put out, said half-jokingly: 'I bet he was sorry he promised you the alarm clock, that's why he didn't come.' Pavlo had the reputation of being somewhat stingy. We soon forgot the incident, but a few nights later Ludwik came in and sat down silently. This was most unusual; he always had something to tell me when he came home from work. That evening he kept quiet for a long time. I asked if something had happened and he answered: 'Yes. Pavlo has been executed!'

I was stunned at first. Had he said that he had been arrested I would have been shocked but might have understood. But executed! This was inconceivable to me, such things did not happen. 'Executed?' I asked. 'Why? By whom?' The 'by whom', of course, was foolish. I knew very well by whom and I did not repeat it. But I asked again: 'Why?' Ludwik said Pavlo had been arrested the night before he was supposed to come to dinner with us, and executed some days later. He said: 'They had to drag him down to the cellar. That big, husky fellow kept sobbing: "What are you doing? I am completely innocent!" '

Ladan, a Ukrainian, was an American citizen, the son of a Galician peasant who had emigrated to the United States before the war. He had become a journalist and when the revolution broke out he went to the Soviet Union, joined the Communist Party and worked for the Comintern. He had become a member of the politburo of the Ukrainian section of the Communist Party of Poland. His private life had suffered

[1] Swierchiewski at any rate survived the purges; a General Swierchiewski was killed in Poland in 1947.

and his marriage was broken up by the constant travelling he did for the Comintern.

He had been accused of working for the Polish intelligence service and of having prepared an uprising in the Soviet Ukraine. This was of course a complete untruth, as Pavlo was loyal and devoted to the Soviet Union. The truth was the N.K.V.D. needed a link between Poland and the Ukrainian comrades who had been made the scapegoats of the famine in the Ukraine. Ladan's frequent foreign travel on behalf of the Comintern came in very handy. And having served the purposes of the N.K.V.D. Pavlo Ladan was killed.

These events hastened Ludwik's decision to begin negotiations with Slutsky, and to accept a position abroad. The consultations were prolonged and had to be carried out with the utmost discretion, for an important transfer such as this could only take place with the approval of the Central Committee of the party. Although the Fourth Department knew perfectly well where Ludwik was heading, it was very much in their interest to pretend not to know or not to explain why a valuable and very senior staff member was leaving them. Nor could I.N.O. simply hire a man who held a key position in military intelligence. A way was finally found which suited both agencies: Ludwik was given an innocuous-sounding post as director of a factory. The general manager of the factory as well as the secretary of the party cell were told that the appointment was temporary and fictitious, but Ludwik was uneasy. He felt that the staff of the factory could not help but wonder at a director who knew nothing of his job and showed so little interest in it.

On the surface our life continued unchanged. We remained in the Red Army housing unit and continued to be members of their co-operative. As far as we knew, none of our neighbours was aware of the change, and if they knew anything about it, they certainly never mentioned it. There was never much shop talk in the house anyway. Whenever one of our neighbours went away on a trip it was always said that he was on official business inside the Soviet Union, and most probably he was. Only once during our stay in the house was a man's true destination revealed, and that was through his own carelessness. The man's wife told everyone he was in the Ukraine, which nobody questioned. A few days later on the table where our post was placed was a postcard from him showing the new German liner *Europa*, post-marked Bremen. This of course attracted a great deal of attention and everyone knew that 'the Ukraine' was in reality the United States.

Ludwik went to his plant in the mornings and in the evenings consulted with Slutsky and Felix Gorski. He also began to make the acquaintance of some of the other N.K.V.D. men. Eventually, with the transfer arranged, he was sent abroad. I was to follow him a few weeks later.

Before he left Moscow Ludwik introduced me to the N.K.V.D. officer, Theodore Maly, who was to help me with preparations for my own departure. Whether Ludwik himself selected Maly or whether the choice was an accident I do not know, but it would have been difficult to find a better man. Teddy, as he was called, was in his forties, a handsome, tall Hungarian with blue eyes and the charming smile of the naturally shy. He had been a priest before he joined the Cheka. I saw little of him in Moscow, but later on, when he was transferred to I.N.O. and was sent to London and then to Paris, we became good friends. In the summer of 1937 he proved to be both loyal and trustworthy. His character combined extreme sweetness and a great deal of determination, so that one felt at ease and protected in his company.

Maly told me it had been decided that I should travel on a Soviet passport, rather than a foreign one. The N.K.V.D. felt that, given our long stay in Moscow, foreigners who had been there might recognize us abroad. This seemed unlikely to me, as the only foreigners with whom we associated in Moscow were friends, either from the Comintern or the Fourth. As a precautionary measure, the family name was altered on the passport from Poretsky to Boretsky, which also struck me as rather childish. But Maly seemed to think the arrangement sound, and as my one interest was to rejoin Ludwik as soon as possible, I did not much care under what name and on what passport I was travelling. The alleged purpose of my trip was to go to Vienna for medical treatment, but as it was much more difficult and took much longer to get an Austrian visa than a

German one, plans were changed so that I was to go to Berlin. This suited me much better, for I knew Ludwik would be coming to Berlin but that he seldom had any business in Vienna.

Although my departure was not going to take place for some weeks, Maly told me to get ready and so I began distributing all our valuable possessions. Willy, naturally, got the phonograph; he had defended it often enough against our prying neighbour Z. to have earned it. Willy helped me pack some of our books in a trunk which went into storage. Most of the other things went to Fedia. The beds and furniture I left behind, to the great delight of the next occupant of our room.

One day at noon Maly stopped by the room to tell me that he would fetch me that evening at eleven o'clock and put me on the midnight train for Berlin. We were ready when he came. He had a car waiting outside. It all happened rapidly; the people in the house were asleep so no one saw us leave. At the station Maly gave me my passport, some German money, and said good-bye. We were on our way.

We had a compartment to ourselves and I put my son to sleep. As the train began to move, I realized that I was actually leaving the Soviet Union and the farther we went the more I realized how tied I had become to that country. The years of suffering and disillusion had forged a closer link than the early hopeful years which followed the revolution.

CHAPTER VII

Europe in the Thirties

I

Next morning we were in Germany and I ordered breakfast in the compartment. The waiter came carrying a tray with coffee, hot milk, and little rolls wrapped in cellophane. I watched my boy, usually a poor eater, forcing himself to eat roll after roll. I stopped him and asked him why he was doing it. 'But, Mother,' he answered, 'there won't be any tomorrow!' I reassured him, saying there would always be nice rolls, but he did not believe me and when he thought I wasn't looking stuffed one in his pocket.

We stayed in Berlin only a few days. My boy had been ill with whooping cough and a doctor advised me to take him to the mountains to get rid of the traces of his cough. But the city in that short time was an unceasing source of wonder to the child. He marvelled at the ease with which one could buy candy in any shop. One day we went into a large department store and after having taken a few spins in the revolving door— a phenomenon unknown to him— he turned to me and said: 'What wonderful co-operatives they have in this country. Tell me, Mother, when did they have their revolution?'—'A long time ago,' I told him.—'That must be why they have everything here,' was the comment. In that same department store I ran into our snooping neighbour from Moscow, Z. He had been in Berlin only a few days, he told me. He too wondered at the 'marvellous co-operatives'.

To me the city was not quite so enchanting. In the midst of its lighted night-clubs, its opulent window displays of dummies in silly little women's hats, young men out of work pushed their children round in prams while their wives tried to find jobs as domestics. Brown-shirted Nazis paraded through the streets with their flags, and at night there were pitched battles between them and the Communists and Socialists. All this looked like a dance of death. I missed the Soviet Union, grim and hungry, where people were being driven to exhaustion but at least did not know unemployment. I was glad when we left Berlin.

On the train to the little resort in Saxony where I was taking my son I asked the conductor if he could recommend a small pension. He was overjoyed to be able to offer us his own place. At the station he took our suitcase and we followed him. His wife could not believe in the miracle of having a paying guest. She cried and told me that almost everyone in the village was unemployed and that the Nazis were making headway all the time. She and her husband were Social-Democrats and appalled that their fourteen-year-old son was a member of the *Hitler Jugend*. It soon became known that I had come from the Soviet Union, and a number of unemployed young men came to ask me whether they could find work there. They said that the situation in Germany was hopeless and that they would go anywhere to find work. Some expressed sympathy with the Soviet Union, though most of them probably joined the Nazis when Hitler came to power. We stayed in Saxony for about four weeks and I would not have minded staying longer, as it was quiet and restful and good for the child; but Ludwik, who came to see us there, told me it was inadvisable to stay in a place so small that everyone knew where I came from. This was the first of many inconveniences caused by my Soviet passport.

In Berlin I found a good furnished room in the flat of an unemployed actress. The flat was in a housing development known in Berlin as 'the parlour pink colony', in which most of the tenants were intellectuals and artists and many were Socialists and Communists. The majority were unemployed and evictions for failure to pay the rent—with the police putting the furniture out on the street and friends putting it right back in the apartment the minute the police were gone—were a daily occurrence. I enrolled my son in a private school in the neighbourhood and waited anxiously to be contacted by the liaison man who was to help me get settled. Such help was unnecessary in my case, as I knew Berlin very well, but it was the usual procedure.

I did not know who the liaison man would be and was all the more pleased when he turned out to be an acquaintance from Moscow, the son of Michael Borodin, who had been the Soviet representative in China in the 1920s. Young Borodin was a handsome young air-force lieutenant called 'the flyer'; when we had known each other in Moscow I had not been aware that he had anything to do with the N.K.V.D. This was his first assignment abroad and he was tremendously impressed. He was awed by the living standards and found the food delicious, although it had taken him some time to get accustomed to chocolate bars. (After Hitler came to power Borodin left Berlin for Paris, which he found still more enticing and the food even better.) We agreed to meet once a fortnight at a fixed place and time and exchanged telephone numbers in case of emergency.

Since the official reason for my visit was the need for medical treatment, I could only get my visa renewed by showing a medical certificate. I therefore visited a neighbourhood doctor recommended by my landlady, and a dentist whom I really did need badly. The doctor was a Communist, while the dentist—an excellent one and a very pleasant and decent young man—was a Nazi sympathizer. Actually he belonged to the Strasser group which was officially in opposition to the Nazi Party, and was very much interested in the Soviet Union, for he believed in some form of 'national bolshevism'.

Then came the Reichstag fire, and the Nazis were in power. They proceeded to arrest every Socialist and Communist they could find. In the early hours of the morning our 'parlour pink' block was surrounded by Brown Shirts. The S.A. men went from room to room, throwing all the books they found into the street where they burnt them. With them were uniformed and plain-clothes police.

When they came to our flat the Nazi in the team went into my landlady's room while my room was searched by a regular police officer. I could see he did not have much enthusiasm for his job. He seemed reluctant to go through the various boxes filled with my son's broken toys, and made only a pretence of looking over the bookshelves, ignoring volumes by Trotsky and Lenin. Then turning to me he said: 'I suppose you are from the eastern borders of Germany, you roll your r's.' I told him I was not German at all and he asked to see my passport. I produced the large red booklet with the hammer and sickle prominently stamped on it. 'I am afraid I'll have to show this to "him", much as I hate to,' the officer said, and added: 'Anyway you can see I have searched your room very thoroughly.' I agreed and he told me to stay in the room while he went to fetch the Nazi.

The Brown Shirt wanted to know what I was doing in Germany. 'I am here for medical treatment,' I told him. As this corresponded with the entry on my passport he accepted it, but told me to report to the police in the morning. Before he left he asked me whether I was a Communist. I said I was not. What was I doing living in the parlour pink colony then? I told him this was a comfortable room and that I knew nothing of 'parlour pinks' and cared less. He asked whether my landlady was a Communist. 'I don't know,' I answered, 'but I don't think so.' He laughed and showed me a receipt for party membership dues signed by her as secretary of the local Communist cell. Then he added: 'Well, you can't complain of our search methods. They would have been a lot rougher in your country!' To which I replied that, although not a Communist, I was a loyal citizen of my country, and things like this did not happen to innocent people there. He laughed again and left the room.

The policeman stayed behind for a few minutes and asked me what I intended to do. I told him I planned to leave as soon as my medical treatment was over and that I did not like Germany any more. The policeman said: 'Look here, after all, he didn't do anything to you.'—'No,' I said, 'not to me. But look out of the window.' Nazis were throwing books out of all the windows; the square below was a pyre of burning books, and their trucks were taking people off to jail by the hundreds. He nodded sadly: 'I know, but this won't last. New brooms always sweep cleaner.'

When I went as I had been told to, to report to the police next day, and to renew my permit which would expire in four days, no one was the least bit interested in me. I told them I would come back in four days when the permit ran out.

'Why do that?' asked the police official. 'I'll give it to you now.' To my surprise he gave me a permit for three months instead of the usual one month. When I told this to a friend of my land-lady's he said that the police official was probably a Social-Democrat who was using this method to get back at the Nazis.

On my next visit to my dentist I found two husky young Brown Shirts in front of his door, chanting: 'Germans, don't patronize a Jew!' The dentist was of course not Jewish, though his name had a vaguely Jewish sound. When I went in I saw him sitting in his patient's chair with an ashen face. 'Why don't you go out there and tell them that you are not a Jew but a Nazi?' I asked him.—'I am not a Nazi any more, not even in opposition to the Nazis, not after what has happened. I don't want anything to do with them any more. It won't be long now before they lock me up together with the Socialists, and the Communists, and the Jews. Then they will kill me. I am only sorry for one thing and that is that I ever contributed anything to them in the past!'

When the day came for my usual meeting with young Borodin, in the tea room at Wertheim's, one of Berlin's largest department stores, I arrived to find the place surrounded by Nazis carrying placards that read: 'A one-way ticket to Pales-tine'. The store, Jewish-owned, was closed and with it the tea room. I met Borodin in the street and he said: 'Two weeks ago one might have predicted anything, an earthquake even, but not that Wertheim's would be closed!' He was glad to see me, as he had heard that some Soviet citizens had been mis-treated by the Nazis. I reassured him and we fixed another meeting place.

Ludwik meanwhile came to Berlin on a short visit and told me that I ought to leave as soon as possible. As we walked through the streets filled with marching and singing Nazi battalions, I asked what he thought of Stalin's having predicted that this would be a short-lived affair and that afterwards the Communists would take over.

'Don't even repeat such nonsense,' Ludwik answered. 'Stalin is criminal enough to say it and stupid enough to believe it. This is no short-lived affair. They are here for a long time. It is a catastrophe which will lead to war.'

It was weeks before I could leave Berlin. My Soviet passport was now a liability, but unfortunately no one at home had thought of such an emergency and preparing a new passport and getting it to me took time. The school my boy had been going to closed in April; the director and many of the Jewish teachers had left earlier, but the school ran for some time with a skeleton staff. My passport arrived, but time was still required to get the necessary visas. In the meantime, of course, I could no longer stay in my room in the actress's flat. I had become friends with my landlady, who was very fond of my boy, and I was sorry to say goodbye to her. I saw her again in Paris where she went as a refugee. During the war, when the Germans occupied Paris, she was arrested and perished in a Nazi concentration camp.

I could not register at a hotel, as for all practical purposes I had no papers at all, so when I left the flat I found shelter for a few days with a German Communist family in the working-class district of Wedding. We stayed there illegally, that is without registering with the police. Then at last we left Berlin and Nazi Germany for good. We crossed the border into Switzerland without incident and rejoined Ludwik.

2

In the years after Hitler came to power we spent most of our time in Paris, or at least I did; Ludwik travelled a great deal. We were considered fortunate, for an assignment in Paris was of course much coveted.

For the many German Communists who had fled there from Nazi Germany, however, there was little pleasure in being in Paris. They were too stunned by what had happened in Germany to take part in French intellectual or political life, and a number were driven to suicide. We had known some of these demoralized and embittered men in earlier and better days, and were naturally closer to them than to others we met later. Some of them worked for Ludwik, others he helped out of his own funds. After 1933 he could pay them out of official funds without having to account for it.

Ludwik did not always wish Moscow to know who his contacts were; many of them had been in opposition, and in any case, it was much safer for all concerned if their identity remained unknown. The fact that Moscow did not know these people enabled us to be much franker with them than with others. With some friends at least one could talk, ask questions and answer them.

Those we knew less well seldom asked questions about what was happening in the Soviet Union, whether because they did not wish to embarrass Ludwik or were afraid of jeopardizing their connection with us we never knew. But we were never afraid these people would denounce us to Moscow for being critical of its policies. In any case they would not have known whom to denounce us to. Most of them knew they were doing some kind of work for the Soviet Union, but they never knew what organization they were working for. They only knew Ludwik, whom they saw occasionally, and me, whom they met when Ludwik was out of town. He encouraged me to see them, for he knew how cut off and lonely they were, and he felt responsible for them. I soon learned that even those who never asked questions had their doubts; they had confidence in Ludwik, however, and felt that as long as he was willing to stay on his job they were morally justified in doing so. Whenever I mentioned their feelings to Ludwik he would answer: 'They'—he meant Moscow—'force one to lie, to wear a mask, never to be one's true self not only with the world but with one's own comrades. I know how these people feel, and I also know where the responsibility lies. But I do not think I have the right to take away even a shred of their faith. Only what am I to do when I am ordered to send them to Hitler's Germany to risk their necks?'

Among the Germans who worked for Ludwik was Paul Urban, a husky, blond Bavarian, a painter from Munich who had worked as book illustrator for various left-wing publications, including the Muenzenberg publishing houses. Through friends in the Comintern he came to know Brun, who was then trying to recruit German fellow-travellers and sympathizers. When the Nazis seized power Paul had to leave Germany. He went to Amsterdam where he ran into Ludwik, whom he had known slightly in Germany. Paul earned very little money in Holland, working for a publisher, and when Ludwik thinking he might be useful asked him to come to Paris, he accepted gladly. In this case Ludwik did notify Moscow that Paul was working for him; there was no risk in doing so, as Paul had practically no political past and had never been mixed up in the opposition.

Paul's artistic activities gave him an entrée to various circles, and, as he was a handsome young bachelor, he had many girl friends, some of whom were useful to us. Paul was not a communicative man and at first was rather difficult to get along with, but we soon became fond of him. I saw a good deal of him when Ludwik was away from Paris, and Ludwik, although Paul and he were not personal friends, appreciated his qualities. 'Paul really is a wonderful co-worker,' Ludwik used to say. 'He does all you expect him to do and never asks questions like "Why does the Soviet Union supply oil to Mussolini to make war on Ethiopia?" '

Our relations with Paul were not always completely smooth. He clearly resented the fact that he could not get in touch with us—an obvious security precaution—while another German, Paul Massing, could. Massing, who later had the good fortune to get out alive from a Nazi concentration camp, was a close friend of long standing, but Paul Urban was none the less jealous and resentful of this mark of favour.

Urban never discussed politics with us, and we had come to the conclusion that he knew nothing about the subject and cared less. But when I encountered him once at the home of the journalist Egon Kisch I discovered how wrong we had been. Paul was asking all kinds of shrewd and very embarrassing questions about conditions in the Soviet Union, where Kisch had been recently, and was not at all satisfied with Kisch's stock reply: 'I do not think. Stalin thinks for me. I am Stalin's soldier.'—'I know all about your being Stalin's soldier and his doing your thinking for you,' Paul was saying. 'What I want to know is do you like the things that are going on there?'

One of the things Paul resented most was the fact that he had never been invited to the U.S.S.R. He asked me to intercede with Ludwik to arrange a trip there for him. Evidently he wanted to see for himself what was going on and not to be told about it by Kisch. He also felt he deserved this reward that so many others had already been given. Ludwik was greatly disturbed by Paul's request. It would have been easy enough for him to arrange the visit, but he was reluctant to do so, as he did not think it was at all safe for Paul to go to Moscow. Paul, on the other hand, became increasingly depressed and insisted on going. Finally, much against his judgement, Ludwik made the necessary arrangements.

Paul left, supposedly to spend only a short time in the Soviet Union, a vacation in the Crimea and a few weeks in Moscow. But months went by and in spite of Ludwik's repeated inquiries, Paul did not return. Ludwik could not forgive himself for having yielded to Paul's insistence. 'They will keep him there,' he told me, 'because he will come in handy as a Nazi spy. It's not every day they get hold of such a perfect Aryan type.'

Not many people in those days were clamouring to go to the U.S.S.R. The political refugees knew better than to ask such favours. Ludwik, on the other hand, had trouble trying to keep those in whom Moscow suddenly showed some interest, and whom it 'invited', from having to go. One such case was Marco Bardach, whose existence Moscow learnt of only when it became impossible to keep it from them. A Galician Socialist, he had gone to the Soviet Ukraine after the revolution, and in 1919 was sent by the Soviet government to Denmark to buy horses and agricultural machinery. He never returned, and Moscow of course put forward the classic accusation that he had made off with the money. Marco, however, claimed that he had not been given any money to carry out the transaction and that this was the reason he never went back. Moscow in any case was no longer concerned with Bardach, although he obviously had a bad record from then on.[1]

Ludwik had helped Bardach privately without mentioning to Moscow that he was doing so and that he occasionally used him. After Hitler came to power Bardach emigrated to France. Ludwik felt he should be on the payroll, as he had excellent connections among the Germans—among them Berchtold Jacob, a journalist whom the Nazis later kidnapped in Switzer-

---

[1] In such cases the Soviets did not really mind if someone defected with a considerable sum of money. It was argued that this gave the man something to live on, whereas if he had no money at all he was much more likely to go to the police and try to sell such information as he had.

land, and the former Chancellor of Germany, Dr. Wirth—and the Ukrainians, notably Sevriuk, a man of considerable value to us.

Sevriuk had represented the Ukrainian *Rada* at the Brest-Litovsk peace conference and although he never went back to the U.S.S.R. had remained very friendly towards the Soviets. He stayed in Germany after the Nazis took over and soon occupied a responsible position in the aircraft ministry. While working there Sevriuk used to come to Switzerland once a month to see Ludwik. Ludwik was worried by these frequent trips abroad; he reasoned that German intelligence must know of Sevriuk's contacts with him and be letting him go abroad for purposes of their own. He continued to meet Sevriuk in spite of these misgivings, however, as the information he brought was important enough to be worth the risk.[1]

It was because of the Sevriuk link that Bardach's existence had to be made known to Moscow. Some time later Ludwik was instructed to 'invite' Bardach to Moscow. We were certain that Bardach would refuse but, to our great surprise and alarm, he was not only willing but extremely anxious to go, or at least so he said. It therefore became my task as discreetly as possible to talk him out of making the trip. This proved difficult. I mentioned his earlier troubles in the Ukraine and he answered that those were an additional reason for going back, as he would have an opportunity to clear them up. Furthermore, he argued, the Ukrainian State Publishing House owed him money for a translation into Ukrainian of the works of Karl Marx, which he had done under the pseudonym of Ivan Sokyra. When I told Krivitsky[2] of my lack of success, he suggested that the wisest course would be to stop trying to dissuade Bardach. He argued that he would go anyway, and that as soon as he got to Moscow he would tell people we had tried to stop him from going. This would not help him, but would get us into trouble. Ludwik was furious at Krivitsky's cynicism and kept repeating: 'I still don't see why that poor old fool should go and get himself shot.'

[1] Sevriuk was not caught, and continued to live in Germany until he was killed in a train crash in 1943.

[2] He too had by then left the Fourth Department for the N.K.V.D. and frequently came to Paris from The Hague where he was based.

There was no doubt in our minds as to what Bardach's fate would be. We reasoned that he was needed to testify against various prominent Ukrainian Communists whom he had known intimately. Some of his former friends, Ladan for instance, had already been executed; others had simply disappeared. The prominent writer Khvilovoi had committed suicide and Grinko was to be one of the defendants in the third Moscow trial. However, we made no further attempts to talk Bardach out of his visit, and in the event, Krivitsky's advice turned out to be right. No sooner had we stopped arguing than Bardach seemed to lose interest in going, or at least stopped talking about it. After a while it seemed safe to ask him how his preparations were going and when he wanted to leave. He began to offer all kinds of excuses: his wife was ill, he was not feeling well, he had urgent business to attend to. Ludwik reported to Moscow that Bardach had decided not to go, and there was no reaction whatever. As far as they were concerned the whole affair was finished, and Bardach was forgotten.

Strangely enough, it was at that stage—when the N.K.V.D. had lost all interest in him—that Bardach panicked. He began to tremble for his life, saw assassination plots everywhere, told all and sundry—including the police—that the N.K.V.D. was out to kill him. His reaction was not unlike that of other fellow-travellers who had taken money from the Soviet services and played along with them while the going was good, and who after that lived in a constant state of panic or at least tried to make everyone believe they were in mortal peril. Bardach was in his late fifties at the time. During the war he was in a German concentration camp and by a miracle survived. When I last saw him, some years after the war, he was an old, lonely man. His wife Lucie, who had spent much time in a mental institution, committed suicide, and he died in Switzerland shortly afterwards.

We had met Egon Kisch through Fedia years before. They had known each other in the Socialist Youth movement before the war. Kisch, born in what became Czechoslovakia, had served as an officer in the Austrian army, but after the war renewed his old contacts and was one of the first to join the Austrian Communist Party. He contributed a great deal towards building the Soviet apparatus in the early days in Austria and elsewhere, but never took part in any of the work itself and never belonged to any of the networks. He went to the Soviet Union soon after the war and remained faithful to its cause ever after. Nothing that happened in the Soviet Union or abroad seemed to shake his fidelity; his motto remained: 'In spite of everything; everything for the Soviet Union.'

We saw a geat deal of Kisch in Vienna, Berlin, Moscow, and now in Paris—or more accurately, in Versailles, where he settled after leaving Germany in 1933. Apart from the fact that he was useful—as a reporter and writer he had been everywhere and seemed to know everyone—he was an engaging companion and an extraordinarily good story-teller. Admittedly it was hard to know which of his stories was true, but this did not matter very much as we enjoyed them all. Some were about his grandmother, who was apparently a holy terror. Others were about his tattoos. He had one on his wrist, some sort of Chinese dragon, but his pride and joy was one he claimed to have on his back. It had been put there by a cell-mate in an army guardhouse—where he seemed to have spent the greater part of his military career—and as it was on his back he said he had not at first known what it was. At a medical inspection however the tattoo turned out to be a very good likeness of his regimental commander in a most unflattering posture. This of course resulted in his speedy return to a cell. Naturally everyone was keen on seeing this masterpiece, but no one ever did.

When pressed on one of these stories Kisch would turn to his wife Lisl for confirmation. She never had much choice but to back up his statements. The last time I saw him he was quarrelling with his wife on a Paris street—Lisl was silent and he was shouting at her. When I spoke to him he shouted at me: 'You probably think you know who Lenin's widow is.' Somewhat taken aback I said: 'Why, yes, it's Krupskaia.'—'That's what you think,' he roared. '*She's* Lenin's widow, she knows everything.' I never did find out what it was all about.

Kisch seemed to like everything about Stalin's Soviet Union except that he himself had never been received by Stalin. He bitterly resented the fact that Henri Barbusse should be celebrated in the Soviet Union as a proletarian writer, while he, a fairly well-known writer and a Communist of long standing, was completely taken for granted. He seemed quite incapable of understanding that the Soviets had a political purpose in cultivating a renowned French writer, while to them, Communist or not, Kisch was only a homeless exile who impressed nobody.

Our earlier friendly relations with Kisch were strained after 1935, when he was in Moscow at the same time as Ludwik but avoided contact with him and with his old friend Fedia. Ludwik learned from Fedia that Kisch had shunned him ever since Fedia had tried to discuss the political situation in the Soviet Union with him. From then on we felt that he could not be trusted.

Shortly before the Nazi invasion Kisch left France for Mexico, where he spent the war. After the 1948 Communist *coup* he went to Prague, where he had the good fortune to die quietly in his bed. Had he lived a few years more he would doubtless—in spite of being 'Stalin's soldier'—have joined Rudolf Slansky and Otto Katz on the gallows.

Among the other people we saw and were friendly with in Paris in the thirties were Alexander and Lene Rado. Rado was a Hungarian Communist who had spent considerable time in the Soviet Union: he had worked for a press agency and was also a highly competent draughtsman and cartographer. When he and his wife and two small children first arrived in Paris in 1933, however, they were cut off from the apparatus and penniless. Ludwik helped them financially as best he could. By the winter of 1934 Rado had been reintegrated into the apparatus, and was sent to Geneva where he was to organize a network using a cartography and reproduction shop as his cover. Rado's genuine professional qualifications enabled him to build a legitimate cover—which was not always easy— and there was already at hand a skeleton staff, organized by Ludwik and others, for him to develop. When the war came his cover firm became the centre of Soviet espionage against Nazi Germany.[1]

The Rados were a close and devoted couple, although

[1] Rado's operations in war-time Switzerland have been described in detail in *Handbook for Spies* (London 1949, 1964) by Alexander Foote, one of his men there.

completely different in character. Lene, a German, was the more intelligent and enterprising and certainly the more devoted Communist, while Rado gave an impression of easy-going sleepiness. They complemented each other very well, however. Rado was apparently ordered back to Moscow after the war, while Lene remained behind in Europe. I tried to get in touch with her in 1950, without success, but Ruth Fischer, who did see her, reported that she was ill and desperate and did not know what had happened to Rado. Later it was reported—though not confirmed—that Rado had returned to Hungary, where he became a teacher, and that Lene had succeeded in rejoining him in Budapest, where she died of cancer.

Another person who was forced to leave Germany—being Jewish as well as a member of the German Communist Party—when the Nazis came to power was Gertrude Schildbach, whom Ludwik had known since 1917. I shall be telling her story elsewhere; it will be enough to say now that when she arrived in Paris in 1934 Ludwik felt obliged to help her. He had often done so in the past but without mentioning her existence to Moscow. In Paris, however, where she was a *bona fide* refugee and could establish herself legally, he thought she could take an apartment which he could use for work and for meetings which could not be held in cafés. He therefore arranged with Moscow to pay Schildbach's rent and a small salary, so that she would be free of the immediate problem of making a living. This was how she first became known to the N.K.V.D.

Ludwik made sure that Schildbach never met any of his contacts; she left the apartment before he and his visitors arrived and returned after they had gone. I saw her very often, as I did some of the other German refugees, at Ludwik's urging, and would occasionally use her address to receive really private letters from friends who could write me safely there. But Schildbach never knew where Ludwik and I lived or the name we used in Paris, and she never met any of our friends, or anybody connected with Ludwik's work. She was much too unstable emotionally for him to make any use of her except for renting the apartment.

Through Paul Urban we also came to know several young

women refugees from Germany who—though not party members—were willing to help fight the Nazis, although they never knew just what it was they were doing. One of these was Gerda Frankfurter. She came from a wealthy family, was financially independent, had good connections, a legal passport, and what was perhaps most important, no political past whatever. Her only link with any of us was that she was Paul's girl friend. Ludwik saw no harm in using her as a postal address and as a courier, and informed Moscow that he was doing so. It was politic to tell them of occasional staff changes, especially as mentioning someone as apolitical as Gerda helped camouflage the use of more effective but often politically compromised people. In this case, however, Moscow immediately considered Gerda their 'own' person, and issued instructions and orders to her.

German refugees like Gerda could be used as couriers in Switzerland or Holland, but it was quite out of the question to send them to Germany. It was in fact very hard to find anyone who could go there, as they could not be German, Jewish, or known to be a Socialist or Communist. One person who could go was the mother of Noel and Herman Field whose cases were to become famous after the war. Mrs. Field, by then fairly advanced in years, a devout Quaker, felt it her duty to do anything she could against Hitler, and her American nationality made her useful as an occasional courier. I had met her a few times in Paris and spoke admiringly to Ludwik of her joy in being able actively to oppose the Nazis. He did not share this feeling, knowing that every such act endangered the lives of people in Germany. He did his best to keep communications to a minimum, and preferred dealing directly, through Sevriuk and other contacts in Switzerland, although he realized that in doing so he himself ran a considerable risk of being kidnapped by the Nazis.

Ludwik's actions also exposed him to criticism from Moscow, where Stalin's idiotic notion that the Hitler regime could not possibly last was giving way very gradually to a realization that the Nazis were there to stay. To undermine them Moscow began to evolve hare-brained and desperate schemes, such as recruiting the Kaiser's son to form an aristocratic opposition. Ludwik was not in the habit of taking orders blindly; moreover he knew perfectly well what kind of opposition the Hohenzollerns could provide. This particular idea must have occurred to the N.K.V.D. because Ludwik once told them he had become friendly with a Hohenlohe, whom he liked and helped financially in the vague hope he might some day prove useful. It soon became apparent that this impoverished aristocrat had no political connections; 'our prince', as we called him, spent his time writing poetry and an autobiography which I read. Ludwik wrote back to Moscow that he knew no Hohenzollerns, had no way of meeting any, and that in any case the whole thing would be a waste of time and money. He then inquired 'whose sick brain had had this brainstorm'. He thought at the time it must have been Artuzov, a Sovietized Swiss on whom such schemes were always being blamed, fairly or not. The plan was not mentioned again, but Felix Gorski wrote to us privately: 'By God, you could not have written a more stupid letter if you tried. The "sick brain" was Stalin himself!'

Several other preposterous schemes were worked out in Moscow which Ludwik was supposed to execute. One day he was advised to get in touch with Putzi Hanfstaengel, a prominent Nazi who had fled Germany. Ludwik told Moscow if they insisted on this they had better send someone else to make the contact, as he would not. He was sure Hanfstaengel's flight had been carefully prepared, and that he was by then in contact with British intelligence. Hanfstaengel was in Belgium, so Krivitsky was instructed to get in touch with him; but the German refused to have anything to do with Krivitsky's emissary, and eventually went to Canada. Felix wrote that the N.K.V.D. had been angry at Ludwik's refusal, but had later to admit he was right. One reason Ludwik wanted no part of such adventures was that he knew Stalin, while ostensibly working against the Nazis, was already trying to enter into negotiations with them.

Some of the delicate work inside Germany was entrusted to the Berlin resident, Zarubin (known as Rudolph), who later occupied several ambassadorial posts abroad. Zarubin, whom we called by his nickname Vasia, was already a high-ranking official in the N.K.V.D., a pudgy, jolly, rather likeable man.

He was the type of the 'trusted ones': Russian, with no past associations with suspect European parties or oppositions, no deep ideological commitment, and having had little to do directly with past party affairs. We used to see Vasia socially when he came to Paris alone, but not when he was accompanied by his wife Lisa, whom everybody avoided like the plague. We had known Lisa Zarubin when she was still Lisa Rosenberg and was Zaporozhets' secretary at the Embassy in Vienna in 1925, and had distrusted her even then. Since that time she had always worked for the N.K.V.D. So did most of her family, including her brother Victor, a photographic specialist, and his wife, who in 1935 was saved *in extremis* from a suicide attempt.

Lisa Zarubin was another of those whom we called 'theirs'—people Moscow entrusted with tasks their European Communist agents, most of them recruited from the Fourth, would never have performed. These were the people in the N.K.V.D. whom Moscow relied on for burglaries, kidnappings, and murders. They were also the ones who recruited and directed a special section of former White officers about whom nothing was known outside the N.K.V.D.[1] But the particular reason everyone avoided Lisa Zarubin was because of the role she had played in the betrayal and eventual death of Jacob Blumkin.

Blumkin, a most unusual figure, had been a member of the extremist wing of the Social Revolutionaries, and was implicated in the murder in 1918 of the German Ambassador to Moscow, Count Mirbach. Perhaps because of his youth, he was released and shortly afterwards admitted to the party. He then joined the G.P.U. and worked for it in Russia and abroad. On one of his foreign journeys he visited Leon Trotsky in exile, in Prinkipo in Turkey. Why he did so is not quite clear, but it was probably out of romantic admiration for the creator and leader of the Red Army. It was generally believed in the party that Trotsky had entrusted Blumkin with a letter to Radek, and that Radek, knowing Blumkin had told several people about this message, had no choice but to denounce him

---

[1] Krivitsky hints in his book (op. cit.) that he had been told all about these activities, but neither he nor Ludwik nor Maly was ever officially told anything of the kind. Of course they had their suspicions, gleaned from newspaper items and hints dropped by Slutsky. But to be privy to this kind of information one had to be one of 'theirs', and Krivitsky, as he often told Ludwik, was not.

to the N.K.V.D. in order to save his own skin. If one knew Blumkin's character, it was not too difficult to believe that Radek had acted in this perhaps sensible if scarcely honourable way. Blumkin had been shot, and as no one would have believed Trotsky or Radek if either had denied the letter's existence,[1] there the matter rested for most people.

Some of us found it hard to believe this version, however. Blumkin may have been careless and adventurous, but Trotsky was not, and it seemed inconceivable that he would have chosen so unreliable an emissary as Blumkin. What had actually happened was simpler and more sordid. The N.K.V.D. knew of Blumkin's visit to Trotsky, either from his own talkativeness or through other agents. They were beginning to suspect Blumkin anyway, for other reasons, and apparently feared he might defect. It was therefore decided to lure him back to the Soviet Union. Lisa Zarubin, with whom he had once been in love, was assigned the job and did it very well. Perhaps the romantically inclined Blumkin invented the letter, and told the story to Lisa Zarubin who passed it on; perhaps the N.K.V.D. invented it to compromise Radek. In any case, it is obvious why no one liked or trusted Lisa Zarubin. I might add that the distinction we made between Lisa and her husband was a rationalization on our part. We knew we could not avoid seeing him and thus unconsciously tried to make our encounters a bit more palatable.

It is not too surprising that the Zarubins survived the purges. Others of the 'trusted ones' no doubt survived, among them perhaps Boris Bazarov, also known as Bykov (his real name was Shpak). Bazarov's career had been quite different from that of Zarubin, an old party member who had been with the Cheka since the Civil War. Bazarov had been a Tsarist officer and had retreated with the White troops into Turkey after the Civil War—a record which would have made him unacceptable to the Fourth Department. Some time in the 1920s he returned to the Soviet Union, after having worked for the Soviet trade mission in Vienna, and joined the G.P.U., which was not quite as firm on principles as the Fourth. He married a

[1] As I was to learn much later from Leon Sedov, Trotsky's son, there was never any such letter.

widow with a small boy whom we referred to as young Bazarov.

We liked Bazarov very much and saw a good deal of him when he and his white-haired wife Nadia were in Paris. But our fondness for them never let us forget that he was one of 'theirs'. A quiet man, made even more so by a chronic liver ailment, Bazarov was never uncompromising in his stand on anything. If one commented on a bungled operation or criticized someone's action he had a stock answer: 'These things will happen, you know.' I remember telling him about the inept way the defendants in the Lydia Stahl espionage trial in Paris had answered the judge's and the prosecutor's questions; they should have had better stories ready to explain how they had met and what they were doing, he said. Surely stories ought to be prepared well before one's arrest. 'Tell me,' Bazarov answered, 'what would you say if someone were to ask you how you had met me? I bet you would sound just the way they did. What difference does it make in the over-all situation? These things will happen, you know.'

Bazarov and Zarubin, both of whom had powerful backing in the Soviet Union, were the really 'trusted ones'. Yet neither of them was 'Chief of Military Intelligence' in Western Europe.[1] In fact, neither the Fourth Department nor the N.K.V.D. ever had a centralized control post in Europe. The resident in each country had an area for which he assumed full responsibility. He in turn was responsible only to 'the centre', or headquarters, in Moscow, not to any West-European section chief. The residents of course collaborated with one another and exchanged information and even personnel, but only when the need arose and then only after getting approval from the centre. Even Ludwik and Krivitsky, so closely linked, did not exchange information regularly. If one of them needed specific information or help, it could always be got through the centre.

Slutsky, as head of I.N.O., was closer to the residents abroad than any of the other officials in the centre, perhaps because he had been a resident abroad himself. Ludwik at least considered him different from the others, and used to say dealing with him was like dealing with someone who had come from the Fourth, even though Slutsky had always been with I.N.O. He was intel-

---

[1] See Krivitsky, op. cit., p. 7, where he claims to have held that position himself.

ligent and broad-minded and, what mattered most to us in those days, loyal. In the letters he wrote Ludwik after he could have had little doubt of Ludwik's feelings about what was going on, he still tried to reassure him. And he never gave him a direct order to come home, but was still writing in the summer of 1937 of Ludwik's coming to Moscow to 'talk things over', 'straighten things out'.

I met Slutsky several times in Paris, and found him a curious mixture, in part dutiful N.K.V.D. official and in part sentimentally attached to the past as a Communist and revolutionary. He could refer in an official letter to the Trotskyites in Spain as 'counter-revolutionary bandits' and yet say to Ludwik with awe that young Communists in Leningrad had gone to their deaths shouting 'Long live Trotsky'. He circulated many admiring legends about Trotsky, among them the story of an N.K.V.D. agent sent to steal documents from Trotsky's home in Prinkipo, whom Trotsky surprised trying to break into his desk. The man tried to flee but Trotsky insisted he stay, saying 'I will leave you alone in this office, comrade, to find evidence of any anti-Soviet work I am doing', and left the room. It was not a true story, as I learnt later from Trotsky's son. The N.K.V.D. fabricated such legends to show Stalin how necessary they were to him in his struggle against Trotsky. Stalin probably did believe them, I know many others did, and if Slutsky knew they were false he certainly did much to make them believed.

Slutsky was a person of many contradictions. We knew of cases, after 1936, when he interceded courageously to save someone from arrest, and he would weep while telling of the interrogation of some of the defendants at the trials and bemoan the fate of their families; in the same breath he could denounce them as 'Trotskyite fascists'. Ludwik and Krivitsky both thought of him as a decent, kind-hearted man, loathing what he had to do and holding no illusions about his own fate or that of his friends. But it is possible, of course, that he was what the Russians call 'two-faced', and only hoped that Ludwik and Krivitsky would betray themselves when he feigned sympathy for the victims of the trials.[1]

[1] Early in 1938 *Pravda* published his obituary, saying this 'faithful son of our party' had died suddenly. Slutsky had had two heart attacks; quite possibly he did die a natural death.

By the summer of 1936 Ludwik's and Krivitsky's own position was becoming clear. We were on a short holiday in Czechoslovakia with our German friend Massing when the first Moscow trial, of Zinoviev, Kamenev, I. N. Smirnov, Mrachkovsky, and others, opened in August. When it ended on the 24th with the death sentence for all sixteen defendants, Ludwik telephoned Krivitsky who was in Geneva, asking him to meet us urgently in Paris. When the two men talked a few days later, Ludwik insisted they must make an open break with Stalin as a protest against the execution of the old Bolsheviks.

Krivitsky advanced two arguments against this. The first was the classic one, that a victorious revolution in Spain, where civil war had broken out a month before, would save the remnants of the October revolution in Russia and would sweep Stalin away. Any assistance one could give the Spanish Republicans was more important, he argued, than a gesture of solidarity with the old Bolsheviks who had been executed. His second argument against a break was its technical impossibility.

The problem of how to break and the more important one of whom to turn to, was to be the topic of many conversations between the two men over the following months. The possibility of betraying their ideals and turning to any of the Western intelligence services was not even discussed. But it was equally out of the question to turn directly to the logical person, Trotsky. To do so would have been to risk compromising Trotsky, for Soviet propaganda could well have pictured them as Fascist or Nazi agents seeking shelter with the arch-fascist Trotsky. But also, Trotsky himself could not be expected to trust two unknown men unless they were introduced to him by known socialists or oppositionists. And at the time Ludwik and Krivitsky had no such contacts.

Krivitsky's second argument had too much weight to be ignored, and though we had few illusions about the help the Soviets might give the Spanish revolution, it was decided to wait, and in the meantime give what support we could to Spain.

3

Until 1934, when Kirov was assassinated, visitors from the U.S.S.R. had brought news and messages from friends, and one felt one was still in touch with 'home' however infrequently one went there. After that, it became much more difficult to find out what was going on, and the only people with whom we could talk openly were old friends such as Krivitsky, or Maly who was by then in London.

The disturbing term 'fatherland' began to appear, first in official statements and then in the few letters one still received from friends.[1] One no longer heard of going 'home' or to 'Mecca': one went to the 'fatherland', *na rodinu*. In 1936 these precious letters from friends stopped; only official communications were received and even these became rarer. It had once been possible to learn something from those who had gone on holiday or on business to the Soviet Union, but as business trips became longer and longer and people often did not return at all, this source of information dried up. No one who did not have to go to the U.S.S.R. now volunteered to spend his holidays there. Once the Soviet Union became 'the fatherland of the toiling masses' where, as Stalin said, 'life was happy and full of joy', a trip to Moscow, whether on business or in answer to an invitation, became ominous.

So when, in late October 1936, we received a letter from Felix Gorski, saying only that it 'would be nice to see one of you here after such a long absence', it was not easy to decide what to do. Felix suggested I might spend Christmas and New Year's in Moscow. I had not been there since 1932, and Ludwik had paid his last visit in the summer of 1935. For some time there had been talk of sending Ludwik to the United States, to replace Bazarov as resident there, but nothing was being done about this now. We tried to read between the lines of Felix's message to see what he really meant. There was no doubt in my mind that he felt uneasy at Ludwik's prolonged absence and believed that a spontaneous expression on my part of a desire to visit the U.S.S.R. might allay the apprehensions of some of Ludwik's superiors. We had only a vague idea of the situation in the Soviet Union, but we

---

[1] These of course came through official channels. There was no correspondence by the regular post. Conspiratorial addresses, so-called 'letter-boxes', were reserved for collaborators or correspondents in Europe, and it was quite impossible for security reasons to receive letters from the Soviet Union at such addresses.

never doubted Felix's friendship and sincerity, and were convinced he would not have suggested I come unless he felt a visit 'home' was safe.

Se we began to make preparations, and I went to ask our liaison man, Grozovsky, to transmit my request for a trip to the Soviet Union. He said only: 'Oh. Going on vacation? All right, I'll take care of it,' although he knew that winter was neither vacation nor visiting time. Grozovsky was a typical lower-echelon Soviet official of the years of the terror and reflected the changed attitude of the Soviet Union towards European Communists and their intellectual sympathizers. A very unattractive cross-eyed man, he would probably not have appealed to us even in those earlier times when anyone from 'home' was automatically treated with sympathy and indulgence. Our relations with him were strictly business ones. At the time, neither Ludwik nor I knew that Grozovsky was already watching us.

Grozovsky was officially a clerk in the Soviet Embassy. His wife Lydia had a job in the Soviet trade mission, and to make it easier for her to be absent from work occasionally without attracting attention she was also supposed to be visiting Soviet children's homes in Paris. She was so busy deceiving her own colleagues and keeping up contacts with the illegal apparatus that she had no time to learn even to look and dress like a Western woman. The Grozovskys' real work of liaison with the illegal apparatus meant attending to routine matters such as delivering letters to us once every ten days or so, and money perhaps once a month. Ludwik used to meet his legal colleagues for conferences on an average of once a month, or oftener if the occasion warranted—for instance, if a visitor arrived from home. (If anything occurred in the interval, a meeting would be arranged by telephone according to a prearranged plan. An innocuous-sounding call was made to fix a time and place to meet. If either party failed to show up, the other was to return to the meeting place the following day at the same time, taking precautions to be as discreet as possible. In such cases no further telephone calls were made for fear of attracting attention.) Ludwik avoided Grozovsky as much as possible; I kept in contact with them, occasionally with Grozovsky but mostly with his wife.

Grozovsky had been in the N.K.V.D. from the beginning and had always been assigned to inland services, police and counter-espionage work, where he held unimportant positions. This was his first assignment abroad. As far as the N.K.V.D. in those days was concerned, he had all the requirements for a foreign assignment: he had no knowledge of Europe, spoke no foreign languages, and lacked connections abroad which could conceivably have helped him in the unlikely event that he should ever decide to break away. Not that he would ever have entertained such an idea. He was unquestioningly and servilely devoted to his superiors and, in any event, there were solid guarantees for his behaviour: both he and his wife had relatives in the Soviet Union who would answer with their liberty and possibly with their lives for any disobedience on his part.

Grozovsky had been thoroughly indoctrinated before leaving the Soviet Union; he had been taught to hate the capitalist world and to distrust the Communists abroad whose loyalty to Moscow was, often justifiably, considered suspect. This suspicion extended to the foreign residents, who, in spite of the almost unlimited authority granted them, were somehow never considered completely Moscow's 'own' people. An important element in this was the fact that none of the residents then abroad had relatives in the Soviet Union. A few years earlier men like Grozovsky would have felt honoured by the slightest sign of friendship from a resident, but by 1936 they kept themselves aloof. Each mistrusted the other, and rightly. The liaison man suspected the resident of being critical of Soviet policies at home and abroad, and of harbouring feelings of independence, while the resident suspected that the liaison man reported his own observations and the opinions of the resident to his superiors.

Between the end of October and the time I actually left for Moscow, in late December, we learned from those on their way to Spain that many of our friends and acquaintances had been arrested, but by then it was too late to cancel the trip. Once a request had been made it could be postponed for a few weeks on one pretext or another, but it was out of the question to abandon it altogether. Arranging a trip to the U.S.S.R. for an illegal person, a member of a Soviet apparatus, was quite complex, and had been made more so by the coming to power of the Nazis. Usually these complications were faced only if a trip was absolutely necessary and if it was to be for long enough to warrant all the technical work involved. I was going supposedly for a fortnight, but the requisite steps were taken none the less.

One of the steps involved was securing a passport good enough to get the necessary transit visas and still not so valuable that it would matter if it were spoiled for ever by being stamped with a Soviet visa. Only a bona fide tourist or business man could afford to have such a visa in his passport. The choice of passports was at the time restricted by political conditions in central Europe. During the 1930s the passports most frequently used were Czechoslovak. They were easier to come by because of the number of Comintern agents and German Communists who had emigrated to Czechoslovakia after Hitler came to power. The fact that the Czech Communist Party was legal and even enjoyed a certain popularity, helped these émigrés to obtain identity cards, residence permits, and similar documents, and the Comintern could get such papers not only for itself but for other agencies as well. As a result, however, anyone travelling to Moscow on a Czech passport was looked on with some suspicion. Also, anyone who was Jewish, or looked Jewish, could not travel through Germany. It was equally unwise to travel through Poland with a Czech passport, especially as relations between Poland and Czechoslovakia were tense; and the 'northern route' through Scandinavia was usually reserved for the return trip. There were Soviet ships in French and Belgian ports, but these were now being used solely for transport to and from Spain.

Given the difficulties, we hoped we might be told it would be better if my trip were postponed. But eventually, in December, Grozovsky brought me a passport and visa. It was a Czech passport belonging to a woman who had been in the United States and whose French visa had been issued in Chicago. The passport may have been genuine but as it had a Soviet visa, also genuine, issued by the Soviet consulate in Paris, it could only be used for this one trip. Grozovsky also gave me money for the ticket which I was to buy myself at Intourist in Paris. He was very friendly, wished me a happy journey and a good stay, and asked me to give his regards to his friends—without however naming any. He was also visibly relieved to have the matter settled.

With passport and tickets in hand, I had only to be on my way. I left our son with his father, and set off by what had been the standard route before Hitler came to power, via Germany and Latvia. I left Paris after midnight and arrived in Berlin on the following day. The train I had been on was continuing its journey via Warsaw, which I had to avoid, and so I spent the night in Berlin. I registered at a hotel, strolled about the city, bought chocolates and toilet soap—always popular gifts in the Soviet Union—had dinner in a restaurant and went back to the hotel. None of the difficulties I expected arose: the hotel clerk gave me back my passport after only a casual glance, no one asked me any questions, I was not followed in the streets. My train left for Moscow the next morning.

We crossed the Latvian border at Eydkhunen, a name that—with Niegoreloie, a town on the border of Poland—will evoke memories in any Western Communists who had to flee their own countries, or who at last succeeded in visiting the U.S.S.R., and who may have survived this period. I saw that this last outpost in Europe before the Soviet Union was unchanged. Not so the Europe of 1936, Germany now was ruled by the Nazis and Poland was a semi-fascist country. And the Soviet Union was no longer the country of the October revolution; it had become a ruthless dictatorship, a country where Communists were imprisoned, accused of collaboration with Poland or Germany, deported to slave labour camps, or executed after summary trials or no trials at all. Eydkhunen or Niegoreloie now meant uncertainty, the fact that one might never return. At Eydkhunen there were still signs on the Soviet side proclaiming, 'Proletarians of the World, Unite'. I wondered whether I would see them again.

CHAPTER VIII

Moscow, 1937

I

My train arrived in Moscow before noon and I was agreeably surprised to find Felix Gorski at the station. I had known I would be met, but I had expected a woman. Felix's coming was a mark of personal friendship which I appreciated very much. I noticed immediately that he had changed a great deal. We embraced, then he turned to a plump woman next to him and said to me: 'Shake hands with comrade Bella.' I had never seen her before, but she would have had no trouble in recognizing me, as she had my photograph and in any event I was the only passenger on the international train.

Felix told me a car was waiting outside, but that because the telegram announcing my arrival had been delayed he had been unable to get me a room in one of the international hotels where tourists stayed; I would have to spend the night in a hotel used by Russians. This was unfortunate, because of the danger of attracting attention, but it was only for one night, as a room was available in a tourist hotel next day. Then, 'I am going to take you to my place,' Felix said, 'and you can wash up and we will have plenty of time to talk'. Changing the subject he added: 'I suppose you must have had trouble at the border, for the wire sent there can only have arrived today.' He seemed very surprised when I told him I had had no difficulty at all: my luggage had been inspected only casually and I had not been questioned. Felix said to Bella: 'See how they work there, they let anybody in, just like that.'

I was to hear again about that unfortunate telegram which I assumed had notified the border of my arrival but which had never got there. Everyone was amazed at my having crossed the frontier without trouble. Personally, I was inclined to attribute it to simple bureaucratic inefficiency, combined with the luck I have always had crossing borders. In many years of travel I cannot recall my luggage ever having been seriously searched, but I had to admit such luck in this instance was most unusual. A few weeks earlier Maly and his wife had come home on a visit, and then too the wire had been late. The border official did not believe Maly's story that they were tourists, largely because their Russian was so good. He not only searched their luggage but told Maly he would not let them enter the Soviet Union until a thorough investigation had been conducted. This would have meant a long and unpleasant stay at the border station, and forced Maly to reveal his connection with the N.K.V.D., by giving the border official a number to call in Moscow to verify his story. The officer took his time about this, and when the train finally left, with Maly abroad, a plainclothesman was sent along to watch him. This was done so discreetly that Maly did not notice and only learned of it when the policeman filed his report. This stated that Maly had been met at the station by an 'ugly, elderly woman' and driven to N.K.V.D. headquarters. The report aroused a good deal of amusement in Moscow, especially as it went straight to the woman in question, the former wife of Sokolnikov, who was to be a defendant in the second Moscow trial; she was only in her early fifties and by no means ugly.

The incident also led to a tightening of the usual procedure, which was that headquarters, having been informed of someone's arrival by a liaison man abroad, would wire the border not to investigate that particular passenger. This was better than having the liaison man get in touch with the border directly, as had once been done, and much safer than another early method of slipping a special note into the passport to show at the Soviet border, rightly considered dangerous, for this potentially incriminating document might be found by the police of another country.

Felix drove me from the station to his flat, in a new building across the street from the N.K.V.D. offices. When we arrived I said at once: 'Ludwik told me to ask you how to behave here, whom to see and whom not to see, and to keep you informed of everything I do.' Felix answered that this was precisely why he had brought me straight to his place, adding: 'Bella is supposed to do these things, but I wanted to talk to you first in private.'

I looked round the flat which Felix and his new wife shared with Boris Bazarov and his son. It consisted of one large room for each family and a common kitchen and bath. Since Bazarov was in the United States, and only his son there, this meant privacy for the Gorskis—a rare thing in Moscow, especially valuable in those days of terror. Of course, these apartments, belonging as they did to the N.K.V.D., might have been wired. We acted as if they were, though in fact it might not have made much difference. At the height of the terror not many confidences were being exchanged and any confidential news that Felix might have given me would not have changed his or my situation in the slightest.

After saying that I looked to him for guidance and would follow his advice, I ventured to ask Felix: 'How are our friends? Could I see them?' He looked at me gravely and repeated: 'Friends? Friends? Whom do you want to see?' The way he pronounced the word 'friends' and his expression froze all the questions I had wanted to ask. He went to the kitchen to prepare some lunch, leaving me to think about his attitude. Had the word 'friend' lost all meaning in this 'fatherland' of ours, or did his response mean that all our friends had perished?

True, everything had a different meaning in this country. Abroad, for people living an uneventful existence, a friend could be someone very close to you, or a friendly neighbour; even a pleasant acquaintance might be called a friend. But those of us who were bound to the Soviet Union were more than friends; in a sense we were a family some of whose members were close, others more distant, but who nevertheless always knew what happened to each other and after long separations met with our feelings unchanged. We kept in touch, just as those who had come from the Polish party, even if they later transferred to the Russian one, kept up their ties with the Polish Communists. As sometimes happens in families, we had black sheep whom nobody mentioned but whom we all thought about. We also had ties with our collaborators abroad; in the old days anyone working with us, and especially coming from the Soviet Union, had been considered a friend.

Felix came back from the kitchen. I thought again, as he sat across the table from me, how much he had changed. The ebullient friendliness so characteristic of him had vanished, and while his mop of red hair was still unstreaked with grey, and his face round, all the liveliness that had once sparkled in his blue eyes was gone. He did not move about exuberantly as in the past. He had always been a great talker, a man who liked a drink and a girl, who would dance Russian folk dances with fire and enthusiasm. He used to coin expressions and was very good at inventing nicknames for people which usually stuck. He and Ludwik got along very well and were fond of each other, and out of this affection Felix had adopted all Ludwik's friends and considered them his own.

In spite of enormous differences in their personalities, their education, and their opinions of the Soviet Union, Felix and Ludwik had one great bond, their attachment to the Polish party. Felix stayed in close contact with the Poles and through him we had remained close to them. His first loyalty, however, was to the Soviet Union. Possibly this was because, unlike Ludwik and his friends who came from the Austrian part of Poland, he came from the Russian territories. Felix did not want to leave the U.S.S.R. and never felt at home in a European city. Whereas Ludwik considered himself as belonging to an international movement, of which the Soviet Union was but one part, Felix was not only a russified Pole but a Sovietized one, who saw not just the international Communist movement but even the Polish party through Soviet eyes. To him whatever happened in the U.S.S.R. was good, and when Ludwik had talked openly to him, during his last visit in 1935 after the assassination of Kirov, about the wave of arrests of totally innocent people and the ruthless suppression of the opposition —of which Felix was fully aware— he answered: 'Yes, yes, the Soviet Union is going through a sea of blood and mud. But everything will come out all right in the end, in spite of everything.' Under 'everything' he included Stalin, whom he considered as a temporary evil, not one that could destroy the Soviet Union.

The Soviet Union was also a personal haven for Felix where he could hide from his own grief. When his wife Justina left him for Milan Gorkić, and took their little boy with her, Felix came to feel that he could lead a meaningful life only in the U.S.S.R. While Justina and Gorkić were in Vienna and later in Prague, the child was left with friends in Paris, and at that time Felix had accepted an assignment in Paris, perhaps to be close to his son. But he soon decided that he was useless in Europe and that the only place he could get back on his feet was at home. He asked to be sent back, knowing his friends and his superiors might accuse him of cowardice. Ludwik knew very well that Felix was no coward, but believing that one should not let personal feelings, however strong, interfere with one's job, tried to dissuade him from leaving.

Felix's mind was made up, however. He told Ludwik, 'It will be a good thing for you to have me in the office back home, where you have no friends and are relatively new. You know that it will be good for you, or maybe you don't know it, but you will see it will be a good thing.' He had been right, at least as long as things remained relatively normal, that is, until 1935. At first Felix kept Ludwik informed of developments at home. But by 1935 letters were being opened and read at headquarters and correspondence, naturally enough, stopped. Ludwik however always knew where he stood with Felix and he also knew that Felix worried about him. The extent to which he trusted Felix was clear from Ludwik's having told me to follow Felix's instructions to the letter, while I was in Moscow, and to keep him informed of my actions.

As lunch proceeded I waited for Felix to ask me about Ludwik, but he never did. He knew very well how Ludwik felt and what he thought. I then brought up the subject of Justina and his child whom I had seen before I left Paris. I expected him to ask questions about them, but he merely said: 'Still seeing each other? This is hardly the time for socializing, it can only lead to trouble.' I knew he was referring to the rule prohibiting contacts between members of the various apparatuses. But he knew perfectly well that these rules were always being broken and he himself had never obeyed them when he was abroad. I could not help wondering at his lack of reaction to news of his child. Was he truly not interested or was he so engrossed in the thought of his own doom that nothing mattered any more? Or did he still believe that everything would turn out all right in the end, and even that the rules were sound and had to be obeyed? It seemed to me that he had even lost his sense of humour and I remembered how, a few years earlier when I told him I thought Stalin ugly because he had no forehead, he had answered: 'I am not a woman, so I cannot tell you whether he is ugly or not, but as for his forehead, such a trifle could lead to one's being thrown out of the party.'

I could not tell from his expression what went on in his mind. I could only see how changed he was and that he was extremely tired, on the verge of collapse. Since it seemed he would volunteer nothing, I asked again about friends, adding that in this matter I would act as he told me to. 'How is Willy?' I asked.—'Oh, I have not seen him for some time now, but I guess he is all right. When I get back to the office I will call him and he will get in touch with you.'—'And Fedia?'—'I ran into him the other day, but I really don't know how he is. But you will want to see him anyway. I am sure Willy will be able to reach him, they probably see each other.' This meant I could see them with his approval, but I wanted to know more.

He told me, when I asked, that he did not know whether Misha was in Moscow but he did not think so. As for Brun: 'You will see him anyway. He lives next door. I saw him in the corridor of the office the other day and stopped to talk to him. I had hardly closed the door of my office when there was a knock and Slutsky came in and said: "I saw you talking to Brun. This must be the last time that happens." Can you imagine Slutsky talking that way to anyone?' Felix said to me. 'I was furious and told him: "Don't speak to me in that tone; after all I am the chief of a department." He just looked at me and said: "I don't give a damn what kind of chief you are and of what kind of department which may be abolished tomorrow. I am simply telling you, and you've heard me." With this he left the office. What do you make of it?'

I knew perfectly well what to make of it, and understood what this meant for Brun and—as Felix also knew—that Slutsky was warning him. Perhaps for the sake of having something to say I told Felix I knew Slutsky had had a personal grudge against Brun ever since they worked together in 1928.

Felix merely said: 'There has been plenty of time and many opportunities since then for Slutsky to get even had he wanted to, or to have Brun transferred elsewhere. Anyway, Slutsky is not a vindictive man. No, there is another reason for that scene in my office and you know what it is. But, as I said, you will be seeing Brun anyway.' Felix knew that a meeting was unavoidable, and he probably thought in the long run it would make very little difference.

I then asked him about Anna Mikhailovna Messing. Felix smiled. 'It is a long time since anyone has asked about her. I myself have not seen her for over a year. She will be very happy to see you. I am sure she is alone in the house with Frossia, her *nania*. The girls must have left Moscow because they were not there last time I saw her.' Then he added: 'You know, of course, that Messing has been removed from his position?'—'I know, it was in the papers.' Felix continued to smile and said: 'You know he has not lived with her for years. I am sure Anna Mikhailovna will be very glad to see you.' With that he leaned back in his chair and fell asleep. I myself was exhausted and felt that quite a bit had been said for one day.

A few minutes later Felix's new wife came in. She was a very pretty young girl who greeted me heartily and loudly, took one look at her husband, and said she had got quite used to his falling asleep in the middle of a sentence. I remembered that when Felix first wrote to us about his new marriage he added: 'My wife, thank God, does not speak any foreign language. I don't think they will ever send me abroad now.' I thought of this as I watched her set the table for tea without paying any attention to the sleeping man whom nothing seemed to disturb. Suddenly the telephone rang, and, instantly awake, Felix stumbled to it. Answering it, he turned to his wife and said, 'It is for you,' adding, to me: 'I thought it would be "Comrade Gorski, come to the office immediately." That's how it begins, and no one knows how it ends.'

Over tea Felix seemed relaxed, joked with his wife, commented on the little presents I had brought her, especially the lipstick. 'How did you know it is her favourite shade?' I told him it was easy to guess the shade that would suit a young and pretty girl. Felix said in a bantering, seemingly easy tone, to his wife: 'See, she is smart, she knows a thing or two.' In fact, I felt anything but smart, and nothing I had learned that afternoon had enlightened me particularly. Felix however continued in the same way: 'We will go and visit friends, you wearing your new lipstick, we will look at the town. They say there is a lot of building going on. Soon this town of ours will look like Chicago or New York, only a lot prettier. Then we will go and look at the Christmas tree in Red Square, it is tremendous.'

'A Christmas tree,' I asked, 'in Red Square?' – 'Yes, right across from the Lenin mausoleum.' While I was digesting this information he said: 'Well, I am off. I will send Bella to fetch you, but before that you will have a visitor, Gravpen. I understand that you two know each other, at least that is what he told me this morning. I don't have to tell you how to act with him. Don't worry, he will do all the talking, he is only too glad to have an audience; after all nobody ever listened to what he had to say before. But now he is deputy chief and by God has his urine hit his brains.' concluded Felix, using a popular Russian expression meaning that my visitor's new rank had gone to his head.

His wife went out shortly after to an evening class, and, left by myself, I tried hard to remember something about Gravpen. I had met him during the winter of 1932 in a rest home some twenty kilometres from Moscow.[1] The home, beautifully located amidst pinewoods, belonged to the N.K.V.D.; in principle only the families of government officials could go there, and of course N.K.V.D. staff had priority, though some factory workers were admitted. As Ludwik was not yet connected with the N.K.V.D., it would have been impossible for me to go there, in those famine days, except for the fact that I had a medical certificate for my son, who had been ill. Gravpen had then just returned from the United States, where he had accompanied a group of engineers studying oil wells in, I believe, Texas. He never stopped talking about the United States and was forever showing off the luggage, ties, and shoes he had bought there. Naturally enough, he was soon being called 'the American', and he seemed very proud of the nickname.

---

[1] It was there that I also met Orlov-Nikolsky, who was later head of the N.K.V.D. in Spain. See Chapter XI, pp. 258–9.

I rather expected to see him in this role again, with a bright tie and new brown shoes, but to my surprise he arrived in the new uniform of the N.K.V.D. This was a dark blue affair with brass buttons and looked rather like a cross between a navy uniform and that of a doorman in an expensive hotel. The uniform was rarely seen in the streets; the N.K.V.D. was very unpopular, so employees wore it as seldom as possible. It was the first time I had ever seen it. Gravpen wore it with considerable dignity but explained that if the Gorskis' apartment had not belonged to 'us' he would have had to go home and change into civilian clothes. He lived some distance away, in Tretia Meschanskaia ('Third Bourgeois Street'), where there were some flats reserved for less important functionaries in the N.K.V.D.; Bella also lived there. The higher-ups or 'operatives', as they were called, lived near the offices in new buildings such as this one, surrounding the old Cheka building which had once been the headquarters of an insurance company. This still gave rise to sad jokes about 'life insurance'.

I had hoped Gravpen would resume where he had left off and talk about America, but instead he spoke immediately about the telegram that had never reached the border. He regretted that he had not been notified, but unfortunately, he said, Comrade Gorski considered my visit as 'his private affair.' He knew of course that Gorski and I were old friends, but still it was up to Gravpen's department to handle such matters; he was Bella's boss, he would have had no trouble getting me accommodation, and so on. He insisted that had he been handling things I would have had a room at the Savoy 'where we could see each other easily' and I would not have had to spend the night at a Russian hotel which 'was unfortunate, to say the least'. He then asked about Ludwik, whom he did not know, about his work and his 'staff' —about which he knew nothing. I noticed that not only did he never wait for an answer, throughout he used 'we' rather than 'I'.

Suddenly he asked a question and for once waited for an answer. How were the German couple, the Massings, Ludwik had on his staff? 'We hear the man is very good, but we understand that she is a gossip.'—'Well, she doesn't gossip with me.'—'We know you are no gossip,' he reassured me, but then went on in the same way about Gerda Frankfurter. Gravpen obviously considered her his own property and added: 'We know a great deal about Gerda, a lot of it good, but we also know that she drinks a good deal.' I did not like the turn the conversation was taking. 'You need two to drink,' I told him; 'she doesn't drink with me.' Gravpen seemed to find this very funny, laughed and answered: 'You always have an answer ready. We know you don't drink, but I think it would be nice to invite her here for a while.'

I knew he had no power to make such decisions—or at least I fervently hoped he did not—but I was greatly worried, and made up my mind to tell Gerda and the others, should I ever see them again, not to accept any invitations of this kind. As they had been hired abroad, I felt they could get away with refusing. I wondered who might be sending them reports about our people. Gravpen provided me with the answer—though I did not know it at the time—when he told me there was 'a very good organization of White Russian émigrés in Paris.'

Gravpen excused himself saying that he still had a lot of work to do that night, as it was 'a busy time' and every man was needed. He told me that Bella would be coming shortly, and that he would send me theatre tickets at the Savoy. He gave me his unlisted office number, as a mark of confidence, and said that he would see me soon.

I never saw him again, he was in none of the offices I visited, and I never heard from him again. I know however what it was that kept him busy. This was the time when Radek was being subjected to intensive questioning, and as Gravpen was an investigator, it was highly probable that he was part of the 'conveyor belt' system of interrogators. I speculated on how a man like this could ever have become an interrogator of Radek.[1]

---

[1] I knew another of Radek's interrogators, Kedrov (Krivitsky called him 'one of the most skilful' of N.K.V.D. investigators), whom I met in 1932 in the same rest home where I met Gravpen. Kedrov must have been less than thirty in 1936, for when I met him he was a pimpled youth with a stupid expression and a half-open mouth. His parents, who were staying at the rest home, had been close collaborators of Lenin in Switzerland, where their only son was born. The elder Kedrov was arrested during the purges and later executed; his son was probably executed also.

2

It was past eight o'clock when Bella came to fetch me. She had a car and took me to my hotel on the other bank of the river, the Zamoskvareche. She left me in front of the hotel, saying she had a quick errand to do and would be back in a minute. Inside, things went badly, as expected; this mistake was much worse than not having sent a telegram to the border. The manager, although he had kept the room for me, wanted my passport and said we would have to go immediately to the militia as he could not let me in without their authorization. I protested and stalled for time, at least until Bella came back. He asked me numerous questions: how had I got into the Soviet Union, whom was I visiting, what was I doing here, and so on. I told him I was a tourist, visiting no one at all. He said there was no such thing as a visitor on his own, no matter what I pretended. Finally Bella returned, but she had no better luck than I in keeping him quiet. In the end she had to give him a telephone number to call at the N.K.V.D. office, which is what we had been trying to avoid all along. The manager called the number, was reassured, and gave me back my passport, and I was finally able to go up to my room.

The manager had of course been quite right. Any visitor from abroad was supposed to go immediately to the militia, who gave him a temporary permit, while they kept his passport for investigation, and eventually gave him permission to stay, usually for thirty days. The N.K.V.D. followed these instructions to the letter, the only exception being that they went to the militia and obtained the permit before the visitor arrived. This they could do easily enough, as they knew his nationality and name, the number of his passport and all the other information the militia needed. The permit was thus in the hotel before the visitor arrived, and the manager of the hotel, an N.K.V.D. employee, never asked questions. In my case everything had been done the wrong way round; it was no wonder the manager was worried. After the telephone call it was Bella's turn to be upset, though as far as I know the incident caused no repercussions.

I had scarcely reached my room when I was called to the

telephone. This of course was in the hall, since this was a Russian hotel, but I did not care whether anyone overheard. It was Willy, the same old Willy, full of pranks and jokes— sometimes amusing, sometimes exasperating. As in older and better days, he tried to disguise his voice, pretending to be a woman. I recognized him immediately, and told him to stop fooling and come over.

He came at once, wearing his Red Army uniform as always— this one was very popular in the streets—and as always, lifted me high in his arms pretending to be looking for a tall piece of furniture on which to perch me. He had not changed much except that he had lost some more hair, of which he had little enough. He was still as strong as a bear, and as jolly as ever. When Bella left, Willy took me to a restaurant to get something to eat. We did not say much there, expecting to talk more freely afterwards in my room, for we assumed that a 'Russian' hotel would probably not be wired, as we supposed all the international hotels were.

Willy had always belonged to all of us. I thought he looked completely undisturbed, a human being perhaps so good as to be simply incapable of conceiving of evil. One night in Berlin he had broken up a fight between two men by separating them and pushing each on his way. I asked him then whether he would have fought them had they turned on him, and he had answered: 'Oh, no. There are better ways of doing things.' Willy was responsible for communications in the Red Army engineer unit to which he was attached, and was the unit's party organizer. He had been promoted to this post after the successful expedition to Mount Elbruz, the highest peak in the Caucasus. His men had become quarrelsome and violent in the rarefied air, fighting among themselves and even killing a mule carrying equipment. One night Willy removed all their weapons while they slept. They attacked him in the morning and he fought them off with wet towels, telling them that this was a much better way to fight than with knives. He had established his ascendancy over them, brought them safely to the top, planted the red flag, set up the radio equipment, and was awarded a decoration.

Willy asked after Ludwik, and wanted to know whether my

son still remembered him. Did the boy still want to kill White officers, he asked. This was a reference to a 7th November parade to which he had taken my son, carrying him on his shoulders, when we lived in Moscow years before. As the boy watched the almost unending parade he saw the uniforms of the foreign military attachés—German, Polish, Japanese. Like all good Soviet children, he believed that anyone not in the Red Army was 'White' and an enemy. He turned to Willy and said: 'What are these Whites doing here? Why don't they kill them?' When the march-past ended Willy explained that we were not at war and that Red Army officers abroad also attended parades. 'In that case,' said the boy, 'it is good they should have been here. Now that they have seen our tanks and planes they know they cannot attack us.'—'That is correct,' said Willy.

I reassured Willy that my son had not forgotten him or his explanations. Then, in a bantering mood, I asked Willy whether he was still Hinkemann. He laughed. 'I am not, and what is more, rest assured, I never was!' Hinkemann, the hero of a play by Ernest Toller, was a soldier in the First World War who had been wounded and made impotent. In the days when Willy was making regular journeys between Berlin and Danzig, loaded with illegal literature for Poland, he always carried a camera with him. Cameras were then rare, and Willy used his to further romance. Whenever he met a girl who appealed to him, or even talked to a telephone operator whose voice he liked, he would offer to take her picture and send it to her, thus having a pretext for meeting her again. On one of his trips the camera was stolen, and Felix promptly dubbed Willy Hinkemann, another nickname by which he was known to all his friends.

Back at the hotel, where we could talk, Willy said he had told Fedia of my arrival, that Brun knew about it also, and that we were expected at Brun's for dinner tomorrow. Misha would be there too and I would have an opportunity to see everyone. He said all of this as if nothing serious were going on and as I looked at him I wondered whether Brun had not been right to call Willy a 'blockhead': nothing around him appeared to affect him.

I asked him about Fedia and he began to talk of his wonder-

ful children, two girls and a boy. 'They look a bit like their
father, they have the same slanted eyes. His wife too looks a bit
like him. She is a strange girl, never says anything, not even to
her husband. Do you know that those two say "you" rather
than "thou" to each other?'[1] I interrupted this social chatter
and asked Willy outright: 'Tell me about Fedia. What is his
position?' Willy suddenly became serious. 'I don't know, he
does not know, nobody does. Still, as he is not working for any
special service he might survive. It is really a case of *kto kovo*
[who gets whom]. If *HE* were only to die, Fedia and so many
others might survive.' As Willy said this there was in his eyes a
look of unadulterated hatred I would never have expected to
see there: there was nothing 'stony' about it.

'In Fedia's case,' he continued, 'there might be a chance, but
I know you are going to ask about Brun, and there it is a question of weeks, perhaps only days, unless there is a miracle and
HE kicks off tonight.'—'Is there a chance in your case?'—'Not
too much of a chance, but there are some favourable factors.
One is that I came from the German party. You people from
the Polish party were sponsored by Unshlikht; that is bad. I
was sponsored by Thaelmann and by no stretch of the imagination can they accuse him of being a Nazi; he is in a Nazi prison.'
When Ludwik was arrested in Poland in 1922 Willy got out by
the skin of his teeth; he had not had time to get a mandate
from the Polish party, and was admitted to the Soviet party only
later via the German party. 'Who knows,' he said, 'that may yet
turn out to be a blessing.'

'But trouble might come from somewhere else altogether,'
he went on. 'Look, as party organizer for my unit, I have to
vouch for the political reliability of my people and for their past.
They are young, they have no past, or so I thought. But the other
day the secretary of the cell called me in and said: "Did you
know that one of the two women in your group is a Trotskyite?"
I asked him which one, and he told me. I told him I did not
think so and he said. "Didn't you know her husband had been
deported as a Trotskyite?" I told him I hadn't known it and
that the girl had been divorced for quite a while. He just
looked at me and said: "You ought to know, comrade. Where

[1] In Russian the intimate form of address is translated as 'thou'.

is your watchfulness?" Do you remember what Fedia once said: "May our children and their children never know the word watchfulness"?'

I remembered it perfectly, as I remembered what Fedia had told Ludwik the day he was readmitted to the party on Ludwik's recommendation. 'There are only two things in store for us. Either the enemy will hang us, or our own people will shoot us.' I reminded Willy of that conversation. 'Tell me, did you believe it then?'—'Believe, no. But I feared it.'—'Willy, will they arrest Fedia because he was once thrown out of the party?'—'No. Not because he was thrown out of it, but because he has been in it too long.'—'Or do you think it is his marriage he will have to account for?' Both of us remembered Ika saying, of Fedia's marriage to an 'ex', 'I hope they will hold it against him.' But Willy said sadly now: 'Fedia knew better than Ika.'

By then it was late, and Willy left, saying he had a day off tomorrow, and would come and fetch me in the morning. 'We can take a stroll through town and look at the Christmas tree', he said. 'Then in the evening we will go over to Brun's and see everybody.' I told him I was glad Misha would be there as well, since Felix had told me he was away. Willy explained: 'Felix might not know. You see, Misha does not go to the office very much these days and as he does not live in the same building, Felix may not have seen him for some time. He probably believes he is away on some special assignment.'

Unlike Brun, who had scarcely left Moscow since his return in 1929, Misha travelled a great deal. I had not seen him for a long time. Even when we lived in Moscow, Misha was always off on some foreign assignment. Because he spoke several European languages he often accompanied Soviet diplomats to international conferences, and when distinguished foreign visitors came to the U.S.S.R. he acted as press officer of the Commissariat of Foreign Affairs or else as an interpreter. Thus, he was present when Anthony Eden came to Moscow, as well as on the occasion of Pierre Laval's visit. The French premier was accompanied by his daughter who was soon to be married. Misha gave Laval's daughter some truly regal wedding gifts such as fur coats and oriental rugs, and Laval reciprocated with a gold watch inscribed '*A mon cher ami, le capitaine Oumansky*'.[1]

Misha was remarkably successful in such assignments, but for all his good looks he had no luck with women. He had married a well-known Soviet singer and whenever possible he took her along on foreign assignments. Once when he had to go to Japan for a few months, she could not accompany him, as she had a singing engagement to fulfil. When he returned his singer had gone, and with her all his belongings: Misha's well-cut foreign suits were now gracing her new lover's shoulders. Most men would have kept such a misfortune to themselves, but not Misha. He told everyone who was willing to listen, and we had even heard of it abroad.

Next morning I moved to the Hotel Savoy a few blocks away from the Lubianka. Bella brought me 1100 rubles for my expenses, the equivalent of a month's salary. Willy came to get me, we had some lunch in the hotel restaurant, and then we were in the streets. It was good to mingle with the crowds, the same old shabby crowds, hurrying along, seemingly unaffected by anything. One could feel secure in this crowd. Probably the terror had claimed its victims there too, but basically it was aimed at the élite, the old party members, and the crowds looked as they had in the past.

We walked to the entrance to Red Square and there, in the dusk, was the mausoleum and a gigantic Christmas tree. There had never been one there before. It was unusually warm for Moscow and the snow which had fallen a week ago had turned to a black mess on the sidewalks. 'It looks like a black Christmas,' said Willy and as I looked at the streets I remembered other Russian winters, with the snow crisp underfoot and the golden cupolas of the churches glistening in the sun. Had the climate changed as well? As we were standing looking at the tree, we noticed an old woman, white hair showing under her fur hat, eyes hidden by dark glasses, coming out of one of

[1] In *I was Stalin's Agent* Krivitsky refers to Misha as 'Oulansky' rather than Oumansky—a pointless change, since the identity of the agent who carried out the assignment in Odessa in 1936 which Krivitsky describes would have been well known to the Soviets. Moreover Krivitsky knew that Misha had been arrested long before his book appeared.

the buildings. 'Look,' said Willy, 'there's Krupskaia.'—'I am sorry for her,' I answered.—'Why be sorry for her? She didn't have to do what she did. You know that she begged *HIM* on her knees for the lives of the Sixteen in the first trial. He insulted her and forced her to sign a statement condemning Lenin's old companions as counter-revolutionaries, spies, and mad dogs. She didn't have to do it. What could *HE* have done to her now?'

We turned round at the sound of clattering cavalry. A troop of Cossacks, resplendent in their colourful uniforms, trotted by. 'Cossacks?' I said. 'Since when?'—'Oh, yes,' said Willy, 'they are Cossacks, all right. They recently had their privileges restored, the ones that were abolished by the revolution.'—'Isn't that an odd sight for Moscow?' I asked. 'Is there no one who still remembers their traditional role under the Tsars? Doesn't anyone remember what they used to do, or that they are the traditional guard of the monarchy?'—'Maybe,' said Willy, 'it's the times we live in. They say around the Kremlin that *HE* brought them back, to guard *HIM*.'

As we entered the building where Brun lived, the guard, the very picture of a Tsarist gendarme, waxed moustache and all, asked no questions of Willy but bowed to me and—most unusual in the Soviet Union—actually opened the door to the elevator, saying: 'At your service, madame.' (Next day, I learned, he said to Shura, Brun's wife: 'You had a visitor last night, a lady.' Shura told him it was not a lady but a comrade, but he merely repeated: 'I have been around a long time, I know a lady when I see one.')

When we rang at Brun's everyone rushed towards us and I was passed from one pair of arms to another while Willy slapped his thighs with joy. Brun and Misha did not seem to have changed much since the last time I saw them, and Shura, who had been slim, was now plump but still very pretty. None of them seemed changed except Fedia. At forty-five he looked like an old man. His thin rat-like hair had gone grey and his face was yellow. His slanting eyes were glistening; it was the only time I had ever seen him weep.

As soon as we entered the room Willy took Brun aside and I soon heard Brun's familiar cursing and shouting: 'So you want a recommendation for your dear kid brother, a written recommendation from me so your darling kid brother can apply for Soviet citizenship, so he can get a job? He's out of work, is he? Hell, there are millions of people out of work all over the world. Let him starve, for all I care! I will never live down the fact that I helped him come to this country in the first place. I bet you he has dear friends in America who send him packages. He will be the nail in my coffin yet!' Brun kept on muttering 'recommendation', while Willy tried to calm him down. 'Look, I only asked whether you could do it. You don't have to.' I could see that Willy's young half-brother was as much of a responsibility as ever.

Brun shouted and raged at everyone—at his wife, wanting to know why dinner was not ready, and at the help. When dinner finally came he pronounced it 'lousy', although it was in fact a perfectly good meal. The sardines it started with were frankly mediocre, however. Fedia tasted one and said sadly: 'They are not French sardines, you know.' Brun blew up. 'These are Soviet sardines, and a damn sight better than your lousy French ones.' While dinner went on in this fashion, Misha asked me about Ludwik and my son and said: 'I suppose you have heard about my broken marriage?' I told him that I had, but one look from his brother cut Misha's story short.

Then the mood changed as the friends began reminiscing about the past. I was never to hear as much of their little town in Galicia as I did that evening, so that I, who had never seen it, began to feel part of it. Brun spoke of the river and of the beautiful woods along its banks. 'Three crazy-looking, shabby, half-dead trees,' said Fedia. 'To him they look like a forest now. You know, Brun, I knew an Italian Communist who died a short time ago. He was still in his fifties, and he hadn't been ill; he died of nostalgia. He came from the Bay of Naples, how could he possibly have survived here? God knows, our little town is no Sorrento, but now it looks good, you are right, Brun, the river was fine.' They would have gone on all night in this vein had I not interrupted to ask Fedia about his children. I said I had been told they were beautiful and resembled him. 'Yes, they are beautiful,' he said, 'and they do look like me, but they are like flowers. They remind me of my sister Lia.'

After dinner Willy and Misha settled down to a game of chess and Fedia watched, while Shura helped the girl clear the table. I took advantage of this to talk to Brun alone for a few minutes. 'How are things with you?' I asked him. Looking away from me he answered: 'I won't be here much longer, I will be transferred to a provincial town. I think that will be better, anything is better than here. We may not be so comfortable, but I think I would like to live in a little house in a little town, like the one I came from. Here it is unbearable.' He put his arms round me and then looked at me. 'What does Ludwik think? Why did you come? If you ever get out of here, tell Ludwik that I told him never to come back. Do you understand? I said never, not under any circumstances, never, never. I know what they can do abroad and Ludwik knows it too, they will kill, but he knows as I do that that is better for the likes of us than a Soviet prison.' He turned abruptly and joined the others round the chess board.

When Shura came back from the kitchen we spoke about her sister Lyda, who had killed herself. I asked if it was because of Pavlo Ladan, their brother-in-law who had been executed. Shura cried a bit and said: 'No, it was much later, it was because of something else, I think a love affair. I did not see much of her, she lived outside Moscow.'

The others had finished their chess game and it was time for us to leave, especially Fedia who worked at night. He told me he would like to see me the next afternoon, as his days were free. As Willy and I were looking for our coats Brun turned to me and said: 'Listen, I want to take you to the theatre, to the premiére of the new Caucasian opera. I will get the tickets. But you must come here again. Promise.' I did, and left shaking hands with Misha and Brun. That was the last time I saw Misha; he and Brun were both arrested soon after I left Moscow.

Fedia came to fetch me at my hotel next day around noon. While waiting for him I tried to buy a newspaper. In this respect Moscow had not changed: one day there were no newspapers or else they had all been sold out early; on another

day there were enormous stocks of them around because no one
had coins to buy them with. Something was always in short
supply in Moscow. During the collectivization drive the lack
of coins had been blamed on peasants' hoarding; I do not
know what the explanation was at this time.

When Fedia picked me up we went to the Hotel Metropol.
The enormous café was empty, except for one person sitting
by himself in a corner, Gerhard Eisler. He and Fedia nodded
to each other, but Eisler made no move to join us. I asked
Fedia what he thought was going on in Eisler's mind. 'How to
get out of the Soviet Union,' Fedia replied promptly.

I asked Fedia about his wife, whom I still had not met, and
reminded him that it was from Ika we had first heard of his
marriage. Fedia grimaced and said: 'I know Ika did not
approve. In principle, of course, he was right. A Communist
ought not to marry a "former". He was also afraid it might get
me into trouble, and there he was wrong. He did not understand it, and I hope he does now. No, it won't get me into
trouble. Who knows? Ironically, it might even turn out to be
a good thing. But nothing is ever that simple.

'I am doing what I can,' he went on. 'Yesterday I went to
the savings bank and took out some money. I have been doing
that for some time, a small sum each time so as not to attract
attention. I hope I can get all the money out before they get
me and "confiscate" all my "property". If they do, my kids
will starve; maybe this way I can hide something for them.'
I pressed him to speak about his wife and he answered with a
smile: 'Can you imagine a young woman, not yet thirty, who
has lost all her teeth and would never think of doing something
about it?' I told him I had brought some presents for her and
that I wanted to leave her the one good dress I had brought
with me. 'Don't bother,' he said, 'she could never get into it,
she's much too fat.' As Fedia described his wife I remembered
an incident Krivitsky told me about. One day in Vienna
Fedia and he were sitting in a café, when Fedia suddenly got
up, left the café and came back a few minutes later with a
bunch of violets which he presented to a very pretty girl sitting
at another table. Then without saying a word to her he rejoined
Krivitsky and said: 'One must render homage to beauty.'

On our way to the Lux Kindergarten to pick up Fedia's children we passed the Lubianka. 'Look at it,' Fedia said. 'At night the windows are blazing with light as they were in 1917, when the White Army was at the gates of St. Petersburg. Then they were trying to save the revolution by working day and night. Now they are burying its corpse.'

With the children, we went to Red Square to look at the gigantic Christmas tree I had seen the day before. It had an enormous red star at the top, and underneath it was a picture of Stalin holding a pretty little Uzbek girl in his arms. 'He adores children,' Fedia said. 'You read the story of that desperate father in a small town whose son was dying far from medical help and hospitals? Why, as soon as Stalin received a telegram from the father, he sent an airplane full of drugs and doctors and the child was saved.' Turning to his own children, who were indeed beautiful—frail, rather exotic-looking, as he had said, somewhat like flowers—he repeated: 'Comrade Stalin loves all little children.' As we watched the crowds that had come to look at the famous tree, I asked Fedia whether he still remembered the days when shabby-looking 'formers' used to bring a few wretched trees to town, keeping a nervous lookout for the *bezbozhniki* (the 'godless ones') who would have denounced them for this act. 'Certainly,' said Fedia. 'But now every Soviet child must have a Christmas tree. Why, just the other day they sold a hundred thousand rubles' worth of Christmas decorations.'

On the way to Fedia's home we passed through Kuznetsky Most, a main shopping street with many book shops. Pictures of the German novelist Leon Feuchtwanger were prominently displayed in their windows, along with the usual portraits of Marx, Lenin, and Stalin. I knew that Feuchtwanger had been invited to the Soviet Union in the hope that he would write a book which would erase the disastrous impression produced by André Gide's earlier account. The French writer had declined the honour of being received by Stalin, and maintained that life in the U.S.S.R. was worse than in Hitler's Germany. 'No, this is not what we wanted,' he wrote, 'and one more step in the same direction will create the exact opposite of what we wanted.' Gide's book had had a great influence on liberal intellectuals in the West; something had to be done to answer it, and although Feuchtwanger, whose novels had previously been completely ignored in the Soviet Union because of their national-Jewish emphasis, was by no means the government's first choice, much better known and more progressive writers having been approached with little success, in the end the Soviets settled for him. He must have been surprised by the evidence of his popularity in the Soviet Union, a popularity that had been carefully engineered.

While gathering material for *Moscow, 1937*, his disgraceful book justifying the trials, Feuchtwanger had a good opportunity to become acquainted with Soviet reality, to compare the living standards of Stalin's panegyrists with those of the ordinary people, to see the innumerable pictures of Stalin holding smiling children in his arms. Fedia, who was present as an interpreter when the novelist had his first meeting with Stalin, told me he acted with a certain courage. After the usual handshake and exchange of politenesses, Feuchtwanger told Stalin rather bluntly that he was shocked at the massive adulation of him. Stalin became visibly angry, retorted that he could not help it if his own people saw him in this light, and ended the interview. Feuchtwanger left the Kremlin pale and shaken. The story now making the rounds of the party was shortly to be followed by a rhyme whose puns make it almost untranslatable. The Russian

> *I okazalsa u dveriei*
> *Z kakimto strannym vidom.*
> *O, kakby etot evrei*
> *Ne okazalsa Zhidom*

contains a series of plays on words, the crucial one hingeing on the derogatory Russian word for 'Jew' being *Zhid*, which is the closest phonetic equivalent in Russian to 'Gide', while the normal term for a Jew is *evrei* (Hebrew). In translation the verse ran something like this:

> And there he appeared at the door
> with an odd expression on his face.
> Oh, let us hope that this one Jew
> Does not turn out to be a Gide.

Fedia and I laughed over this as we walked along. Then he began to speak about the Spanish civil war. After a long initial silence, he said, the party cells had suddenly begun to discuss the war. The other day the secretary of his cell had asked how many would volunteer to fight in Spain. A few members raised their hands and the secretary looked at them: 'What do you have in mind, comrade, the Spanish revolution or just a nice little trip to Europe?' Fedia said that although he wanted to go he had not volunteered. 'If I did they would undoubtedly ask me: "Do you want to help save the revolution in Spain or are you only anxious to get out of the Soviet Union?" '—'Why do they do this, Fedia?' I asked. 'Watchfulness, watchfulness,' he answered.

After I had been to Fedia's and at last met his wife, a rather nice but sloppy-looking young woman, I went in the evening to see Felix. He asked what I had done during the day. I told him I had been to Red Square with Fedia and the children to see the Christmas tree and that Fedia wanted to go to Spain. 'Ah,' said Felix, 'his old revolutionary heart beats faster again. Pity he won't go. It's a pity.' Then he added: 'I suppose if you have been with him you have heard the rhyme about Feuchtwanger. Don't worry, this Jew will turn out all right. Did you know that Firin has been removed from his position?' I was not surprised at this news because earlier, without asking Felix who would certainly have told me not to, I had tried to call Firin at his office in the N.K.V.D. construction department in the outskirts of Moscow. After a very long wait on the telephone a woman's voice answered: 'Comrade Firin is not here.' When I asked whether they expected him back, she simply said 'No' and hung up.

Firin had been appointed by Yagoda to carry out the building of the White Sea canal. When the canal was completed he was photographed shaking hands with Stalin and receiving a decoration from Yagoda. I saw this scene in a film in Moscow a few weeks after Firin's removal and probable arrest.[1] Not

---

[1] Firin's picture also appeared in Streicher's *Stürmer*, the most rabidly racist Nazi sheet, among a group identified as 'Jewish Bolshevik Plutocrats, the Real Rulers of the Soviet Union'.

much later Yagoda, Firin's chief, whom Stalin had called 'the sword of the revolution', was in turn arrested, and a huge statue of him marking the entrance to the canal had to be destroyed. As it was carved out of the rock, the whole rock had to be dynamited.

Firin had not been very popular with us. He was an arrogant man, and an unreliable one, given to intriguing, as his association with Markin had shown us in 1932. Although naturally aloof, Firin sometimes visited us on his trips abroad. He always seemed to have a soft spot for me and perhaps this is why I called him, knowing that he was a bit more vulnerable than the others. It would never have occurred to me abroad to go and see him, but a few days in Moscow had taught me that normal caution or even the intelligent consideration of problems simply had no meaning. I was however careful enough not to mention my intention to Felix and this was the only time I did not do so.

Felix had a way of dropping hints so that I did not have to ask whether it was all right to see so-and-so or whether he should be avoided. More often than not he would simply mention a name carelessly and add the information that he was in town. Sometimes he added a little remark that made his meaning quite clear. Thus he told me, 'Louis Fischer is here, but there is no need to see him. He is going to Spain. You'll see him abroad. Anyway we are not completely by ourselves in this town, there are plenty of foreigners too. It would be better if you were not seen together.' This time I followed Felix's instructions to the letter and when I passed Louis Fischer in the lobby of the Hotel National I did not speak to him.

Louis was an old friend of ours[1] and we saw a lot of each other abroad. He was very well informed and often had interviews with heads of government, ministers, and other important political figures, which he would tell us about. In Moscow, for instance, he interviewed Uritsky, chief of the Fourth Department, before going to Spain. This was completely in line with his work as a newspaperman, but I knew the N.K.V.D. had its

---

[1] He later devoted a chapter of his *Men and Politics* (New York 1941) to Ludwik, of whom he was very fond.

own ways of interpreting things and I therefore avoided him in Moscow.

I was by then getting very used to Felix's ways of warning me. 'Did you know that so-and-so has been removed from his post?' meant 'So-and-so will be arrested at any moment, don't go and see him.' He in turn was pleased with the way I had caught on to his technique, and was grateful that I did not ask him any embarrassing questions or for instructions on how to behave. 'Wait until Christmas,' he told me, 'then we will go and see our friends together.' There were not many left whom we could see, but if Felix were still alive I would thank him for giving me an opportunity to see the few people we did visit before their liquidation. I do not know whether he did it for my sake or because he, too, wanted a chance to see them for the last time. He also had realized that when terror is at its height danger becomes meaningless and it is pointless to take precautions.

I told him Brun had asked me to go with him to the opening of the Caucasian opera. 'The Caucasian opera? Good!' said Felix. 'Stalin will be there and the government too.' He had scarcely said this when Brun burst in. His face had the look of a cornered animal. 'I thought you might be here,' he told me. 'I have come to fetch you. Let's have dinner, then we will go to the opera.' Then, turning to Felix, he asked: 'Has Firin been arrested yet?' Without waiting for an answer, he turned to me. 'Let's go.'

We went first to his flat, where we were alone, as his wife was out. He threw his coat over a chair and started to pace the room. 'I had got the tickets and was planning to leave the office early to get some rest before the opera, but just as I was ready to leave I got a call from the inner building, from the prison, that Kippenberger wanted to talk to me. I could have put it off till tomorrow, but I had not seen him for over a week, so I thought I had better have him over and tell him I would see him tomorrow. I know why he called me. He probably wanted to confess, but I am not particularly anxious to have him confess now. I know he will, after all that is what I have been working on. But as long as he doesn't confess I've still got a case. After that . . . Slutsky knows damn well what he is doing, entrusting Hans Kippenberger and Werner Hirsch[1] to me. What would his Kedrovs do with Europeans, with German Communists? Threaten them, mistreat them? That's all they know how to do. But Slutsky wants a confession and he won't get it that way and he knows it. He needs these confessions. Even though he is not yet in a great hurry, he is under pressure. He will get his confession, I will get them, the Kedrovs can finish the job. It makes no difference anyway. There will probably never be a trial. Maybe after they get the confessions they will keep these German Communists for some other purpose in the future. Anyway, it won't do them or me any harm to drag the case out as long as possible. This is why I let ten days go by without interrogating Kippenberger. And do you know what he said the minute the guard left us alone: "Brun, I called for you to find out what had happened to you. As I hadn't seen you for ten days now, I was sure you had been arrested. I kept looking for you on my daily walks in the prison yard, but you weren't there either. Let's get it over with. You can have my confession. You yourself told me that there is nothing else I can do. I would rather you got it than one of your successors. You know, of course, that any dealings I had with General Bredow were on behalf of the Fourth and on orders from Thaelmann. Ludwik knows it, Krivitsky knows it, and I know that you were not in on that assignment but you can ask them. But of course these people don't want the truth, it is no use. You are welcome to my confession, maybe it can help you!" '

Brun laughed to himself and there was a mad gleam in his eyes as he said aloud, to himself: 'No, Kippenberger, it won't be of any use to me, nor will anything else.' He caught himself up and resumed the story: 'I said: "Good. I have deliberately left you alone for a while. I would have seen you tomorrow anyway. Let's leave it till then and not talk about it now. Tonight I am seeing a very dear friend, probably for the last

[1] Kippenberger was head of the German party's military apparatus. Hirsch, a newspaperman, one of the editors of *Rote Fahne,* was the son of a Jewish father and an aristocratic German mother, daughter of a high-ranking army officer. The Nazis arrested him, but thanks to his mother's connections and the personal intervention of Emy Goering, he was released from a Nazi concentration camp and extradited to the U.S.S.R. There he was liquidated.

time. I am taking her to the opera. I will see you tomorrow."
I rang for the guard and had him taken away. You know, I
wanted to go with him. I used to look like him, unshaven,
collar turned up. Well, all that is behind him. For me it's still
to come.'

I was relieved when Shura came back and put an end to the
conversation. Brun shaved and when we went out looked very
respectable. He drank a good deal at dinner. Our seats at the
opera were good, right next to Stalin's box. The audience was
brilliant: diplomatic corps, low-cut evening dresses, military
uniforms everywhere, Stalin in his grey military uniform. At
the interval we had an ice cream in the ornate hall. Mrs.
Sokolnikov joined us and pointed out Berman, a high official
in the N.K.V.D. 'Well, this will give him something to report
tomorrow.' The opera began again, long and colourful. To me
it seemed endless. I was happy when it was over at last.

3

Anna Mikhailovna Messing's telephone did not answer,
perhaps because it was out of order, or had been removed, so
I went to her apartment. Anna Mikhailovna and her maid,
Frossia, answered the bell and looked at me as if I were a
ghost. 'When did you get here? You came to see me! It has
been almost a year since anybody, but anybody, has done that.'
As she talked she pushed me into a chair as if afraid I might
leave as suddenly as I had come. 'You know that your phone
is out of order, Anna Mikhailovna, do you?' I asked. 'I know,'
she answered, 'but what of it? No one ever bothered using it
before. They just dropped in. You remember how many
people used to be here, staying, coming, going, and now there is
nobody, although I am so close to the offices.' Her big apartment, in a luxurious building that had belonged to a rich
Moscow merchant, was in the centre of town on the Miasnit-
skaia, in what had once been a fashionable part of Moscow.
Messing had been able to secure the place for his family,
although he no longer lived with them.

'The only one who still comes is Messing,' she continued,
'and it won't be long before he stops coming too. I don't know
what is going on here. Under the Tsar it didn't matter what they

did to us, it did not affect our personal relations. The Tsar could throw us into prison, lock us up in fortresses, send us to Siberia, but he could never sever the ties that bound us together. On the contrary, whenever we suffered a blow we moved closer together, helped each other. But now? What is happening to us all?' She told me that Sophia Unshlikht had been arrested in bed, after she had had a heart attack, and that when her sister Stefa went to the cadre department of the Comintern where she worked to ask for permission to send her some clothes and medicine, the official there said: 'What? Your heart bleeds for an enemy of the people?' A few weeks later the same man came to her and said: 'How odd that you care so little for your sister. Why don't you send her a parcel?'

I immediately thought of Fedia and 'watchfulness'. Had the official been told to act in this way or was the first answer he gave her the one he was supposed to give and his suggestion that she send a parcel caused by his feeling sorry for her?

Listening to Anna Mikhailovna I began to feel sorry for the first time, sorry for her, sorry for all of us, sorry for myself. . . . Abroad, our conception of things was different. We were more terrified than those living in the Soviet Union, we spent our time combing the papers for news, we were expecting something to happen. What we could not conceive of is that life simply went on. Anna Mikhailovna was right; Stalin had succeeded in doing something the Tsars had never done. The terror had destroyed the bonds of humanity, and had made those who were directly affected go on living in a void, accept this void, and create it around themselves.

Did Messing come to visit his wife more often because she was so very much alone or was it because he felt the void growing around him and his friends who were being 'removed from office'? The night before when I went with Brun into his house, we had met several of his neighbours; they seemed to hurry by, nodding slightly. Yet they were the same ones who would drop in, in other days, for a game of chess. I also thought that the guard, who had been so friendly to me a day or so before, now looked the other way. Or did I merely think so?

'The other day,' continued Anna Mikhailovna, 'I called Joseph Unshlikht and asked him to do something for a girl who was once my maid. This young woman is now a streetcar conductress in Kharkov. After working for me, she went back to her village, became a party member and then went to Kharkov. Now I get a letter from her sister-in-law telling me that the girl and her husband have both been arrested. What could they possibly have done? She is an intelligent and good girl, and her husband is intelligent too. They are true children of the people, both good party members, and now they are arrested.' She had felt quite justified in asking Unshlikht to do something for them, she said, although no one had expected him to intervene when his sister was arrested; for they had always been political opponents and he disapproved of her stand for the opposition. 'But these people', she said, 'he could have done something for them. You know what he said? He said he couldn't do anything. I will never call him again, and you know how close I used to be to him and to his wife.'

I thought of another link broken: Anna Mikhailovna who would never call again, thus deepening the isolation around Unshlikht, an isolation he had himself helped to create.—'After all,' I said, 'maybe he really couldn't do anything.'—'Maybe,' she answered. 'But in that case what is going to happen to that girl's two small children? Does anybody think of them?'

Evidently no one did. It was simply accepted, what could one do? Willy had told me that many committed suicide, and mentioned a friend of his who had recently killed himself. 'That is a silly thing to do,' Willy said. 'There is always time to do it when they come to get you. They don't prevent you from doing it.'—'Is that true?' I asked him.—'Yes,' he answered. 'The only ones they watch are the important people whom they want to keep alive for a trial, they don't care about people like us.' I was thinking of this earlier conversation as I said goodbye to Anna Mikhailovna, promising to return. I did not keep my promise. I forgot her, as all the others who had frequented her house had forgotten her. I never saw her again.

I wandered through the quiet, black streets. There was still no snow. I went down the escalator into the new subway. The Dzerzhinsky Square station was resplendent with marble and rare granite brought from the Caucasus, but for all its grandeur, it was still a means of transportation, showy but useful. The trains were crowded, of course, but not with people hanging in bunches on the outside, as they had on the trams in the collectivization days.

When I got back to Felix's I found Max Maximov-Friedman there, lying on the couch. We were very happy to see each other. When I came in Max was telling Felix that one of their friends had been arrested that morning. 'Why'? asked Felix.— 'Connections with Lyova,' Max said, using the nickname for Trotsky. 'By the way, did you know that Alex Borovich has been called back to Moscow and that he is going to Spain?' Felix frowned at this piece of news. 'You mean to say they are going to send him to Spain? What for?'—'He is an officer,' answered Max. 'They need military men in Spain.'

I was pleased that I might get an opportunity to see Alex Borovich whom we all liked very much. Borovich had been on numerous assignments abroad, as a colonel in the Red Army.[1] At one time, in 1929, he had been military adviser to Radek, who was then head of the Sun Yat-sen University in Moscow, among whose students was a son of Chiang Kai-shek. Radek got along very well with Borovich, partly because they were both Poles, and partly because Borovich, a soldier rather than a politician, was a very pleasant, unassuming, quiet man with whom Radek, then already quite isolated politically, found he could talk freely. Alex knew of Radek's connections with his friends in the opposition as well as of the contacts he had made with the Right opposition, and through Alex we thus had a pretty good idea of Radek's thoughts and his assessment of the situation. In spite of his capitulation and reinstatement, he was bitterly critical of the government, and was credited with inventing most of the anti-government jokes then circulating in Moscow. It was said that when Radek returned to Moscow from exile, Manuilsky of the Comintern asked him: 'Well, comrade Radek, can one or can one not build socialism in one country?'—

---

[1] Borovich and Alfred Tilden were the only colonels among our friends, and the only ones except Willy to bear active military rank. Ludwik and Krivitsky both had the rank and received the pay of captains in the N.K.V.D., as they had in the Fourth Department, but had otherwise the status of civilians.

'Certainly,' Radek is supposed to have answered, 'but God help the country. Anyway, why in one country, why not in one town, or one street? Never mind, there will be a fair in our street too!'[1] It was also said that, when Stalin told Radek to stop making up and circulating anti-government jokes, Radek answered: 'Yes, comrade Stalin, but the latest joke, the one that you are our leader, is not one I made up.' Such jokes, whether correctly attributed to Radek or not, had endeared him to everyone in the party—except, presumably, Stalin.

After having worked with Radek, Borovich was sent to China in 1933. Now it seemed he was being recalled. When Max had gone, Felix said: 'So they are bringing Alex back from the Far East and they even have a new assignment for him in Spain? Not Spain. They need him here, for the Radek trial!'

I was never to see Borovich, though I had looked forward to hearing from him about Ika in China. When *Pravda* on 4 September 1964 published a eulogy on Richard Sorge, it mentioned that Sorge's two superiors in Moscow, Berzin and Borovich, had been liquidated. Borovich was probably arrested the minute he arrived in Moscow.

4

One morning I received a visit from George Mueller, head of the passport division of the N.K.V.D. A Viennese and, like many of his compatriots, taken prisoner by the Russians in the First World War, he had remained in the U.S.S.R. and fought on the side of the Bolsheviks. After the Civil War he joined the G.P.U., and had served in various departments of the N.K.V.D. before he was given his present post. He and his one-time counterpart in the Fourth Department, Ludwik's old friend Locker, also Viennese, were jokingly known to us, from their work of preparing forged passports, as 'the consuls'.[2]

Mueller, who was very friendly, knew Ludwik quite well and said that he had been anxious to meet his wife. After chatting for a while he said he would like to show me his office and that

---

[1] A popular saying in Russia, meaning 'Some day we too will have our say'.

[2] In 1937 Locker was in the Far East, and his friend Nebenfuehrer in Spain. It is possible that these two Austrians survived the terror, but I have never heard from them.

several of his colleagues would also like to see me. We arranged to meet at three o'clock outside the hotel.

Before leaving Mueller asked to see my passport, examined it closely, and put it in his briefcase. 'I hope,' he said, 'that you are not disturbed at my taking your passport along. I want to photograph the border stamps, they keep changing them and we have to keep abreast. We do this with everyone who comes from abroad.' He spoke in a very kindly tone and I answered: 'No, I am not disturbed at being without my passport. After all, even if I had it in my pocket, could I leave here without your permission?' He laughed. 'You certainly could not, but I am glad to see that you understand why I do it.' (I was not to see the passport again till he brought it to me on the eve of my departure—whether he kept it because he had not yet photographed it, or simply because he felt I had no use for it in Moscow, I do not know.)

Mueller stayed for a little while but, as I hardly knew him, we did not have much to talk about. As a mark of confidence, he gave me his unlisted phone number at the N.K.V.D. in case I should be apprehended in the streets. It would have been useless to call him through the regular number, since the N.K.V.D. switchboard was busy day and night. As he was leaving he asked me whether I had seen Fedia, whom he knew well. There was concern in his eyes as he spoke, but he said nothing except to give Fedia his regards.

When I came out of the hotel at the appointed time that afternoon Mueller was nowhere in sight, but I saw a rather shabby-looking man watching me. He nodded and turned on his heels, and I followed him. I had never seen him before, but he must have been shown a picture of me because he acted as if he knew me. We entered the N.K.V.D. office building, passing a sentry who asked no questions, and stepped into the lift; when we got out Bella was waiting for us. She introduced me to some officers in the room and when one, a bearded man, became altogether too friendly, she asked him whether he had never seen a woman before. He answered: 'Sure, but not like this one.'

This went on until Spiegelglas, Slutsky's deputy, whom I had not met before, entered the room. Why had I been kept waiting, he asked. Then, turning to the bearded officer, he said, 'I don't blame you.' A small, stout, blond man with protruding eyes, he continued to pay me compliments, to tell me how happy he was to meet the wife of Ludwik, whom he so much respected, although he wished he had got closer to him in the past, and how much he was looking forward to seeing us abroad where he would soon be going. But for the absence of Slutsky, he said, he would not have had the opportunity to meet me in the office, but now that we had met we should see more of each other. Then, as had all the others, he asked whether there was anything I needed or that he could do for me. He said he would send me some tickets to the theatre, though he could not very well escort me, as it would be imprudent for us to be seen together. Our chat was interrupted by Mueller who came to take me to his office. As I left, Spiegelglas said: 'Well, I see they are taking you away, but you are in good hands. I hope to see you soon again.'

George Mueller showed me his office, two big rooms full of photographic equipment, and introduced me to his assistant Kaminsky, a Ukrainian who knew Ludwik quite well. Kaminsky talked of mutual friends, Ukrainians, some of whom had been arrested and two of whom had killed themselves. He spoke as if they were still alive, although he must have known they were dead. After a while he said: 'It is time to go home. You know, we work almost regular hours here, not like the others, isn't that so, George?' Mueller agreed, but when Kaminsky added, 'And what's more we are irreplaceable too,' he merely shrugged.

Mueller took me back to the front entrance but when I tried to pass through it the guard stopped me, saying: 'Where are you going?' He explained that I could leave the building only in the company of the person who brought me in. It was the same guard who had seen me enter and had seen me with Mueller, but he insisted that he had strict orders and I would have to wait for my escort. The man was a driver, he said, and was probably on an errand, but would be back. He offered to go to the garage to look for him as soon as his relief came. After I had waited more than an hour in the lobby my escort appeared and the same scene was repeated. He turned on his heels wordlessly,

I followed him to the door of the hotel. There he waited until I had passed the reception desk, then left.

The incident added to my discomfort and unease, although I knew that it was of no importance, and I decided to call it a day. I rang up Felix to tell him I was staying in. He simply laughed, saying no doubt I had other boy friends, and I went to bed.

One day I went to visit Paul Urban at his hotel, the National. As I walked in I recognized the manager as an old acquaintance a Latvian who had worked in the Embassy in Vienna in 1926. We were glad to see each other and he showed me round the brand new hotel. I asked him whether the large cracks and fissures in the walls were due to sabotage, as was generally believed. (The new N.K.V.D. buildings also showed these cracks through which rain used to seep.) He told me that it was quite possible that some of the German builders hired for the job had worked badly on purpose, but that he didn't really think so. No doubt there was an element of ill will, but generally it was simply lack of skill on the part of the Russian labourers.

There was however plenty of petty sabotage going on. He showed me one example. All the beautifully painted white doors in the hotel had large glass plates round the handles and locks to keep the paint from getting smeared. The glass, of course, was easy to wash and it was always clean, but the paint round it was smudged. Since some of the stained areas were almost impossible to get at, because of the protective glass, the smudging was obviously being done on purpose by the hotel staff, but no matter how sharp a lookout the manager kept he had never been able to catch anyone in the act. When I asked why his staff did this he answered: 'They are underpaid and overworked, and they live under the constant strain of having to report on their guests and on each other.' As he was an N.K.V.D. employee, he knew what he was talking about. When at his trial Radek said the entire Soviet people was behind the police apparatus, he was stating a fact; he certainly did not intend it as a compliment, although Vyshinsky, the state prosecutor, took it as one.

Paul Urban did not know I was in Moscow; when he opened

the door and saw me he was speechless for a few minutes. Then he began to cry, something I would never have expected from him. He told me he was completely isolated in Moscow, that he had nothing to do, no one to talk to, and that he did not even have anything to read as he did not understand Russian. 'I can't reach anybody, it is worse than in Paris. I understand that one has to be cautious there, but I never expected life here to be so conspiratorial.'

Since he had come in the spring, expecting to stay a short time, he had only a light suit. Now it was deep winter and he had no overcoat. When he said this to the man who came every two weeks to bring him money the man answered: 'What do you need a coat for? You don't have to leave the hotel, it is nice and warm here and you can get your meals in the hotel restaurant.'[1]

Paul told me that once in a while he did go out, to the Hotel Lux where the Comintern people stayed, to visit some German friends, Johannes Becher and Lilly Corpus. Becher never said anything of interest; Lilly told him she was doing housework, but secretly, as she was not allowed to work, not being a Soviet citizen. In spite of Nazi rule she was holding on for dear life to her German citizenship.

In the restaurant at the National, the waitress mistook me for Paul's sister—we did look a bit alike—and said: 'I am so glad you are here, he won't be so lonely any more, the poor man.' Among the other lonely people in the room was Dr. Wolf, a prominent German physician who had had to leave Germany because of his opposition to a law forbidding birth control. Now Soviet women, who had had the right to decide whether they wanted a child or not, were calling for the abolition of this privilege. But in the Soviet Union Dr. Wolf could not protest, and sat alone in the restaurant, waiting for a miracle or for something to put an end to this endless waiting.

Not realizing the true state of affairs, Paul was convinced I would be able to find out why he was being kept in Moscow, and when he might leave. That evening I told Felix the condition in which I had found him, without even an overcoat, and said that

[1] In his *Handbook for Spies* Alexander Foote describes an identical experience. He was occasionally visited in his hotel room but never saw the inside of an office.

Ludwik wanted to know why Paul was being kept here when he was needed abroad. Felix said it was not his business to find this out, but that he would get him an overcoat. 'He will have his coat tomorrow, and then he won't have to sit in his room all day. But why does he have to go visiting the Germans at the Lux? Is he that dumb? Do you know what he told the man who visits him? He said he wanted to go to Leningrad to see Rakovsky's adopted daughter. Tell him, for God's sake, to keep quiet.'

Felix kept his promise, and Paul got an overcoat the very next day. It was a short, miserable coat of the kind that comes only to the hips and is called a *kurtka*. It was at least two sizes too small and the material was incredibly shoddy. Still, such things cost 700 rubles in a department store. Paul was overjoyed, as it meant he could move about a bit.

The first thing we did was to go to the Museum of the Revolution. It had not changed much since the last time I saw it. There were not nearly as many pictures of Stalin there as in the town. Lenin's coat with the bullet holes dating from Dora Kaplan's attempt to assassinate him was still on display. There were even a few pictures of him with Willy Muenzenberg, although the latter was no longer in the party's good graces.[1]

As we were about to leave, a group of factory workers on one of the usual compulsory cultural tours came in, guided by a young woman with a red kerchief. The faces of the workers showed quite clearly that they would have much preferred to spend their day off with their families or resting. The guide was explaining the meaning of one of the pre-revolutionary cartoons showing the old Bolsheviks at a party conference in Copenhagen. Lenin was depicted as a cat, the others as mice. Evidently there was some disagreement, for the cat seemed to be chasing the

[1] When Muenzenberg later declined an 'invitation' to Moscow to 'straighten things out', he was expelled from the Party, but he was too well-known a figure to be killed at the time. With other German political refugees he was interned by the French government at the outbreak of the Second World War. As the German forces advanced, he and some other internees known to be in danger from the Nazis were released by the French authorities and allowed to find their way out of France. Two weeks after he left the internment camp Muenzenberg's body was found by the French *gendarmerie*, hanging from a tree. It was not suicide; he had been strangled on the ground before he was strung up—thus providing a variation on Fedia's prediction, by being both murdered *and* hanged by 'his own people'.

mice. One of the mice was Kamenev, and the young woman asked the workers: 'Comrades, who is this man?' There was silence. She repeated the question, and still received no answer. Then she lectured them: 'That man is Kamenev, the great traitor who wanted to kill comrade Lenin and comrade Stalin.' There was no reaction from the workers, who were marched off sullenly to another exhibit.

Later I asked Paul why on earth he wanted to visit Rakovsky's daughter in Leningrad. I pointed out how dangerous this was, not only because she was Rakovsky's daughter but because her husband, a well-known writer, had just been arrested. 'What of it?' said Paul. 'Of course, I told the man who comes to visit me. Who else could I tell? He is the only one I ever see. I told him why I wanted to see her. I met her abroad, we became friends and we are both artists.'

Paul's neglect of the elementary principles of 'watchfulness' was quite different from the attitude of Fedia or my other friends. They knew how little it mattered, in the circumstances, whether they were careful or not. But Paul had never realized there might be a need to be careful. He resented being left out of things and while he vaguely knew that people were being arrested, it never occurred to him that he might be in any danger. He was merely furious at not being allowed to leave when he wanted to.

Felix told me some time later that there was a good chance of Paul's being sent to Spain, but I could not mention this to him till it was certain. When I was finally permitted to tell him I wanted very badly to suggest he stop off in Paris and talk to Ludwik. But I did not dare; his orders were to go directly to Barcelona via Czechoslovakia. I don't know what advice Ludwik would have given him, but I knew it was much too dangerous to tell him anything here. In Paris we would have taken the risk, a real one, since Paul simply did not understand, but in Moscow in 1937 it was out of the question.

Paul was enthusiastic over going to Spain, and grateful to me, as he was convinced I was responsible for the assignment. I had of course nothing to do with it, though I may unwittingly have played a part by reminding the N.K.V.D. of his existence. In fact, Paul's leaving for Spain did not change his situation much;

in Barcelona one was just as much in the hands of the N.K.V.D. as if one had never left Moscow. It was the job of Orlov-Nikolsky, N.K.V.D. commandant in Spain, to see that anyone Moscow wanted returned alive got there. Soviet ships were standing by in the harbour of Barcelona to take those who were needed to Moscow or to dispose at sea of those who were not.

Had Paul understood what was going on in Spain he could have saved himself; all he had to do was get off the train at Prague and go to Paris. But he wanted to go to Spain. Anything was better than the eternal waiting in Moscow, he thought, and besides he was genuinely convinced he would do something useful in Spain. We never saw him again, and received only one cryptic note in the summer of 1937, sent to a cover address: 'It looks as if heads are rolling in Red Square.' Perhaps he understood by then, much too late. After the war I made inquiries among his friends and relatives. In vain. No one ever heard of Paul Urban again.

5

On Christmas Eve Felix, his wife, and I had gone to visit Bortnovsky, the only friend I had not yet seen and wanted to see. A member of the politburo of the Polish Communist Party, in his years as a section chief of the Fourth Department Bortnovsky had gathered many Poles around him, some of whom followed him to the Comintern, while others joined the N.K.V.D. In his forties, a slightly built, blond man with a receding chin, Bortnovsky (also known as Bronkovsky; his Christian name was Bronek) had been severely wounded during the Civil War: he could not use one arm and dragged the leg on the same side. He had married, late in life, the former wife of another Polish politburo member, Henrykovsky, and they had a little girl about two years old. At the time I saw them his wife's former husband had just been recalled from abroad and arrested.

We had our main meal at midday, as our hosts wanted to take their child to Red Square and show her the Christmas tree. Bortnovsky was rather a shy man who did not talk much, and I was not too surprised at his rather subdued greeting, especially since we had never been very close. His coolness towards Felix surprised me more, as they had known each other well, especially in the years when Justina had worked for Bortnovsky. But Felix did not seem taken aback, and I thought how Felix himself, so exuberantly friendly in earlier times, had become short-tempered.

Bortnovsky showed Felix the census form he was supposed to file, and that even I had had to fill out, though I was merely a visitor to the U.S.S.R. 'How am I supposed to answer this question?' Bortnovsky asked Felix. 'What nationality am I supposed to put down for the child? I am a Pole, and so was Stella until now. But she is Jewish, and I guess that is what I am supposed to put down. But this is silly, she has no religion, and, as far as we are concerned, we always thought of her as Polish. And what about the little girl? What is she supposed to be? Polish? Jewish?' I suggested that, since the child was born in the Soviet Union, the answer ought to be Soviet. 'Yes,' he said, 'but according to this, she is supposed to have the same nationality as her parents.'

While we pondered this, the telephone rang. Everyone froze for a moment, as one did in Moscow when the telephone rang. We watched Bortnovsky as he answered in a muffled voice. He talked for a few minutes and I heard my name mentioned before he hung up. 'That was Madame Stachevsky, she wants us to come to a New Year's Eve party. I promised that we would come and bring you as well.'

The invitation was welcome, for it solved the problem of what to do with oneself. It was after all essential to be seen somewhere. I asked Felix if I could take Paul. He saw no objection and even promised to come himself and bring Max.

Soon afterwards we all left the house and went to Red Square. Felix said he was going home to sleep and I was alone. It was a terribly lonely Christmas Eve. Fedia was with his family and, as nobody called on me, I went back out into the streets. They were beginning to empty, with only a few last-minute shoppers rushing home. I remembered a Christmas a few years earlier, when I had walked with Alex Borovich through Red Square. Alex was in uniform, and a few young men who were passing seized him in their arms and tossed him high up in the air, in Russian fashion, shouting: 'Hurrah, the Red Army!'

Regina Stachevsky was a vivacious Frenchwoman who spoke the most amazing mixture of Russian and French. She was delighted to see me on New Year's Eve and asked all sorts of questions about Paris where her daughter Lolotte was going to be working in the Soviet pavilion at the 1937 World's Fair. She told me she would soon be joining her daughter in Paris and that her husband Arthur, then in Valencia, would come there as well.

It was the first time since my return to Moscow that I had heard anyone speak so enthusiastically, as if things were completely normal. She told me that her daughter was now in good health after an accident got while parachute-jumping, and expressed great pleasure at Paul's presence, as a young Russian girl friend of Lolotte's was staying with them. The other guests arrived, including a man whom she introduced as 'a comrade from the Central Committee'. Someone put on a record and Paul asked the young Russian girl to dance. She looked at him and said: '*Niemiets*, German, I don't dance with Germans,' and she could not be persuaded to change her mind. That little incident, plus the fact that none of the other guests—including Felix and Max—had come, although it was getting late, depressed Madame Stachevsky, and she shut off the phonograph. Finally Bortnovsky came, and since it was obvious no one else would, we sat down to eat. As Bortnovsky was not very talkative and no one knew the 'comrade from the Central Committee', the meal was silent and gloomy.

The party would have broken up much sooner but on New Year's Eve we had to see the Old Year out. Just as midnight struck, and before we finished exchanging the traditional 'Happy New Year' the telephone rang. It was long distance from Valencia. Madame Stachevsky's husband wanted to wish her a happy New Year. Overwhelmed with joy, she began to tell him who was at her flat, what they were doing, giving various names, until Bortnovsky brutally tore the telephone out of her hand. I would never have thought him capable of such fury. 'Doesn't the damn fool know better than to call this country from Spain in the middle of a civil war, with every intelligence service in the world listening in?' He grabbed his coat and went out, slamming the door behind him. Madame Stachevsky looked at us. 'Why, he is impossible, what on earth is wrong with Arthur calling me?' The 'comrade from the Central

Committee' was also looking for his coat. 'The comrade is right,' he said, 'this is no time to be calling Moscow from Valencia.' With that he also went out, leaving me with the weeping Madame Stachevsky and the young Russian girl.

I do not know what the atmosphere was like at other New Year's Eve parties in 1937. Usually such parties lasted well into the small hours and were gay affairs. but I doubt if there were any like that among the people I knew. When I saw Felix next day I mentioned Stachevsky's call from Valencia and Bortnovsky's anger. 'He was absolutely right,' said Felix. 'That idiot ought to know better. I am glad I did not come. I went to sleep and then dropped in at our club.'

New Year's Day was a holiday and I learned from Willy, who visited me, that he had taken Brun and Brun's wife to a party at the Red Army House the night before. In the old days Brun would never have gone, and would have made fun of Willy for going, but now he needed Willy to take him as he could not have got in otherwise. I saw Brun later that day and he asked me where I had been. When I told him, without mentioning the telephone call, he said it was too bad I had not gone to the Red Army House with them. Henceforth he was going to go there for all celebrations.

When I told Fedia about this he said: 'The silly fool. Why didn't he stay home and go to bed? He still thinks he should be seen in public. Nobody knows him there anyway. He used to try to impress others and now he tries to impress himself. You know, it's the same when he speaks about our town. All he talks about is the river, a nice little stream. He never thinks of the people. No one exists but himself. I bet you he doesn't remember our teacher. I bet you he has even forgotten Krusia! Maybe she was right when she refused to see me, that time in Berlin. I had no right to happiness. It is good that she married that decent fellow who wasn't one of us but took good care of her until she died.'

He continued to reminisce: 'When I used to spend my furloughs in Vienna on leave from the Italian front, strolling with Krusia through that beautiful, hungry city, it was full of young soldiers, children really, whom they forced to grow moustaches so they would look like men instead of kids. There were young war cripples, and Red Cross ladies leading the blind who had left their eyesight in the Karst mountains. And many women in mourning. And everyone hoping to get a postcard, one of those pink cards with a printed message in every language of the Monarchy, saying: "I am well". All the soldier had to do was underline the one sentence in his language, sign the card and write the address. It was post-free, of course. By the time the little card arrived, the soldier was often already dead.'

Fedia remembered walking through the Burg one day with Krusia, stopping to watch the changing of the guard. 'In spite of the war it was still the same ceremonial, the same colourful pompousness,' he said, 'as if the Monarchy would last forever. I said to Krusia: "These are their last parades. It won't be long before a new world is born out of this bloodshed." Then a shot rang out. Friedrich Adler had shot and killed the Minister of War, Count Stuergkh. Krusia said that in doing this Adler had betrayed the principles of the Social-Democratic Party, that socialists should never engage in terroristic acts. But I remember telling her that in killing the Austrian Minister of War Adler had killed all ministers of war. I knew that a new world would emerge from all this carnage.'

Lenin, then in Switzerland, had called for a revolution in all the countries engaged in this madness of killing. And in Bern a meeting of the Socialist Youth International had elected Willy Muenzenberg as its secretary. 'We had a strong group in Vienna and we used to meet in Krusia's room,' Fedia said. 'We sent a delegate from there to Muenzenberg. And in St. Petersburg thousands demonstrated in the streets, and the Romanovs were tottering. When my furlough was over I did not go back to the Italian front. I deserted to Russia. That was the last time I saw her, in her little room in the summer of 1917 . . . '

He came back to the present and spoke again about Brun. Fedia talked more about him than about the others, perhaps because he was especially angry with him, or perhaps because of the friends in Moscow Brun was the one we both knew best, except for Willy. But no one could ever be angry with Willy.

'So he spends his New Year's Eve at the Red Army House! He is nothing but a frightened petty bourgeois. He has always been one. If it hadn't been for me he would have become a Marmurek.'

Even now, in his desperate situation, Fedia would never have traded his lot for the uneventful life of a Marmurek. And now, so many years after Krusia's death, amidst the terror, with all his hopes ruined, he felt he had missed something in life and regretted that he had denied himself happiness. He seemed to have forgotten his surroundings. That must have been the last time he ever spoke to anyone about the past.

Breaking into his reminiscences, Fedia told me that a second interview had taken place between Stalin and Feuchtwanger. He was not present at this one but had been told what had happened. The meeting went off much more smoothly than the first. Feuchtwanger had agreed to write an apologia for the trials, he said, but in exchange asked that Radek and other Jewish defendants be spared.[1]

After Fedia told me this I happened to be at the Jewish theatre's production of *King Lear,* with young Bazarov. By accident I sat next to Feuchtwanger and a woman who may have been his wife. Before the performance began an actor came to the front of the stage to greet 'comrade Feuchtwanger who is honouring us with his presence.' Feuchtwanger seemed embarrassed, thanked the actor in German—avoiding the word 'comrade'—and said it was he who was honoured to attend a performance in Yiddish because, while he had an international head, he had a Jewish heart. This remark was a great success. The performance was excellent, as always at the Jewish theatre to which it was very hard to get tickets.

By then it was mid-January and the second trial was about to begin. At Felix's, while we drank our tea, Felix suddenly said, as if it were the most natural thing in the world: 'Why, this Radek is really a whore. He has been torturing the investigators for months. There was no way of getting him to col-

---

[1] Feuchtwanger kept his word, describing the second trial as a peaceful performance at which all the defendants looked rested and well-fed and carried newspapers in their pockets. When the trial was over, Radek, Sokolnikov, and two minor figures, one a so-called 'specialist' and the other an *agent provocateur,* received prison sentences. All the other defendants who were not Jewish, among them Piatakov, were sentenced to death.

laborate on anything. Now, all of a sudden, he tells the interrogator to go away and go to sleep while he writes out his own confession. He's confessed that he is a Polish spy and that he has been working for Polish intelligence for years.'

We sat in silence until Felix's wife suddenly said: 'It's unbelievable. Where else in the world could Radek have reached as high a position as in this country? After all people spy for something. What did he need to become a spy for?'

Felix turned crimson and shouted at her: 'Idiot!' She burst into tears and left the room. 'Why did you say that?' I asked Felix.

Without looking at me he went to his desk, opened a drawer, and took out a gun. Then, turning to me, he said: 'They won't take me alive!' Then he put the gun back and, in a calmer tone, said: 'Why did I say that? Well, old girl, we have had some hard times together, but don't worry, I won't have to confess, I will have time to take care of myself.[1] Yes, we have had hard times, but we have had some pretty good ones too. Do you remember when the Chinese Communists took Shanghai in 1927 and we celebrated in the Rathaus Keller in Vienna? We were shouting: "Long live Red Shanghai!" I danced a Cossack dance on the table. You have not forgotten that, I hope.'

I did not want to think just then of that celebration ten years earlier in Vienna, or of how the Shanghai Communists were slaughtered a few weeks after their victory. I was thinking of Felix and his wife. Why had he told the story of Radek? Was it for my benefit or hers? Had her sane reaction to the story brought him back to his senses and was that why he showed me the gun? It was clear that the deal Stalin had made with Feuchtwanger for Radek's life had left a terrible impression on Felix, who had known Radek well, partly through Borovich, and had still been seeing him occasionally.

No one would have been surprised to see Radek emerge as the leader of some opposition to Stalin, in spite of his earlier capitulation. He was witty and courageous enough; on the other hand, he was also known to be opportunistic and cynical, and one might even guess that, if the news of a deal had been long in coming, it was because of Stalin's reluctance, not Radek's.

[1] Felix was right. He did not have to confess. When they came to arrest him, so a friend of ours learned from Slutsky, he shot himself.

The second trial, ending 30 January 1937 with death sentences for Piatakov, Serebriakov, Muralov, and others, created an ominous atmosphere which this time went far beyond the ranks of the Party. In factories the workers were called on to vote resolutions calling for 'death to the mad dogs'. Raising their arms, the workers remained motionless and silent. The N.K.V.D. was well aware of the feeling in the country, and so was Stalin.

It was a time when people did not believe in natural death. When Sergo Ordzhonikidze died in mid-February everyone took it for granted he had committed suicide, some said over his failure to persuade Stalin to spare the life of Piatakov, his former deputy. According to one story he died at home; others said it was while confronting Stalin. I asked Felix where Sergo had in fact died, and he answered that it had been in the Politburo. My face must have shown some scepticism, as Felix repeated: 'Yes, in the Politburo, of a stroke. Wouldn't you have a stroke if you were face to face with Stalin?'

Of course people did die naturally in the Soviet Union. Occasionally one would see a funeral cortège, with a red-covered coffin if the corpse was a Communist, or just a plain coffin. But there were no obituaries in the press except of very important persons, just as there were no reports of crimes or acts of passion or drunken brawls, no court reports. The big morning papers and the popular evening tabloids were all alike, full of plan overfulfilments, victories on the grain front, happy Stakhanovites and, of course, Stalin.

One day Felix told me that Molchanov, an N.K.V.D. division chief, had been arrested. To the usual charges of the period was added a new one: Molchanov was said to have deliberately created disorders in the N.K.V.D. This seemed to indicate that Stalin, afraid of the extent of the purges and their effect, was looking for a scapegoat, and that a thorough purge of the N.K.V.D., in the wake of Yagoda's dismissal the year before, was in the offing. I did not know Molchanov, and his arrest meant nothing to me personally, but I badly wanted to ask Felix's opinion of it. As I did not dare ask him I asked Fedia instead.

Fedia explained that Felix had told me the story only because it was about to appear in the papers. In fact, Molchanov and his deputies had been arrested several weeks before. I asked Fedia whether he thought Molchanov's arrest might not mean an end, or at least a shift, of the terror, but he did not think so. He had expected Molchanov to survive the terror, as he was known as a staunch Stalinist. He thought that, while Molchanov had fallen victim to a thorough housecleaning by Yezhov, Yagoda's successor, the case against him had probably been prepared much earlier by Yagoda himself, in an attempt to save his own skin. Fedia said that by now even Stalin was powerless to stop the terror. 'Once you start sliding there is no halting. The terror will not ease up; it will get worse as long as there is anyone left who was around in October.'

His analysis was soon to be confirmed; Rykov and Bukharin were arrested together with many others of the Right opposition, and a wave of suicides followed.

6

My Christmas visit had by then lasted more than two months, and still nothing was said of my going back. Winter had set in in earnest, and it was now too cold to stroll about the city. Willy still came by occasionally, but we had little left to talk about, since I did not know his circle. As for our mutual friends, we had already said as much as it was possible to say about them. It was no use asking: 'What will happen to you?' Willy did not know, nor did anyone else, and all he could answer was: 'Who knows, as long as one stays alive . . . '

I sometimes walked past the house we had lived in five years before on the Smolensk Boulevard. I did not go in, there seemed to be no point. One day I met the neighbour I mentioned earlier. I inquired after his wife but did not ask about any others. He did not volunteer any information, nor did he ask me in.

Every morning at ten o'clock I went round to the dispatching office of *Izvestiia* to buy a paper, a tip Fedia had given me, as there were always plenty of papers there. Eventually I became friendly with the man there, who had only one arm—I never discovered whether he had lost the other during the war or in some accident. One day, as I was paying for my paper, he held out a red booklet, saying: 'Here, citizen, only half a ruble for all the latest Soviet songs.' I knew what these were. They all began and ended with 'Stalin, our great father, our sun, our Soviet tractor . . . ' I put the booklet down on the counter. 'Come, citizen,' the man said, 'don't be stingy, half a ruble isn't much, these are Soviet songs.' I told him I knew but I didn't want them. 'Of course you want them, don't you want to sing? Life is happy, life is joyous, of course you want to sing.' I told him I could not sing. 'You can talk, can't you? You have a voice, that is quite enough for these songs,' he said as he put the booklet back on the shelf. The next morning, and those following, he still greeted me in a friendly fashion, but we never chatted any more.

I stayed in my room most of the time, reading Russian books and papers. I received no letters from abroad, nor did I write any. The staff in the hotel were quite used to me by now. The girls were friendly and had probably stopped reporting on me. I had stopped going to the Café National, where I had been with Paul Urban, but I sometimes stopped by the hotel to chat with the manager. He too, after all was an old-timer and I would not have been surprised to see a stranger behind the desk when I came in.

I visited Brun only rarely. I still dropped by Felix's, but no longer every evening, as there was no more need to get instructions on how to act and whom to see. I knew all this by now, and there was no one I wanted to see any more. The void that Anna Mikhailovna had talked about was all around me.

The only person I still saw was Fedia. We would talk in my room, as the big cafés were empty and one felt exposed and naked sitting in them. Our conversations could, in any event, have been overheard with impunity, for they were all about the past. 'Fedia,' I would say, 'do you remember Pudra?'— 'Certainly,' he would answer, 'I remember her, and the Baron too, and Larissa. It is good that she died . . . ' Yes, it was good to have died of typhus when not yet thirty. It was a good thing for Stakh Huber-Wrzos to have died in a plane crash. All this was good . . . how good, and how lucky . . .

One day I asked Fedia to accompany me to the warehouse where I had stored a trunk long ago, before going abroad. There was a pressing iron in it which Fedia wanted, and some blankets I wanted to give him. A warehouse employee stood alongside us as we opened the trunk. To my horror the first thing that turned up was a book of Trotsky's. I looked at the man but he paid no attention and I rapidly turned the book face down. I took the blankets and the iron and we left in a hurry. Outside I told Fedia that such books could probably only be found in old trunks in warehouses. 'No,' he said. 'I have them on my shelves, and so does Willy. That way, when they come to arrest you, they can take them along. It does not make the slightest difference.' Abroad we used to hide such books when we had a visitor of whom we were not entirely sure. Here they were left in the open. Terror, evidently, has its own kind of freedom.

One morning George Mueller dropped in to see me. Was it out of kindness or curiosity? I do not know. He claimed he had dropped in just to see how I was, and he asked me whether I could do a French translation for him. He would send a man to bring me to his office to do the job there. I knew that use was made of such pretexts to detain people in Moscow, but I did not really see why they should go to this trouble. There were after all much simpler ways. They could also have asked Ludwik to come and fetch me. He would have come and then we would both have been in their hands. Next morning, however, George called me. There was no need for the translation any more. He would come and see me again soon, however.

The days dragged on, and no one came to see me. Bella never came, nor did anyone send me theatre tickets; everyone had already done his share in entertaining me. One evening I succeeded in getting a ticket for myself. I had seen Bulgakov's play *Dni Turbinikh* (The Days of the Turbins) several times, but it was a good play and as always very well acted. It dealt with a family during the Civil War which could not adjust to the new order. I thought less emphasis was being placed on ridiculing White Army officers and members of the dying upper classes than in earlier performances, but perhaps this was just an impression. It was good to be in a theatre, in any case. The actors, some of whom were 'deserving artists of the Republic', helped one forget reality. They were perhaps the only group relatively untouched by the terror, although many of them were party members. The audience was also somehow reassuring. They were ordinary people I did not know.

Towards the end of February, on a bitterly cold day, I went to Felix's again. There was Max, stretched out on the couch. He was glad to see me but I felt as if I had interrupted a private conversation. I told them I had been to the theatre, we talked of the play and Max reminded me that I had once seen it with him and his wife, Anna. The conversation continued in this fashion, until Max said that he had to leave. At the door he said: 'If I don't see you here again, give my regards to Ludwik. Anyway I will see you both abroad soon.'[1]

Max's farewell reassured me, as I thought Felix might have told him earlier that Ludwik was coming to Moscow. After he had gone, Felix announced that Slutsky was back from abroad, something he had evidently not wanted to tell me in Max's presence.

I knew that with Slutsky's return something was bound to happen. Either he would let me go back, or Ludwik would be recalled, but the long uncertainty was nearing its end. I also hoped to have some news of Ludwik, as I was sure he and Slutsky had seen each other.

A few days later George Mueller called again. He told me that Slutsky sent his regards but was sorry he would be unable to see me; he would certainly see me abroad. This meant that I would soon be going. I did not really believe that Slutsky had wanted to see me or was in fact going to be abroad soon, but I thought I understood that he wanted me out of the country. When George added that he would bring my passport back next day I realized that Slutsky was in a hurry to get rid of me.

[1] Max's phenomenal luck, coupled with the fact that he was never admitted to the party and hence seemed to be apolitical and harmless, led Fedia to say to him at one of our meetings in 1937, 'You will outlive us all, Max. And it is your duty to write down everything you know and what happened to us here.' But Max's luck ran out, after I left Moscow, and he was among the first of the group to be arrested, just as he was on the point of leaving for an assignment in the United States. (Krivitsky gives a somewhat inaccurate account of his arrest in his book, op. cit., p. 270.) The incident only bore out Fedia's sad and cynical dicta: 'No one can predict the future. Anything might happen, including the fact that one might not be arrested.'

Next day Mueller brought my passport and a ticket to the Finnish border. I was to pay my own fare from there, via the northern route through Scandinavia, with some U.S. dollars he gave me. On leaving he told me he would see us in America— thus bringing into the open what I had not realized he knew: that Ludwik was supposed to replace Bazarov in the U.S. Kind and considerate as always, Mueller bade me goodbye and sent his best regards to Ludwik.

I had less than twenty-four hours to say goodbye to our friends. When Fedia rang me that afternoon, I told him to tell Willy of my departure. We all went to Brun's for a farewell dinner. The atmosphere was different; Willy did not slap his thighs with joy and Brun was unlike himself, quiet and not shouting at anybody. I did not ask where Misha was. As I left, Brun looked hard at me and repeated: 'Don't forget what I told you to tell Ludwik.' I promised I wouldn't. Afterwards Fedia asked what it was I had promised not to forget. I told him. 'He is right,' Fedia said. 'Never come back, not under any circumstances. Perhaps one of you will live to tell about us.' He walked with me to the hotel. We kissed and shook hands for the last time.

Next morning Felix rang to say he would take me to the train. This time he was alone. We had only a few moments before the train left. I could see that he was anxious for me to be gone. When we embraced to say goodbye he said: 'Tell Ludwik to come home. The hell with the assignment in America. Let this be your last trip. Come back, all of you.' This time he was quite sincere. He well knew what the consequences would be for him if Ludwik did not come back.

7

The Red Arrow from Moscow to Leningrad is, or was, a very fine train of which all Soviet citizens were proud, although few ever travelled on it; it was mostly used by government officials. Although fairly full the train was far from crowded. Next morning I was in Leningrad. The city was shrouded in a cold fog and the golden spires of the Admiralty and the Cathedral shone faintly in the early morning light. As my case was light—having as usual left all my belongings with my friends—I carried it with me into the street.

I walked down the Avenue of the 25th October, once known as the Nevsky Prospekt, to look up my friend Galina Klinger. I passed by the statue of Tsar Alexander, with Demian Biedny's warning to the monarch '*Sic transit* . . .' and entered what had once been a sumptuous building, now shabby and derelict. It was here that my friend had been living, in a furnished room, when I last heard from her. The doorbell was out of order, but finally a woman answered my repeated knocks. I asked for Galina Germanova. 'Not here,' was the answer.—'Do you know where she is?' brought forth only another 'No'. I took a tram to the Military Medical Academy to look up our friend Doctor K. The story was the same. 'Not here' and 'Don't know' were the only answers to my questions.

These two attempts were enough to discourage me. I reminded myself that Leningrad was a favourite place to arrest those whom it seemed impolitic, for one reason or another, to arrest in Moscow. With this in mind, and aware of the cold outside, I went to a café to wait until it was time to go to the Finland Station.

The train this time was no Red Arrow. It was a local train stopping at every small surburban station, crowded with peasants laden with bundles. As it neared the frontier, however, it began to empty until I thought I must be the only passenger, as I had been in the international train that brought me to Moscow. Then I noticed that there was one other passenger, a young man looking out of the window. My first thought was that he had been sent after me, but then I realized that this was unlikely: it would have been simpler and less conspicuous to arrest me unobtrusively in a Leningrad street. As it turned out, we both crossed the border uneventfully. When my travelling companion handed his papers to the Finnish border official I noticed that he too was travelling on a Czech passport.

I was to see my travelling companion everywhere for the next few days; in the frozen harbour of Helsinki, in railway stations, on the ferry, round the smorgasbord table at the Royal Palace in Stockholm, and in the travel agency where we were both buying tickets to Paris. It was only on the way to Copenhagen that I lost sight of him. I boarded the plane at Abo at six o'clock in the morning and it was still dark when we landed in Copenhagen. There another passenger entered the plane, but I paid no attention. When it became light the stewardess called my attention to Heligoland below. As I turned to look I saw the new passenger. It was Justina, Felix's former wife. She was as surprised as I was. She sat down next to me, pointing to a passenger in front of us. He was my fellow-Czech from the Finnish border, whom she was to meet on the plane.

At Amsterdam, while she waited for another plane, we had a few hours to talk about home, since I was going on by train. I told her Felix had said it was probably imprudent for us to meet, and added: 'But if I were to write that I met you accidentally thousands of feet over Heligoland, no one would believe it anyway.'—'No,' Justina said.

I saw Justina only once more, late in 1938. By then Felix and Milan Gorkić and Ludwik were all dead, but she had remained in the Comintern apparatus. When I passed her in the street in Paris we did not speak, but I thought I saw a sneer on her face—perhaps it was only the horror of seeing her at all that made me think so. According to some reports she went to Mexico with Anna Seghers when the war broke out; she was also reported to have stayed in Paris, and after the war returned to Poland where she now lives.

CHAPTER IX

Paris

I was back in Paris. Spring had come exceptionally early; the warm weather made all the parks and gardens burst out in bloom. Children playing with their boats round the fountains, the exquisite flower markets, young people embracing in the métro and the cafés: everything seemed natural here, life had good things in store for mankind, but I did not feel part of it. I saw a flower girl offer a bunch of violets to a man. He brushed it away and to my surprise said in Russian: 'I am not in the mood for flowers.' I sympathized with him, I felt the same way. In my mind I was still back in Moscow in the atmosphere of the terror.

All those I had left behind somehow blended into one person in my mind; Piatakov, who had been promised he could see his family if he would confess, and when he had done so, been told that the family were no longer in Moscow, saying at his trial: 'Here I stand before you, a man who has lost his family . . . '; Felix Gorski playing with his pistol and saying: 'Don't worry, they'll never take me alive'; Fedia drawing out his meagre savings so his children would have something to eat after his arrest . . . I had become more aware of the terror in Paris than I had been in Moscow, seeing one of our own disappear every day.

I told Ludwik every detail of every conversation and everything I had seen. He sat in silence not interrupting my story once. The episode at Felix's, when he told me of Radek's confession and showed me his pistol, affected me more in Paris than when I actually lived through it in Moscow. I asked Ludwik why he thought Felix had put on this show in front of me. 'Who knows?' he answered. 'Who knows how one would behave in such circumstances? Radek's confession, which Felix helped prepare, may have broken his resistance. I am sure that he will kill himself if he has the time. A gun isn't enough, he needs time too.

'One knows, or at least one thinks one knows, how to cope with an enemy against whom one has fought,' Ludwik went on, as if to himself. 'But how is one supposed to behave when faced with one's own people, for whom one was ready to give up life and freedom? I don't know. I only know one thing, a Soviet prison would be impossible. Would I have the strength to refuse to play their game, would I have more strength than those they put on trial? They were better men than I am, and their services to the revolution were much greater than mine. I might not have had the courage of a Friedmann[1] who refused to play their game.'

A few days after my return, in March, I had rung Krivitsky in The Hague. I knew he would be anxious to hear the latest news. He told me he would be in Paris shortly, and we agreed to meet in a café. He told me he had been summoned back to Moscow for consultations and was extremely nervous. He hardly listened to what I said and asked no questions about our friends. The only thing that seemed to interest him was my flight back. He was going to Moscow by the same route and since he had never been in an airplane before, he asked how it felt. I told him it was quite a pleasant experience.

His lack of interest in what I had to tell was understandable. After all, he would be in Moscow himself in a few days and

[1] We had heard the story of Friedmann, the only one we knew of who had refused to confess, from Slutsky, who had been one of his interrogators at the time of the first trial. Friedmann, a Latvian Communist, flatly refused to sign a confession saying he had been a Trotskyite and had served as a link between Trotsky and members of the Left opposition then being got ready for trial. After two weeks of intensive interrogation under glaring lights without any sleep whatever, he broke down crying: 'Let me sleep, let me sleep, later we will see!' Thinking Friedmann was practically ready to confess, Slutsky gave him a few days' rest. He then talked to him in a friendly fashion, more or less promising him his life if he would confess. But Friedmann again refused. Slutsky, according to his own account, became enraged and shouted at him: 'You promised you would sign, and I ordered a rest for you and now you refuse to sign. Why, you're a whore!' Friedmann shouted back: 'What? Me, a whore? I am not one, you are one and you can go and tell Stalin that he is the biggest whore of them all! What can you do to Friedmann? You can shoot him but you can only shoot him once. Go ahead and do it, I have nothing to say to you!' He was shot in the cellars of the Lubianka shortly afterwards.

would get much more recent and more important news. It was obvious we were both thinking the same thing: would he ever come back to give me news from Moscow? Before he left I asked whether he could take along an overcoat for Fedia's little boy, and when he agreed I brought the coat to his hotel and left it for him.[1]

Krivitsky's visit to Moscow was supposed to last only two weeks and Ludwik decided to put off any move of his own until his return, provided he did return. He and Krivitsky had again discussed the possibility of a break and, although they still could not see how they would go about it, had decided to do it jointly. Ludwik knew any isolated action on his part would not only deprive him of Krivitsky's support abroad but would also gravely endanger Krivitsky in Moscow.

One argument against a break that Krivitsky had advanced in 1936—that one must defend the Spanish revolution—could scarcely be brought forward now. By the time I left for Moscow in December 1936, Ludwik had no illusions left about the Soviet role in Spain. He had hoped, as had Krivitsky, that a truly proletarian rising there might shake the Soviet control over the Comintern, and break Stalin's power at home. Stalin evidently thought the same thing, and made sure no such revolution took place. His approaches, first to the democratic powers in Europe who were interested in stopping Hitler and Mussolini but not enough to commit themselves seriously, and later to the Nazis themselves, through his fellow-Georgian, David Kandelaki, the Soviet trade representative in Germany, were aimed only at making his own position secure.

Nevertheless, Ludwik clung to his job, the only one he considered worth doing, of supplying Republican Spain with weapons. This meant he was away from Paris a great deal. It was impossible to do anything from France, the Popular Front government having declared an embargo on weapons to Spain, so he had to arrange contacts with other governments or private firms outside France. This was dangerous because Nazi agents were watching such efforts closely, and there were cases of Soviet agents being kidnapped by them. But Ludwik not only considered this work worth doing, he knew he was the only one

[1] The coat was later to serve as a means of establishing his *bona fides* with Sedov, Trotsky's son, after Krivitsky had broken with the party.

able to do it. During his years in Europe he had built solid friendships on which he alone could call. One of his closest friends, a Dutchman, had been willing to risk his whole existence when Ludwik asked him to carry out a particularly hazardous operation, securing a contract with a certain government for delivery of weapons to Republican Spain.[1]

But the events of that spring—the cancellation at the last minute of Marshal Tukhachevsky's visit to London to represent the U.S.S.R. at King George VI's coronation (a harbinger of his arrest and execution), the May Days in Barcelona which were to be followed by the assassination of Andreas Nin, the leader of the P.O.U.M.—were making it more and more difficult for Ludwik to continue this work. Furthermore he had just received an official letter from Slutsky which struck an ominous note. Apart from the usual instructions, the letter stated: 'Our whole attention is focussed on Catalonia and on our merciless fight against the Trotskyite bandits, the Fascists and the P.O.U.M.' Slutsky had never used this kind of language with Ludwik before, either in correspondence or in conversation. The letter also said that 'personal consultations' would be needed soon.

Ludwik told me he was going to disobey orders. He would not return to the U.S.S.R. for 'consultation' and he would emphatically not engage in any activities against the Spanish revolutionaries.

Not long after that we heard that Berzin, who had been head of the Fourth Department and was now in Spain directing the war against Franco, had been recalled to the Soviet Union. With him went Arthur Stachevsky, the Soviet commercial representative in Valencia, whose phone call to his wife had caused such consternation at her New Year's Eve party in Moscow. Neither of them could have had any illusions about what was waiting for them. Berzin was a courageous man whose youth in Latvia had been spent in illegality, fighting against the Tsar, and in years of jail and forced labour in Siberia. He had a brilliant record in the Civil War and as head of Soviet military intel-

---

[1] This is the man, still alive after five years in Buchenwald and as close to me as ever, whom Krivitsky refers to in his book as 'a blue blood'. He says of him: 'An exceptional agent was obviously required, but I had the right man.' Actually Krivitsky had nothing to do with that operation; he had heard of it from Ludwik.

ligence had held a post of the highest responsibility. An officer
of the General Staff, he was never in opposition to the régime. He
trained many officers and was very popular with his staff. As
far as I know, he did not even have a family to consider, yet
he went back to be shot. Had he refused to return, he, with his
authority and popularity, would have gathered round him all
those abroad whom he had trained and who had confidence in
him.[1] He could have saved lives abroad, and perhaps could
have stopped the killing in the Soviet Union. But here Stalin
gambled, as he did with the trials in the Soviet Union, and won.
Berzin was in a position to know how Stalin had got 'evidence'
of the treason of Marshal Tukhachevsky, and the other marshals
and generals of the Red Army, once heroes of the Soviet Union
and the revolution. Yet he went back and went meekly down
the steps to a Lubianka cellar to get a bullet in the neck.
Terror—sanctified by a victorious revolution—destroyed reasoning, loyalty, duty, friendship; it made a man like Berzin
obey. I remembered Anna Mikhailovna Messing saying that
Stalin had destroyed socialist ties and solidarity, a destruction
the Tsars had been unable to achieve.

Arthur Stachevsky, once an assistant to Berzin, was another
fierce foe of all oppositions. Earlier in the year when he was in
Moscow, Stalin had complimented him on his work and let him
feel how highly he trusted him. Stachevsky then criticized the
ruthless terror which the N.K.V.D. was displaying in Spain,
under the eyes of the world, and said that this would undermine
the prestige of the Soviet Union. Stachevsky was very happy
when Stalin seemed to agree and promised he would take care
of it. Stalin no doubt decided not to stop the terror but to
liquidate Stachevsky who knew about it.

Stachevsky, when recalled, knew that all his friends, Poles
like himself who served with him or under him, had already

---

[1] The men who worked closely under Berzin in the Fourth were known as the
'Latvian fraction', just as the Poles who had been in the Department earlier under
Bortnovsky, and who followed him to the Comintern, were called the 'Polish fraction'. The term 'fraction' had no political significance; it merely reflected the fact
that Berzin and Bortnovsky preferred to work with people whom they had known a
long time and whom they considered capable. Naturally such people came from
their own parties. When the time came to liquidate the chiefs, their collaborators
were treated as if they had belonged to a real political fraction, and they too were
liquidated.

been liquidated. But his family was safe abroad, or so he thought: his wife was by then in Paris, and he ignored the fact that his daughter Lolotte had been sent to Moscow a few days before his recall on the pretext of getting material for the World's Fair exhibition in Paris—a precautionary measure to make sure he would return.[1]

I rang Madame Stachevsky after we heard of Berzin's and Stachevsky's recall. She said they had passed through Paris, and that she was to wait for Arthur and her daughter to return. Weeks later, when there was still no news of them and she had begun to worry, she tried to telephone her flat in Moscow. On the fourth or fifth try her maid answered; neither Arthur or Lolotte had been there. It was evident that neither of them had reached Moscow. A few days later Madame Stachevsky received a hand-written note from her husband telling her to come back at once. After making frantic preparations she left for the Soviet Union and we never heard of her again.

Theodore Maly was also in Paris during that spring of 1937. He had finished his assignment in London and was waiting to be called back to the U.S.S.R. I spent many hours telling him all that had happened to me in Moscow, and also the Stachevsky incident. He appeared quite unmoved by these stories, and this surprised me as I had always thought of him as a very kind person, someone in whose company I felt safe. Maly and Ludwik were good friends; no doubt he told Ludwik many secrets he would never have told me. And I realized of course that Maly was as lonely as everyone else, and that the reason he seemed unmoved now was that he knew terror even better than we did.

Though he did not know many of our friends Maly knew Stachevsky and Berzin very well. 'Why did they go back?' I asked. 'They knew what was waiting for them in Moscow.'

For the first time that day Teddy looked up at me and said: 'They had to, they had to.'—'And you, Teddy?' I asked. 'Will you go back?'—'Yes, I will,' he answered.—'But why? You know what is in store for you, they will shoot you!'—'Yes, I

[1] This same daughter, as we later learned, had been able to leave the Soviet Union to come to Paris only because Slutsky had deliberately not issued an order to prevent her departure until he knew she had crossed the border.

know,' he answered. 'They will kill me there and they will kill me here. Better to die there.'

I pleaded with him, saying that in order to kill you abroad they first have to find you, and that here there was still a chance of escaping but there was none back there. 'No, no.' he said. 'They will kill here just as easily. They can do it. You may not know this, but I know how powerful they are. There are some White officers here who do the job for them. They know how to do it. They betray their own people and they will enjoy killing a Communist.'

I realized that by saying what I had I might be giving away Ludwik's plans, but at the moment this did not seem to matter. I said that to me it was preferable to be killed abroad, where at least the world would hear about it, than to be shot, unknown to all, in the cellars of the Lubianka.

'No,' Teddy repeated. 'For me it is better that I die there. For someone else it might be different. But for me, let them do it there.' Then he began to explain:

'During the war I was a chaplain. I had just been ordained as a priest. I was taken prisoner in the Carpathians. I saw all the horrors, young men with frozen limbs dying in the trenches. I was moved from one camp to another and starved along with the other prisoners. We were all covered with vermin and many were dying of typhus. I lost my faith in God and when the revolution broke out I joined the Bolsheviks. I broke with my past completely. I was no longer a Hungarian, a priest, a Christian, even anyone's son. I was just a soldier "missing in action". I became a Communist and have always remained one.'

He had joined the Cheka, the organization created to 'protect the revolution' from the Whites, from the enemies of the people, from the clergy, and fought in the Civil War. 'We would pass burning villages which had changed hands several times in a day. Civil war is terrible. Our Red detachments would "clean up" villages exactly the way the Whites did. What was left of the inhabitants, old men, women, children, were machine-gunned for having given assistance to the enemy. I could not stand the wailing of the women. I simply could not. And what did I do?' He had pretended to have diarrhoea and would hide behind a truck, stopping his ears. Soon he did not have to pretend, he really had dysentery. 'Whenever our side cleaned out a village I was seized with violent pains in my belly. I used to hide until it was over. That is how I protected the revolution.'

When the Civil War was over Maly could have left the Cheka, but he thought he ought to stay on, and did. Then came the collectivization years. 'I knew what we were doing to the peasants,' he said, 'how many were deported, how many were shot. And still I stayed on. I still hoped the chance would come for me to atone for what I had done.'

And then the chance came. On his desk was the file of a man who had been sentenced to death for having stolen and hoarded potatoes—the usual penalty during the famine years. The wife of the man begged to see someone. 'I had no authority to do it, but I took a close look at the man's file,' Maly said. 'He had stolen just one small bag of potatoes and that only to feed his kids. I took the file and went to see my chief, an old friend, a Hungarian like myself who had joined the Cheka when I did. I told him I thought that the man had already been punished enough and asked whether I could have permission to see his wife. My chief looked into the case and agreed. He recommended a prison sentence. I let the wife know she could come and when she did I was happy to tell her that her husband would not die. This case had become my atonement.

'I was ready to do anything to save this one life,' he went on. 'Then I had to go away on a two-week assignment. When I got back the first thing I did was to look for "my case". I could not find the file. I ran to my chief. He did not know what had happened and both of us started to hunt for the file. We finally found it. Scribbled across it was one word: "Executed".

'My chief was very upset and immediately started an investigation, but I just went home. This time I did not get a belly ache, but I found a cat that had soiled my bed. I strangled it and threw it out of the window. Next day I went to the foreign division of the N.K.V.D. and asked for an assignment abroad. That was when you and I first met. Yes, I asked for a foreign assignment, having turned down many in the past. I could not bear to live in the Soviet Union any more. I had to run away somewhere and even resurrect my own past. Don't you see that I must go back to be shot? Shall I hide now also?'

Then I remembered a story he had told us earlier. While in London, he had seen an announcement of a concert by a Hungarian pianist named Maly. It was his younger brother. Teddy went to the concert but left before the end. I asked him why he had not talked to his brother. 'You could have talked to him, Teddy, you could have had news of your family!'—'No,' he had answered. 'I should never have gone to the concert in the first place. I had been dead to my past, I should never have come that close to it. Afterwards I felt like fleeing again, hiding again. I wanted to go back to the Soviet Union and I did, but only for a short time, then I came back to Europe. Now I will go back again to the Soviet Union, but not to hide. This time for good.'

So, I said to myself, Teddy will go back to atone, an unknown N.K.V.D. agent. But the others? Why do they accept an order to return to be shot? In the name of what do they obey? In the spring and summer of 1937 Paris was a stopping place on the one-way road to Moscow. People from all parts of the world passed through on their way home. Almost everyone we knew had been recalled, and since all of them, except those in Spain, had been quite isolated in their posts and left without news from home, each was apt to consider his own case as unique. Meeting others in Paris soon taught them otherwise. It is always more reassuring to be in company than to be an isolated case. The recall could mean a general overhaul of services, they thought—all the more because everyone had been advised to take along his staff, no matter how unimportant they were in the organization.

They had also been advised to reach Moscow as soon as possible, and to avoid Paris. This last was for most of them virtually impossible; and in any case, everyone who had been recalled was hoping to find out something on the way back. Moscow was aware that consultations, which could take place only in Paris, might be dangerous and could perhaps lead to refusals to go home. At the end of the twenties, when the Soviet Union had reorganized commercial concerns like the trade mission in Berlin, where police raids and cases of malversation made an overhaul necessary, and ordered the personnel home, quite a few employees, among them some appointed in Moscow and with families there, stayed behind. In those days, no one who refused to return feared for the lives of his relatives. But by 1937 it was a foregone conclusion that if one refused to go home one's relatives—no matter what their age or occupation—would pay with their lives.

The terror had seized everybody, even those who had only a remote idea of what their obligations towards the Soviet Union were. Foreign Communists or sympathizers, who had never been to Moscow and hadn't an inkling of what organization they were working for, but had had the misfortune to lend their services in one capacity or another, paid or—as was the case with occasional couriers or letter-boxes—unpaid, were suddenly confronted with an order to go 'home'. Most of them could have refused and Moscow would not have bothered about them, but they too were terrified and put up no resistance. They went, and those few who might still be useful abroad were allowed to go on leading a miserable existence. The others disappeared in Siberian camps or, if they were Germans, were handed over to the Nazis, after the Soviet-Nazi friendship pact, and perished in concentration camps.

We saw almost everybody who passed through Paris with whom we had been on friendly, if not intimate, terms. In that atmosphere of doom, after the Tukhachevsky trial and executions and the mass arrests, people sought each other's company. But there was no conversation, even among very close friends. We all read the same papers. The Soviet press reported executions, trials, and arrests of prominent party members as enemies of the people, traitors to the Soviet fatherland, persons who until now had been considered above reproach. The foreign press reported other arrests and commented on the terror. When the rumour that Stalin had been arrested[1] appeared, there was no indignation, only disbelief and a vague gleam of hope that it might be true and that perhaps the madness at home had reached a point where it could be called off, and the nightmare end. But no one really believed that it would.

---

[1] I remember Isourin, Maly's brother-in-law, who worked for the N.K.V.D. in Paris, showing me this report. Though he talked about the rumour guardedly, I got the distinct impression he would have cheered such news if it had been confirmed; but as with others in the apparatus, neither of us dared confide in the other.

One of the most disturbing things was the lack of any communication from home. One day I saw Milan Gorkić, who said how glad he was to have run into me. He had been recruiting for Spain, and for the last few weeks had been left without directions from Comintern headquarters. He took the responsibility in many cases, but his was a very difficult assignment, as he had to deal with an international crowd, among whom were some trying to worm their way into the International Brigade. He had just dealt with a man, a Yugoslav who looked every bit like an agent, but who claimed to have been sent from Moscow. He had no credentials, only some vague recommendation from another Yugoslav who lived in Moscow. Gorkić had tried in vain to get information about him from Moscow, and thought we might be able to help.

Ludwik, when I told him, advised me to keep out of it and to tell Gorkić we could not help him. 'Tell Gorkić,' he added, 'that we have no means of getting the information. The man might well be a *provocateur*. Gorkić will find out and I would not be amazed if this man were to meet with an accident.' When I told Gorkić that we could do nothing, he said he did not know what to do with the man and that they were keeping him locked up.

This was the last time I saw Gorkić before he too was recalled and shot. But at the end of 1937 a man was found badly wounded in Paris. It was Gorkić's Yugoslav. Later the man tried to get in touch with Sedov, who showed me a letter from him asking to meet him. When I told Sedov what I knew, he too had his doubts and did not reply.

Weeks had stretched into months and we had heard nothing from Krivitsky. By now Ludwik was certain he would never return. Then one day we learned that he was back in The Hague.

Early next morning I rang him. I asked about our friends. In every case the answer was the same: 'He is very ill, he is in hospital . . . ' It was obvious that all had been arrested. I was perturbed that Krivitsky should have been allowed to leave, while everyone else was being arrested. Ludwik said he thought that Krivitsky had been 'trusted' enough to be sent abroad to avert a panic in the services, on the calculated risk that he too might not return.

Ludwik was glad he had not acted before and decided that now he and Krivitsky together could take the necessary steps. I reminded him that Krivitsky was a person who alternated continually between hope and despair, and that for the last two years he had shied away from a decision. After all, it was he who in 1935, after Ludwik's return from Moscow, had said: 'They don't trust us.' This sentence became a leitmotiv, often repeated: 'They need us, but they can't trust us. We are international Communists, our time is over. They will replace us with Soviet Communists, men like Zarubin to whom the revolutionary movement means nothing.' But when I asked him whether he intended to wait until they disposed of him Krivitsky would always answer: 'No. But the time is not ripe yet.' I was sure he would find some ray of hope, even now, to hang on to. Ludwik answered that he knew Krivitsky's character well enough, but that his main argument, the Spanish revolution, was gone.

Ludwik met Krivitsky a few days later, and they had a long conversation. Krivitsky told Ludwik of an interview he had had with Yezhov, the new head of the N.K.V.D. He was convinced Yezhov was insane. In the middle of an important and confidential telephone call he would suddenly burst out in crazy laughter and tell stories of his own life in the most obscene language. After a few hours spent with Yezhov, Krivitsky said he had begun to doubt his own sanity. This was the man to whom Stalin had given the task of purging the party.

But Krivitsky had things of greater personal import to tell Ludwik. He said he had been asked why he had not reported to the party that Ludwik's brother had been killed serving in the Polish army against the Soviets. Had he not known that Ludwik's brother had been a Polish intelligence agent, and that the reason Ludwik had kept this secret was that he himself was carrying on his brother's work, had in fact been working for the Polish police during all the years he had pretended to be a loyal Communist? Had Krivitsky misled the party deliberately about Ludwik's brother? Krivitsky said he had answered that he knew Ludwik's brother had been killed during the war but he did not know which war—he did know, of course—and that he had always believed it was the First World War. Krivitsky added that his explanation had not been believed.

Ludwik now realized why Krivitsky had been 'trusted' to return. The old and almost forgotten story of his brother was a clear indication: Krivitsky had been sent abroad with the mission of bringing Ludwik back. At the same time, it was obvious that Krivitsky was deliberately sabotaging his own mission by telling Ludwik the story. Had Ludwik still had any intention of returning, this story alone would have kept him from doing so; it was obvious what his fate would be the minute he got there. Moreover, Krivitsky realized very well the consequences of his loyalty to his old friend. If Ludwik did not come back, Krivitsky's failure would not be forgiven.

There was only one thing to be done now. Ludwik told Krivitsky that he had been awaiting his return before announcing his break, and that now was the time for both of them to make it. Krivitsky, however, could not bring himself to that last step, and here his loyalty to an old friend ended. In his book he says: 'I mustered all the familiar arguments and sang the old song that we must not run away from the battle. "The Soviet Union", I insisted, "is still the sole hope of the workers of the world. It is our duty to stick to our post." '[1]

Krivitsky also adds that Ludwik left him 'with the understanding that he would bide his time and watch further developments in Moscow before making his contemplated break with the Soviet Government.' But he knew Ludwik had no intention of biding his time. He had waited long enough and he knew he had to act, even alone.

Soon after this Ludwik went to Amsterdam and telephoned Sneevliet. He knew that in spite of the many years during which they had not seen each other, he could trust him completely. Sneevliet told Ludwik he had expected his call. It was high time, he said. He had been in Barcelona, looking in vain for Andreas Nin. They arranged to meet in a café. 'I will come alone to this appointment,' Sneevliet added, 'and should you ask me to ride in a car with you, I would. I trust you.'

Sneevliet urged Ludwik to make a public break and publish

[1] Krivitsky, *op. cit.*, p. 276.

it in the left-wing press. Ludwik however believed it was his duty to notify the Central Committee of the Soviet Communist Party first. He intended to wait a week to publish his letter, a week being about the time he calculated it would take the letter to reach the Central Committee through Embassy channels. Meanwhile Ludwik urged me to leave Paris immediately; for, as he pointed out, through me he could be easily detected.

In fact I was the only one through whom he could be traced, since he avoided any other contact. He could move from one part of the city to another and make it harder for them to find him, but I had a permanent address known to the N.K.V.D. Although I was terrified at leaving him in Paris without knowing what was happening to him, I had to agree he was right. I therefore wrote to the mayor of a mountain village in Switzerland which we had once passed through and liked, and rented two rooms. Thus I would have an address when I left, and not have to communicate with him by post. He told me he would join us in about a week, after he had attended to his business in Paris. He did not say what he planned to do, and I am not sure he himself knew exactly how he would proceed.

Ludwik saw Krivitsky again in Paris but did not tell him of his meeting with Sneevliet. They agreed to meet again in a few days. I myself saw Krivitsky once more before I left, but this very old friend had only one thing to say: 'I hope you are not encouraging Ludwik not to return to the Soviet Union. I must warn you against that.' We spoke of the numbers of people passing through Paris now on their way back to Moscow, and I said that their returning there now to be shot reminded me of those soldiers in the First World War who were killed an hour before the Armistice bugle sounded. 'Yes,' said Krivitsky, 'that is true. And yet there were some killed in that last hour.' When I asked Krivitsky what he planned to do, he answered: 'I will go back to the Soviet Union.' He must have believed even then that if he went back the N.K.V.D. would let him live. I wondered whether he really would want to live on after all his friends had been liquidated. Did he want to be the only survivor?

On one of the last days before I left Paris I brought Ludwik some post given me by Lydia Grozovsky. There was a letter from Slutsky, urging him to return to Moscow soon, not to delay any more, and adding: 'Your nerves seem to be on edge, come without delay, it is time we talked things over and straightened things out.' Ludwik showed me the letter without comment.

There was also another letter, or rather a confused note, from Gertrude Schildbach in Rome. She had lost contact with us and was anxious to get in touch with Ludwik, for she badly needed his advice.

This note was a piece of luck for the N.K.V.D. Ludwik had almost slipped through their fingers. He had broken off all contacts, and they really did not know through whom to reach him; and then came this windfall. Although the note—which as I know now was intercepted and read before we saw it—was short and contained nothing of an intimate nature, it indicated clearly that Schildbach was dependent on Ludwik's advice as to how to proceed, and from it they deduced that he felt a similar confidence in her.

Ludwik had known Schildbach, as I mentioned earlier, for a very long time. She could be said without exaggeration to have worshipped him, and she attached herself to me and our son. When she lived in Paris she used to wait anxiously for Thursdays, a free day for schoolchildren in France, to take care of the boy, to go with him to see a Laurel and Hardy film or to the circus. It also became a habit for her to go with me and the boy on vacation. She was very often a burden to me and I would complain to Ludwik, but he said it was our duty to put up with her, for she was so lonely and so devoted.

He naturally had no time or patience to listen to all her stories. From time to time this ugly, ageing woman would tell me about a love affair, some man desperately in love with her, but always somehow unable to marry her. She would then go through a crisis and, so she said, twice tried to commit suicide. We were convinced that no such man ever existed and that it was all invention and neurasthenia. Ludwik said she was one of those desperate, loveless women who write love letters to themselves and then anxiously wait for the morning post to read them. On other occasions she would talk about her achievements at university or her extremely important contacts among writers and politicians; another time it would be her very confidential contacts with representåtives of the opposition to the German Communist Party. Some of these claims could have been true, and indeed Ludwik suspected that her connections with oppositionists were not altogether invented.

That alone was enough to make us keep her far away from our friends. Schildbach, who had practically nothing to do in Paris, may well have contacted some of her old acquaintances among the German political refugees there. This was not reassuring because the opposition groups were heavily infiltrated and it would have been quite possible for Moscow to learn, through its agents, that she was connected with an opposition. Ludwik might then have been asked why he made use of such a person and why he had not reported on her. What he feared more was that, if it became known in Moscow that Schildbach had connections with the opposition, she might be asked to keep these up and report on them to Moscow.

Schildbach, who had never been to Moscow, asked Ludwik in the spring of 1936 to arrange a visit for her. He saw nothing against her going, and as usual, paid the fare and arranged a room in a hotel for her. This was taken care of by the office in Moscow, but no one, not even Felix Gorski who generally looked after our friends when they visited Moscow, came to see her. Ludwik expected this, since no one really knew she was close to us. She did not know any of our friends and could not speak Russian. As far as the N.K.V.D. was concerned, she was a handy contact, a woman who rented an apartment which could be used and who had now asked to spend a holiday in the Soviet Union. Moscow seldom refused such requests.

On her own in Moscow, Schildbach immediately contacted the German refugees living in the Hotel Lux. From this group, isolated and already terrorized, she learned about many arrests and executions. When she returned she told Ludwik of the happenings in Moscow on the eve of the Zinoviev trial, and the atmosphere of doom in the Lux among the Comintern people daily awaiting arrest. We could neither reassure her nor tell her what to do. When we saw her again after the first trial in August 1936, during which we were absent from Paris, she was desperate. She wanted to know whether Ludwik still supported the Soviet Union and said that it was their duty to defend those executed and prevent other executions by joining an opposition. Of course he made no reply.

Schildbach undoubtedly took up contacts with some oppositionists in Paris after her return from Moscow. Ludwik could not do as she did; he had to bide his time, but he did nothing to dissuade her. He only asked her to liquidate her apartment, for he would have no further use for it. She evidently had not expected this, and realized it would also involve a break with him, for which she was by no means ready. Besides, it also meant that without her rent being paid, and the small salary she had received, she would, like so many others, be destitute. In the circumstances Ludwik could not offer her financial help, as he had done often in the past. For the first time he asked himself whether she really did not have anybody in the world, as she claimed.

It was not usual in our circle to ask about a person's family; whatever was told one was accepted. When Ludwik first met Schildbach in Germany, towards the end of the First World War, she had said she was all alone, having just lost her mother and sister in the Spanish 'flu epidemic. She told him her father had died when she was still young, and for that reason she could not finish her university studies. (This did not prevent her later on from claiming doctoral degrees.) She introduced herself as an actress, and ever since had referred to her past as theatrical. Actually, as Ludwik later learned, she had tried unsuccessfully to get into a so-called 'field theatre' which gave performances for troops behind the lines in the last days of the war. She was then already approaching her thirties and was particularly unattractive, with a short, squat body, an oversized head, glasses with very thick lenses, and blackened, protruding teeth. She attached herself to Ludwik immediately and he felt respect for her, for she was a Communist, and could introduce him to Communists; later, when he came to work in Germany, she could facilitate his contacts. He, on the other hand, helped her financially, for she never had a job. In later years we used to wonder how she managed when Ludwik did not help her, for instance, during the years when we lived in the Soviet Union and had no contacts abroad. There was certainly no man in her life to take care of her. By 1936 we knew so many of her stories were pure invention that we hoped her claim to be all alone in the world was also untrue, and that she might have somebody who could help her.

By this time Schildbach had become a real problem to us. She was very depressed and we could not say what affected her more: the terror in the Soviet Union or the prospect of being severed from Ludwik. We began to fear she might, as she threatened, commit suicide. Such a threat had to be taken seriously, for the wave of suicides in the Soviet Union had spread abroad. Lisa Zarubin's sister-in-law, Victor Rosenberg's wife, had tried to kill herself recently. In her case there was a husband to take care of her and to prevent the police from interfering. But Schildbach was all alone and had she tried to take her life, as she claimed to have done in the past, she might have been discovered by a concierge, who would report the case to the police. If she recovered she would have to face an investigation.

We both felt sorry for her, but could not see any solution. Then the resident in Rome, who had been for quite a while in Moscow, passed through Paris on his way back and told Ludwik he needed somebody to help him in Rome. Ludwik would not have recommended Schildbach in normal circumstances, but he was very anxious to get her out of Paris. Rome had practically no German political refugees and so there would be little danger of her getting involved in anything which might compromise the apparatus there. The resident, a Russian whom Ludwik knew only slightly, had been for many years in the Middle East; a distinguished scholar and a specialist in Near and Far Eastern languages, he was a reserved man who had had very little contact with Europeans, and was much less politically alert than his colleagues in Europe. That too was reassuring; Schildbach would not have occasion to reveal herself to him.

Ludwik recommended her, but felt he must warn the Rome resident of certain things: that she pretended to be a sinologist, and claimed an academic career which she had not had. He expected that the resident might reject her for this, for even the innocent lie of a Communist, particularly one connected with an illegal apparatus, should be taken seriously. But, he went on to say, Schildbach never did anything and did not know anybody in the apparatus; and she had a legal German passport, could establish herself as a bona fide political refugee and could rent an apartment which could be used. That was all she had done for him, and he would recommend her for that. He was relieved when the resident said that was exactly what he needed, and that it would be quite natural for a German refugee in her fifties, of independent means, to take an apartment and establish herself legally in Rome. We were delighted, and Schildbach gladly accepted the offer, although she was sorry to be separated from us. Ludwik promised to keep in touch with her and advised her to register for some courses at the university in Rome, pointing out that this would not only be good for her but would be important as a cover for her work. He knew that she did not need a cover, but thought the courses would keep her busy and give her a feeling of her own importance, and thus perhaps keep her from indulging in fantasies.

Now, after some months in Rome, Schildbach wrote that she was in difficulties. Ludwik glanced through the note and said: 'Her boss probably has been recalled and has been told to take her along. She would like to know whether I am going back. She would probably go if I told her to. I know how she feels about Moscow, but I cannot write to her now. Later, when things settle down, I will get in touch with her.'

CHAPTER X

Switzerland

I

The mountain village of Finhaut in the Valais, where Ludwik and I spent what were to be our last few weeks together, was a secluded spot, not frequented by tourists. Such places were not so rare in those days; still we had wondered when we passed through it once why this particularly beautiful village, on the railway, had not a single hotel or restaurant. This now seemed an advantage, as it would be easy to spot surveillance. There were only a dozen peasant families, whose houses were strung along a single road; in a couple of days I seemed to know everybody. Sometimes a group of young people passed by on the road to the mountains, or schoolchildren led by a teacher. Otherwise the road was deserted.

The rooms I had rented sight-unseen turned out to be even more primitive than I had expected. There was only a big peasant kitchen and one other room, though we had electricity and running water. There were three cots, rather than beds, quite uncomfortable and with a tendency to cave in when one lay down; Ludwik used to say being in one was like being already in one's grave. But the rooms were on the upper floor of the mayor's house, so we were not isolated. During the day there were people coming and going, and at night the door was locked and it would have been hard to break in, as we feared someone might do.

I found it difficult to get food, for the nearest shop was in the next village, about two kilometres away. Normally that would have meant only a nice walk, with a chance also to get newspapers and perhaps go to the post office, but in our situation it was not easy because we dared not both leave our boy, and he was not to be torn away from his playmates. So I used to go by myself, hurrying back with the food for fear something had happened in my absence.

Neither did we dare leave the child to go for walks in the mountains. But there was a magnificent waterfall from the foot of which we could survey the house, and there, facing the snow-covered mountains, we spent many hours sitting in silence.

I had an anxious ten days in Finhaut before Ludwik came. At last I received a letter telling me the time of his arrival, and I went with my son to the station to meet him. The boy said immediately: 'Oh, Father, your hair is white.' Ludwik had changed in the last few weeks; he had been greying before and now his temples were indeed white. As our house was not far from the station, and he had only one suitcase, we were soon home. Ludwik found the rooms quite nice and was visibly happy to be there with us, though he said little.

Soon after his arrival he talked about his last days in Paris, and told me he had sent a letter to the Central Committee of the Party. He had spent the nights in a hotel writing the letter and making copies by hand, since he had no typewriter. He had also written to Slutsky, informing him of his decision to break, and assuring him that any Soviet 'secrets' he knew were quite safe. When he had finished he handed the letters to Lydia Grozovsky, to be sent through the Embassy post. He immediately moved to another hotel, giving his address to Maly and to Krivitsky. That night his telephone rang several times. Each time he answered the caller hung up without speaking. He understood that this was a warning. 'Perhaps,' he said, 'the letters were opened on the spot. In any case, I decided to leave early in the morning. I checked out of the hotel as soon as it was light, and came here.'

That was all he said. I did not ask any questions, nor did he expect me to. He was used to my silences; sometimes he would call me 'the mute one'. Besides, what could I have asked him?

I think four or five days must have passed before he showed me a copy of the letter printed at the beginning of this book. We had finished our evening meal and the boy had gone down to play. I was busy with the dishes. Ludwik went into the other room and came back to the kitchen. He put the letter on the table and said: 'Read it.' He himself turned to the window. I stood at the table, gripping it, bent over as I read the letter.

Each word—a blow. As I finished reading I glanced towards Ludwik. He seemed lost in contemplation of the sunset over the mountains. I read the letter a second time. Then he turned to me, and his face was grey. From his eyes I saw that mine must have been the same. 'Have you read it?' he asked. I nodded, and he took the letter to put it back into his suitcase. Then we went down to sit by the waterfall. In silence. There was nothing to say. Our world was gone forever; we had no past, we had no future, there was only the present.

When we spoke, it was about the people in the village, our son and his little friends, the weather. In the afternoon I would get, or someone would bring, the newspapers. Then we would speak about the news.

Once we were together, all three of us, in the village shop, and Ludwik bought himself a heavy mountain stick. I asked whether he expected to use it against an aggressor, and he laughed and said: 'No, that would not be any good. But I hope to make a tour in the mountains.' And indeed one morning he did take his stick and say: 'I am going for a little walk. Don't worry, I will be back before noon.' It was a long time to wait. Noon passed and he was still not back. It was close to one o'clock, and I was standing in the middle of the road when I saw him coming. 'Oh, I am sorry,' he said. 'It was so beautiful up in the mountains. There is a farm there and one can get buttermilk'— his favourite drink. Seeing how very much afraid I was, he said: 'Forgive me, I will never do it again.'

Our days passed very quietly, and with each day Ludwik seemed to get over some of his depression. Perhaps also the rest and mountain air had their effect, for he had been physically exhausted when he arrived. But with physical well-being came a kind of unrest. He complained about sleeping badly, and he would always add, 'That bed seems to be a rehearsal for a coffin.' Most of all he deplored the lack of books. There were none to be had in the village, and he suggested we go down to Lake Geneva, where we could find books and perhaps some better things to eat.

We were all glad of the change in our routine, and I took

the opportunity to visit a pension in Territet near Montreux where I had once stayed and knew the landlady. I asked her to keep me a room for the autumn. This solved the problem of where to go when summer was over and we could no longer remain in our village. I assumed Ludwik would go with me from the mountains to Territet. We would spend the month of September there, and thus have a few more weeks in which to decide what to do and where to go for the winter, a problem we had avoided discussing.

Back in our mountain retreat we continued to live as before, never speaking about the past or the future. One night a terrific thunderstorm broke over the Alps. The whole house seemed to be coming down, the thunder rolled in the mountains, and flashes lit up our kitchen like broad daylight. Ludwik came into the kitchen where I slept with the boy and sat down near my cot, saying: 'I know you don't like to be alone in a thunderstorm. Look how mighty and forbidding the mountains are.'— 'No,' I said, 'I don't like to be alone. It is good that you came.'— 'You don't like to be alone at all,' he said, 'and you know that I always came when I could.'

When the storm abated and the boy went back to sleep, Ludwik stayed for a while, and for the first time since his arrival he tried to reassure me. 'Don't worry so much, you will see that things will straighten out.' I felt he himself was not convinced that they would. But from that night on he did sometimes talk about our friends, and once or twice about our prospects. Once he said: 'I don't know what we will do'; and here he betrayed the real insecurity of the professional revolutionary who has spent his entire life in the service of the Soviet Union, living in many countries but never being part of any country, always on the fringes of life only. What indeed was one to do, suddenly separated from the Soviet Union, from the party, from all one's friends?

I tried to tell him I was much more concerned about his safety now than about life in the future. I too was aware how hard it would be to find employment, in that time of world economic crisis. Still, these were problems it seemed to me we could face, once we had some assurance that his life was not in immediate danger. And once, when he spoke again about the difficulties ahead, I said: 'But you seem much more afraid of life than of death.' He did not reply immediately, and then, smiling sadly: 'Why, it is much easier to die than to live.'

In every passer-by Ludwik discovered some feature of a friend who had been executed or had disappeared. 'Look', he would say of some stranger, 'doesn't that man smile like Misha, he is just like him!' I could never find any such resemblance, but I agreed with him. I knew he was only seeing his friend, not the person who passed. Those friends were always with him, he was constantly remembering certain episodes in their lives or their sayings.

We also talked about those who had returned to Moscow after he left Paris. There was no doubt that Maly had gone back, as he said he would, and Ludwik was convinced that Krivitsky too had returned. I had my doubts. I had known Krivitsky too well not to know that he could reverse a decision just as promptly as he had made it. I said Krivitsky might still be around, and might now even be forced to help the N.K.V.D. find him. But Ludwik believed his own break had made it impossible for Krivitsky to put off his departure; in Moscow's eyes he had failed to persuade Ludwik to return, and they would not trust him now with such an assignment. Then, when I still did not agree, he added: 'Well, if he does that, even if forced to, if he joins the hunt for me, then life is not worth living anyway.'

It must have been on one of the walks he now took alone that he made a visit to the post office and communicated with Sneevliet. One day he told me he had made an appointment to meet him in Rheims on 5 September. We had planned to leave the mountains on the 4th. I would go to the pension in Territet, and he would go on to Lausanne whence he would take a night train for Rheims. After his meeting with Sneevliet he would rejoin us on 6 September. Then he said I could go with him as far as Lausanne, for he had also made an appointment to see Schildbach in the few hours he would have in Lausanne before taking the train, and he thought I would also like to see her. I gladly agreed and did not even ask him when he had got in touch with her, for it seemed unimportant. He would certainly not have arranged an appointment with her now, when she could only be a burden to him, had he not had a few hours' time. He simply did not think much about it. He did not look forward to seeing her but knew she must be in a precarious situation and thought, as he always did, that he owed her some support.

I did not think twice about his seeing Schildbach either. All my fears were concentrated on the meeting with Sneevliet. When Ludwik told me about this I tried to persuade him not to go. Sneevliet was bound to have been watched since Ludwik's break. I asked whether it might not have become known that Ludwik had contacted him and whether it would not be logical for the N.K.V.D. to look for him through Sneevliet. 'Naturally,' he said, 'this is conceivable. But do you think I got in touch with Sneevliet only to save my skin? Had I been anxious only for my own safety I could have thought of other ways. Joining Sneevliet means taking the consequences of my break with the Soviet Union, it means joining the struggle against counter-revolution there and against the slaughter of a whole generation of revolutionists.

'Besides,' he went on, 'you don't seem to realize that there is no hiding from the N.K.V.D. if one stays alone. Sneevliet will bring my break to public attention, he will publish my letter to the Central Committee in his press, and you may be sure that the press all over the world will reprint it. So it will come into the open, and only then will Stalin's arm be too short to reach me. If I don't come into the open, sooner or later his N.K.V.D. will get me. And then the press might or might not carry a small item that an unknown man has been found assassinated.'

I understood his reasoning; what I could not understand was why he did not authorize Sneevliet to publish the letter, of which he had sent him a copy, while he himself was in relative safety. Ludwik said he thought that, while the publication announcing his break with the Soviet Union and the reasons for it might paralyze the efforts of the N.K.V.D. to kill him, it would also provoke interest in him, which he wanted to avoid. 'Yes,' he said, 'the publication of the letter will make it much harder for Stalin to kill me. It is easier to find somebody in hiding and kill him than to reach one who has appealed to the world openly. But the publication will also arouse the interest of others in me. Believe me, all the intelligence services of the world will be after me. Until I know how or where I will live the next few months I cannot come out publicly.' That is why Ludwik wanted to talk with Sneevliet, who would have ideas on how to meet the problem. He thought that through his influential socialist friends in Europe and in his own country Sneevliet would be able to arrange a safe place for him to stay while his break with Moscow was being publicized. 'I don't know what his ideas are or what he intends to do,' Ludwik said. 'We agreed he would do nothing till our next meeting. It is time now for us to discuss the problem and to make the decision.'

On one of our last days at Finhaut a group of people passed us on the road. A young woman smiled and waved. It was Renata Steiner, whom I was to recognize later in a photograph shown to me by the Swiss police.

On the morning of 4 September we left the mountains as we had planned. We went to the pension in Territet and had lunch. It was a short trip to Lausanne and as I was to be away for only a couple of hours, I asked the landlady to keep an eye on our boy.

It was a radiant early autumn day as we travelled along the shore of the lake in a little suburban train. I am sure neither of us gave a thought to the meeting with Schildbach, our minds were so much on Sneevliet who would be waiting for Ludwik in Rheims. We did not speak of this, or of anything else, only Ludwik said, glancing at the conductor when he asked for our tickets: 'Doesn't he look like Maximovich?', a Ukrainian friend shot in Kiev. Again I found hardly any resemblance, but I nodded. Ludwik fell asleep for a few minutes and I looked at his face on which only the sun-tan covered the traces of his ordeal. When he opened his eyes suddenly there was a lonely, forlorn look in them; he must have seen, in his short dream, his friends.

We were in Lausanne. Ludwik bought his ticket for Rheims and a ticket for me back to Territet. He had just time to purchase some stamps for our boy, who was a great collector, before we went to meet Schildbach in a big café not far from the station.

She was there already and waved. We shook hands and sat

down. She was deadly pale and seemed extremely nervous, but perhaps we gave the same impression—the circumstances hardly warranted a relaxed get-together. On her lap she had the handbag Ludwik had sent her for her last birthday, which I had chosen. He never forgot to send her something on such occasions. She was very well dressed and I complimented her on that. I sat next to her; Ludwik, facing us, said hardly a word. He kept on looking at her and perhaps wondered at her changed appearance more than I who was talking to her, answering her questions about our boy, asking how long she was going to stay in Switzerland and what her plans were. She said she was returning to Rome to get married, volunteering the information that her fiancé was a rich Italian industrialist. It was not the first time I had heard such tales.

Beside her on the window sill was a pretty candy box, and I touched it, but she tore it roughly from my hands and said: 'It is not for you.' Only later, much later, did I remember that there was a sob in her voice. Her face was turned towards the window, so that Ludwik could not have seen it. Perhaps if he had been next to her as I was he might have noticed her unusual gesture and the sob. I could not even say that he had been following our conversation. He was somehow far away.

Then he said it was time to leave, if I wanted to get my train back. He arranged to meet her for dinner, and we took our leave. Schildbach said that we had hardly had time to talk and suggested she come the next day, Sunday, at nine o'clock in the morning to Vevey, between Lausanne and Montreux, to spend an hour with me before she left again for Lausanne, and thence back to Rome.

Ludwik took me to the station, asking me on the way whether I did not find Schildbach extremely nervous and what I thought about the fiancé. I had not found anything out of the ordinary in her story and reminded him we had heard such things before. I agreed that she seemed very nervous, but that too was hardly surprising in our situation. I may have calmed his apprehensions. At any rate his suspicion, if indeed one had formed in his mind, did not prevent him from keeping his dinner appointment.

At the station, Ludwik said to me: 'Take good care of our boy and don't worry, I will be back on Monday night.' It was some hours before he was to meet Schildbach again, but we both knew our child must not be left alone too long. I had already telephoned twice to our landlady to make sure everything was all right. I had to go back, and we had to take leave of each other.

The train from Lausanne to Territet winds its way across slopes covered with vineyards, with the blue, glistening lake below. In the autumn-coloured hills, among scattered houses, were cemeteries deep in verdure and flowers; I envied those who would find their peace there. I was not alone on that train. Renata Steiner was on it too. But I did not notice her, my thoughts racing between the pension where my son was and the old French city of Rheims and the appointment there that was never to take place.

My son was disappointed that his father, whom he cherished, had not come back with me, but I promised him Ludwik would be back on Monday. It was Saturday afternoon, so he would not have long to wait. He had his stamps, and I took him for a walk to the Château de Chillon. We were back by nightfall.

From our attic room with its sloping roof one could see the magnificent sunset. Long after the boy went to sleep I was still sitting at the window in the darkness, watching the lights on the other shore of the lake, in France, where all my thoughts were turned. I could not sleep that night, or concentrate on a travel book about Africa that I had picked up; my thoughts were with Ludwik.

On Sunday, I took the train to Vevey to meet Schildbach as I had promised. She was not on the 9.00 train. I let a couple of others pass, pacing the Sunday-morning empty station, and then I hurried back to my son. It was noon already and we would not have much longer to wait.

The next morning, Monday, 6 September 1937, I picked up the first edition of a Lausanne paper. An item in small print told me that on Saturday, 4 September, late at night a man known as Hans Eberhard had been found murdered on the Chamblandes road, near Lausanne. Again I left my son with the landlady and took a train to Lausanne, to go to the police.

The police had already found the bloodstained car at the Cornavin station in Geneva. They had already arrested Renata

Steiner and knew the identities of the killers. They had seized the luggage and the box of strychnine-stuffed candy in the Lausanne hotel room occupied by Schildbach and her companion Rossi. It remained to identify the dead man.

The name Eberhard was not unknown to the Swiss police. Like the French police (as I learned later), they had received an anonymous letter denouncing one Hans Eberhard as an international adventurer and weapons smuggler. The N.K.V.D., the only ones who knew this name, had done this to lead the police on a false trail after the murder, and keep suspicion from the Soviet Union. But I was alive, Schildbach had not fulfilled her mission; instead of giving me the poisoned candy she took the box back to the hotel and abandoned it. Renata Steiner could reveal who were the killers, those who carried out the orders, but I was there to tell the police and the world the identity of those who gave the orders, to accuse the Soviet government of the murder of a Communist who had dared to denounce counter-revolution in the U.S.S.R.

2

Ludwik's murderers must have been in the café at which we met Schildbach; they would have been watching to make sure she did not break down. Now, and many times when I live through that last scene again, I am sure she was on the verge of breaking. She could have cried out up to the very last minute; even that night at dinner, she could have warned Ludwik and prevented his death. But the terror kept her in its grip—and perhaps also a promise of marriage Rossi had made her.

Ludwik and Schildbach had dinner in a restaurant on the outskirts of town. It was already dark when they started back and they were followed by a car. Ludwik must have realized too late that she had led him into a trap. He fought: for in his clenched hands there were strands of her grey hair. The killers had to travel a few miles along the road to find a deserted spot to get rid of the bullet-ridden body. What must Schildbach have felt, riding beside the slumped corpse of the only human being who had shown her consideration? Unlike Renata Steiner, who may not have realized that her role in the affair would lead to murder, Schildbach had known Ludwik would be killed, and that she had delivered, not a traitor to justice, but a Communist to be killed by a gang of Whites and counter-revolutionaries hired by the Soviet Union. And if it was love and the promise of marriage that made her do it, she would have had no tenderness from Rossi from the moment the murder was done: he and the others showed only the brutality of killers, who had now to hand her and themselves over to the N.K.V.D. to receive their reward.

From the Swiss police I learned that Rossi had made love to young Renata Steiner as well as to poor lonely old Gertrude Schildbach. This was the role for which he was paid before the murder. And Renata Steiner, who also was paid for the role she played, was in many respects not unlike Gertrude Schildbach.

The Swiss police were satisfied with Steiner's depositions, and I too am convinced that she was telling the truth when she said that she did not know for whom she was acting, unless it was for the good of the Soviet Union. She may only vaguely have heard of the N.K.V.D. as an organization; the Soviet Union was a place she had visited once as a tourist, and had a good time; and to which she wanted to return.

Steiner told the Swiss police about her childhood but omitted to say that her parents had had her committed to a mental institution in Meilen near Zurich. Asked by the police why they had done so, she said it was because of a love affair of which they disapproved. After her release from hospital she came to know some Communists, who told her about the Soviet Union, and since her mother had died meanwhile and left her some money, she went as a tourist. There she had several love affairs and promises of marriage, though the suitors always disappeared, but she could not get a permit to stay or to work. She promised herself she would go back. When she went to the Soviet Embassy in Paris to ask for a visa she was directed to apply at the Union for Repatriation of Russians Abroad.

The White Russian emigration consisted of several groups, and though they had a common goal—to fight communism in Russia—they were always quarrelling among themselves, intriguing and denouncing one another to the French police. It was easy to recruit among them, for they were poor, uprooted, demoralized, and divided even over their evaluation of what was going on in the Soviet Union. All of them approved of

Stalin's liquidation of the revolution, but each group had its reservations about the future: the monarchists had no illusions that Stalin would restore a Romanov to the throne; nor could the Tsarist officers see themselves restored to their former status. The Soviets had agents of long standing in both these groups, but their main effort was concentrated on the constitutional democratic group, the so-called Gutchkov Circle. Founded by Alexander Gutchkov, a former member of the Duma and War Minister after the abdication of the Tsar, it was the most active and consequently the most heavily infiltrated of the White groups, and from its very beginning the object of Soviet attention.

All these groups converged in the Union for Repatriation of Russians Abroad, at 12, rue de Buci. This organization prospered mysteriously, and some of its members, among them venerable bearded Orthodox priests with heavy crosses on their breasts, must have wondered where the money was coming from, since so few Russians were, or wanted to be, repatriated. The Soviets needed notable émigrés such as Orthodox priests to give the organization a semblance of respectability. A few knew whom they were serving and what was expected of them. The others did not manifest too much curiosity, especially as they were not asked to render active service; it was the younger set the Soviets needed, men who could use women to get into French circles, who would trace Communists suspected of turning against the Soviets, break into apartments where the Soviets suspected there was evidence that might incriminate them, who would kill.

In the rue de Buci Renata Steiner met Serge Efron, who introduced her to Marcel Rollin, alias Dimitry Smirensky, who was a next-door neighbour in Paris of Leon Sedov, Trotsky's son. Efron and Smirensky promised Steiner a repatriation visa, though she was not Russian but a Swiss citizen, if she would render a service to the Soviet Union. She was to get acquainted with the Sedovs, who were on holiday in Antibes in Southern France. She accepted. It was not much to do in exchange for a visa, and it was not unpleasant. She took a room next to the Sedovs. She was given money and clothes, and all she had to do was to report to Efron and Smirensky on Sedov's movements.

She evidently acquitted herself to their satisfaction, and both men began to see a lot of her in Paris. She was in no hurry for the visa now; there were men around and they all seemed unattached. Besides Efron and Smirensky, she also met Kondratiev, a White Russian journalist and member of the Union for Repatriation.

The Swiss police learned from Renata Steiner everything they needed to pursue their investigation of Ludwik's death. She gave the name of the hotel in Lausanne and the names of the two occupants: François Rossi, alias Abiate, supposedly a French citizen but as they found out a subject of Monaco, and Gertrude Schildbach. In adjoining rooms in the hotel the police found their luggage, and in Rossi's suitcase a detailed plan of the house where Leon Trotsky lived in Mexico. Rossi-Abiate, they learned, was not unknown to the international police, and had once been arrested in the United States. The fact that the luggage and the box of strychnine-filled candy that had been intended for me and the child had been left behind, suggested that the killers had not returned to the hotel after the murder. They left without paying their bill.

Steiner told the police she had brought the box of candy from Paris, where it was given to her on 25 August by a certain 'Leo', whom she knew through Pierre Louis Ducomet, and another Frenchman, Etienne Charles Martignat. 'Leo' had enquired whether she could drive a car and, when she told him she had a Swiss licence, gave her the candy and a letter for Rossi, who was to meet her in Berne. When they met, Rossi sent her to the Cassino garage to rent a car, which he then drove off in. This was on 2 September. When he fetched her again Kondratiev, Smirensky, Efron, and Schildbach, whom she now saw for the first time, were in the car.

She and Kondratiev were taken along as far as Martigny, whence she was told to go to Finhaut, our mountain village. She told the police how when she saw Ludwik in the village she smiled and waved. She then went, with Kondratiev, to a hotel in Martigny.[1] On 4 September she followed me from Lausanne

---

[1] On 3 September in Lausanne, the Swiss police—checking papers because Marshal Pétain was coming as an observer at Swiss Army manoeuvres—apprehended Kondratiev. But his passport was in order, and they let him go.

to Territet and phoned to the Hotel de la Paix that 'the Uncle' had left. She was told by Schildbach to go immediately to Berne, where she was to meet Rossi next day. Kondratiev, in Martigny, received on 4 September a telegram to go 'home'; he understood and went to Paris. His task, and Renata Steiner's, was done.

In Berne Steiner waited in vain for Rossi and tried to telephone him in Lausanne and in Paris, but got no answer. She was left on her own. During the time in which she was attempting to reach her friends she read in the papers about a crime near Lausanne, but did not suspect that it had anything to do with her. She became uneasy at being left alone and went to the Cassino garage to inquire about the car. The police meanwhile had traced the bloodstained car found in Geneva to the garage in Berne. They arrested Renata Steiner there.

The killers' panic undid the otherwise well-organized crime, for they left behind a witness who could identify them all and reveal the well-guarded secret that White organizations were used in the services of the Soviet Union. The killers themselves got away. The French police interrogated the Russians, Efron and Smirensky, and released them; according to the French, they went to Spain. Ducomet was in Paris, but the French authorities refused to extradite him, on the grounds that he was a French citizen. Higher political considerations, the Soviet-French mutual friendship pact signed by Stalin and Laval, prevented the French police from co-operating with their Swiss colleagues, and Kondratiev was permitted to get away, thus making possible another crime three weeks later. But the kidnapping of General Miller, in which he figured, was committed in Paris, on French soil, and so the French could not ignore it as they did the murder of Ludwik.[1]

[1] Kondratiev was first assistant to General Skobline, a Soviet agent of long standing, who played Schildbach's role in luring General Eugene Miller, head of the Federation of Tsarist Army Veterans, to an appointment from which he failed to return. Miller left a note implicating Skobline in the kidnapping, but Skobline had time to escape, leaving his wife, a singer, Nadine Plevitskaia, to be tried by the French authorities. Her trial revealed that Skobline and Kondratiev were members of the Gutchkov Circle, which had connections with the German General Staff; it also made clear why Miller had been kidnapped, for he knew that the 'evidence' of the treason of Tukhachevsky and the other Red Army generals had been supplied by the Nazis, acting through Skobline.

As for Rossi and Schildbach, the N.K.V.D. would have prepared their departure in advance, had passports ready and a safe place in which they could wait until they saw how the investigation was going. But after such a botched job they probably had to use the utmost speed to get them out of Europe. The killers could have been taken to Spain and put on a Soviet boat, or put on one in a French or Belgian port, and brought to collect their reward from the N.K.V.D. in Moscow. But Moscow could make no more use of the skills of Rossi-Abiate: the police of the whole world were after him, his identity and photograph had been published. And Schildbach? What could she expect? She had helped to murder a revolutionary, the only friend she ever had, a man whom she worshipped and respected and obeyed—and she had left me alive. She had bungled her orders, and spoilt the whole scheme. Did the N.K.V.D. send her far away to the Arctic regions, as they usually did with compromised persons, so that no European eye should ever see them? Did they do away with her on the spot? Or did they give her an opportunity to kill herself?

By the time Sneevliet, to whom I had sent a telegram, arrived in Lausanne, the Swiss police had all the information they needed and could proceed with the identification of the body and release it for burial. The police looked after my son, so as to enable me and the Sneevliets to attend the cremation. In the vast Columbarium of the cemetery in Lausanne there were the three of us: Sneevliet, his wife, and myself, and at the door, discreetly, two plainclothes Swiss policemen.

Sneevliet and I told the police that 'Hans Eberhard' was an assumed name and gave the dead man a name on which we had agreed, 'Reiss'. Ludwik had once told me that this name was in a remote way a family name, but what made us decide on it was that I was sure the name was unknown in Moscow. Sneevliet thought this might increase my own and my son's security. And so, Ignace S. Poretsky became 'Ignace Reiss', and by that name is now known. We declared to the Swiss police that the dead man was a Soviet Communist, in opposition to the present regime in the Soviet Union. We did not disclose any other information about him, nor did we say to what Soviet organization he had belonged. We were both reluctant to bring everything into the open, so long as Ludwik's letter had not been widely published and his case was in the hands of the police only. We felt that we were acting in accordance with his wishes. He wanted to make his break with the Soviet Union public and bring it to the attention of the world and, as he hoped, of Communists abroad. He did not go to the police for protection and I went to them only to identify the body. It was the N.K.V.D. who had brought the police into the case before anybody but themselves had knowledge of it.

The Swiss police gave me back Ludwik's wallet. It contained French and Swiss bills and a railway ticket to Rheims with a bullet hole through it.

CHAPTER XI

Aftermath: Amsterdam and Paris

I

When the cremation was over, I accepted the Sneevliets' invitation to stay with them in Amsterdam. I was relieved that at least the immediate future was taken care of, as I had no plans and no place to go. I informed the Swiss police of this decision, but agreed to remain a few days longer in Lausanne to help with the investigation; after that we were free to leave. Before we left the Swiss police informed their French colleagues of our passage through France on our way to Amsterdam.

Sneevliet told me he had some business to attend to in Paris and that we would remain there a few days. I did not care, I was in no hurry to get anywhere, and quite indifferent to what was going on. The only thing I wanted was not to meet anyone. I knew the Sneevliets would be very busy in Paris and that, although we had adjoining rooms in a hotel, we would not see much of each other. I had no desire to leave my room; I stayed there with my child and had all our meals sent upstairs.

One day the French police came to see me. It was then that they showed me an anonymous letter, written many months before, denouncing Ludwik as an agent of the Gestapo about to break with the Nazis. The letter must have been written by one of Ludwik's colleagues in the legal services of the Embassy, as they were the only ones who were in contact with him and knew his address. I believe it had a double purpose: first, by putting the French police on the wrong track, to prepare an alibi for the Soviets if Ludwik had eventually to be liquidated; and second, to prompt an immediate surveillance by the French authorities which, it was hoped, would force Ludwik to change his identity and residence and return to Moscow. But the N.K.V.D. did not realize how slowly the French police worked: they were suspicious of denunciations, especially anonymous ones, at a time when refugee groups of all kinds were busily denouncing one another, and had paid no attention whatever to the letter until after Ludwik's murder. By then it was quite clear who the murderers and the informers were, and the myth that Ludwik had been assassinated by the Gestapo was never believed by anyone.

The visit from the police was not unexpected, but when Sneevliet came in to tell me I had a visitor I was taken aback. I said I would much rather not see anyone, but he insisted, saying he fully understood my reluctance, but the interview he was about to inflict on me was by no means unnecessary. He added that I would certainly be glad to see this visitor: Victor Serge.

Before I had time to tell him Serge was the last person in the world I wanted to see, there was a knock on the door and Serge came in. To our dismay he was not alone. With him was a young man I had never seen before and whom, I am certain, Sneevliet did not know either. Sneevliet took Serge outside, and I heard him storm at him for having been indiscreet enough to bring along another person. Meanwhile, the young man introduced himself as Friedman, a friend of Serge and of Sedov, Trotsky's son. This man, whose real name was Marc Zborovsky, was known among the Trotskyites as Etienne. He was then acting as Sedov's secretary.

When Sneevliet and Serge re-entered the room Serge was visibly embarrassed, and Sneevliet looked white and shaken. Serge shook hands with me and said something to me in Russian about my broken life, but was interrupted by Sneevliet who told him not to speak a language that he, Sneevliet, could not understand.

When the visitors had gone, Sneevliet did not try to hide his fury at Serge for having brought Etienne along. But he attempted to reassure me, pointing out that Etienne was after all Sedov's trusted aide. When I asked why Sedov had not come himself Sneevliet answered: 'I understand he is ill.' Sneevliet did not know Serge very well, but he considered him a personal friend and trusted him. Serge had gone to Rheims with him to meet Ludwik. The fact that he had passed on to Etienne the highly confidential word that I was in Paris, and worse, had brought Etienne with him to the hotel, gave Sneevliet a shock that never wore off. After this incident he understood why I had said Serge was the last person I wanted to see.

I did not know Serge well either, but I knew enough about him to be cautious. Serge's natural curiosity had made him keep seeing all kinds of people, party members, ex-party members, former anarchists, every kind of oppositionist, until the very day he was arrested, in Leningrad in 1933. Some considered this showed courage, others irresponsibility. It was probably a bit of both, but carrying on as he did exposed others as well as himself to danger.

More baffling still was the fact that Serge had managed to come out of the Soviet Union in 1936. We knew the press abroad had been agitating for his release, but such campaigns—when they were not instigated by the Soviets themselves[1]—usually came to nothing, and the notion that Serge was released as a result of public pressure and the personal intervention of Gorky did not seem very convincing to us. Ludwik, Krivitsky, and I were sitting in the Café des Deux Magots when we read, to our surprise, that Serge had arrived in Belgium with his family. I remember being excited, thinking it might mean a turn for the better in the Soviet Union. Neither of the men shared my optimism. 'But why should they let him go?' I asked.—'Why?' said Krivitsky. 'Just remember, no one leaves the Soviet Union unless the N.K.V.D. can use him.' Ludwik agreed that Serge's contacts with opposition groups and his entrée to political circles would be invaluable to Moscow.

On his release Serge began to write articles for the mass-circulation French press, accusing the Soviet regime of crimes and appealing to the public and especially to left-wing writers not to accept everything the Soviet Union did. Normally anyone allowed to leave the U.S.S.R. was warned not to publish anything detrimental to it. I asked Ludwik what he thought the articles meant. Less prone to jump to conclusions than

[1] We had heard stories from Louis Fischer of how from his hotel room in the Lutetia André Simon (who, as Otto Katz, was later hanged with Slansky) practically dictated articles on events in Moscow to a French woman journalist jokingly referred to as 'Stalin's inkwell'.

Krivitsky, he said that, while the articles were extremely courageous, they did not prove anything either way. Possibly, in-
tending to use him, the Soviets had not asked him for a pledge,
reasoning that any attacks on them he might publish would
gain him the confidence of opposition groups. We continued to
have doubts about him.

Serge published an account of his meeting with me in the
hotel in Paris quite different from the one I have given. But
Serge was not a professional conspirator, he was essentially a
writer. 'Poets and novelists are not political beings,' he himself
wrote, 'because they are not essentially rational. . . . The
artist . . . is always delving for his raw material in the sub-
conscious. . . . If the novelist's characters are truly alive, . . .
they eventually take their author by surprise.'[1] This insight no
doubt accounts for his version of events.

After our short stay in Paris, I went with the Sneevliets to
Amsterdam. The meeting with Serge and Etienne, to which I
had objected so strenuously, produced a strain between
Sneevliet and myself which he was obviously not ready to discuss. Only in Paris had I become aware how far apart Sneevliet
and Trotsky were. We had known of course that there were
disagreements among the various opposition groups, but we
had believed they were all part of the Fourth International
whose leader Trotsky was. When Ludwik first approached
Sneevliet he took him to be the head of the Dutch section of that
body; now I learned that Sneevliet's group did not even belong
to the International—though I might add that this would not
have made any difference to Ludwik if he had known. Sneevliet
never consulted Trotsky, and though he had informed Sedov of
Ludwik's break and arranged the meeting at Rheims, he did
so with misgivings—partly political, but partly because he was
on general principles suspicious of Sedov's entourage. Unfortunately he felt no need for caution where Serge was concerned.

While the immediate cause of Ludwik's death was his desire
to help Schildbach, there is no doubt that he was surrounded
and could not have escaped. This did not prevent a bitter disagreement between Trotsky and Sneevliet in which Trotsky

[1] *Memoirs of a Revolutionary* (London 1963), p. 265.

accused Sneevliet of handling the matter irresponsibly and not enlisting Sedov's support. It was extremely painful for me to have to be the centre of attention in this kind of dispute and to see Ludwik's corpse become an object **of** contention between two rival factions. As soon as I was physically able to do so I wrote to Trotsky, setting out the facts, but the dispute continued and made life at the Sneevliets' difficult. Sneevliet, who could not read Russian, was irritated by the correspondence between Trotsky, Sedov, and myself; though I offered to translate the letters, he was not satisfied, and the atmosphere remained tense.

Sneevliet had suffered some bad times since we had seen him last. After his wife Sima left him he had remarried, and his new wife, a hard-working, compassionate woman, was devoted to him and her family. But in 1935 his twin sons by his first wife had both died; one had committed suicide and the other was found drowned on a beach. Although a police investigation of the second case found no evidence of foul play, Sneevliet and his friends suspected that the Dutch pro-Nazi party led by Mussert was responsible for the son's death.

Despite our disagreements, Sneevliet and his wife did their best to make me comfortable. Mrs. Sneevliet was especially kind and understanding; she became attached to my son and would play with him, as did, to the boy's delight, their dog. Living with them was Mrs. Sneevliet's daughter by her first marriage, a very nice young girl who was engaged to a member of Sneevliet's group, a strapping young man called Sal Santen.[1] But the household was by no means a restful place. There was a steady stream of visitors, members of Sneevliet's party and his trade union, people from abroad and journalists asking for interviews, and the telephone rang constantly. Most were business calls, but there was at least one call a day from someone in the Mussert Nazi group.

Although we had a room of our own, there was little privacy in the house. I used to take my son for walks in parks that I

[1] Miraculously, Sal survived the Nazi concentration camps and returned to marry his Bep. Mrs. Sneevliet was sent to Ravensbrück after Sneevliet and six of his comrades were executed by the Nazis in 1942; she too survived, and died in Amsterdam in 1965.

knew well from the time we had lived in Holland. One day, pointing to a stationery shop where Ludwik had used to buy stamps for him, I asked my son whether he remembered the shop and his father. 'Mother,' he answered, 'there were other shops too where I bought things with my father. I will never forget him, but please, let's not talk about it any more.' I respected his wish.

Once out of the house, turbulent and noisy though it was, I felt exposed and threatened, not so much by the N.K.V.D., though that danger was real enough, as by the possibility of meeting some of our former friends who might offer me lame and shameful sympathy. None of them had attempted to get in touch with me, though they knew where I was staying. I was sure they did not approve of what had happened, but they were terrorized, and terror killed friendship, solidarity, and compassion. I could never persuade Sneevliet that these people were not Stalinists just because they did not openly condemn this Stalinist crime. They were people who had acted out of personal friendship for Ludwik, who had believed the Soviet cause to be just if Ludwik stood for it. But Sneevliet was all for attacking them in his papers, and even telephoned them at their homes. I found it unbearable to listen to these calls.

The post brought quite a few letters. Some, very few, were abusive. Most of them came from people quite unknown to me, offering help and sympathy. Some of these were no doubt genuine, but a few at least were intended to lure me to some appointment. We never answered these letters and, after an attempt was made to break into the house, Sneevliet turned the correspondence over to the Dutch police. The police were convinced that the several daring efforts to break in were aimed not at getting hold of some papers Ludwik had left with me—in fact they were notes for a book—but at myself and my boy. This greatly shook Sneevliet's faith in the security his home and the several tough dock workers, members of his party, who stood guard, could offer.

One day a letter came from Gerda Frankfurter, who wrote of her grief and offered me financial assistance if I should need it. She also asked my advice: should she give in to the pressure and threats that had started immediately after Ludwik's murder, and go to Moscow? She said she was very tired, but if

I advised her, as Ludwik had done, not to go she would find the strength to go on refusing. I knew the N.K.V.D. did not want anyone even remotely connected with Ludwik to remain free abroad, but I wrote Gerda that she was under no obligation to go to Moscow, and that if she went she would never see Europe again. I do not know whether she got my letter, but much later someone told me she was living in South America. I never heard from her again.

One day, late in October, a letter came for me signed 'Krusia'. Now that Ludwik was gone, I knew there were only two people left in the world to whom that name meant anything: myself and Krivitsky. The letter was short; it said, to the best of my memory, 'I have broken with my employers. It is imperative that we see each other as soon as possible. Tell Sneevliet to be very careful. There is great danger for you and the child. If you receive this letter answer it by inserting an advertisement in *L'Oeuvre* under the "Employment Sought" column and sign as I do. KRUSIA.'

Sneevliet always opened the letters addressed to me, and had read this one before handing it to me. He was watching me as I read it. 'It is signed with a woman's name, but I am sure it is a man—a man who knows who I am. Who is it?'

I did not answer. So he did stay behind after all, I was thinking as I stared at the letter signed with the name of a dead woman. But it was not only Krusia who was dead; so was everything else. Ludwik's blood was between me and Krivitsky now. He was in danger, was asking my help, but I did not want to see him again. We had nothing to say to each other.

'Who is this man?' Sneevliet insisted. 'He is someone important and it is your duty to save him, not just because he is in danger but because he can tell us things Ludwik cannot.'

I finally told him it was Krivitsky, and he immediately placed the advertisement in *L'Oeuvre*. Then he said we must go to Paris. His wife wanted to accompany him, but he asked her to remain behind to keep an eye on my son; he arranged to have two trusted men stay in the house, and two other men were to go with us to Paris as a precaution. I tried hard to convince Sneevliet that he did not need me, but he insisted, saying: 'The man cannot trust us. You must be there to introduce us.'

We arrived in Paris early in the afternoon and went straight to the home of my lawyer, Gérard Rosenthal, with whom I was to stay. I had not met Rosenthal before, and I was immediately impressed by him. He did his best to make me comfortable in the large apartment he shared with his father, a prominent physician, and a brother who was also a lawyer. The household was womanless, but he had installed a bed for me in his office, and brought supper for both of us on a tray.

Tactfully skirting subjects that might be painful for me, Rosenthal told me of a visit he had made to Moscow in 1927, with Pierre Naville, when they had met Trotsky, and we also talked about Sedov, whom I had not yet met. We discussed matters that as my lawyer he needed to know about, such as where I was going to live. I had already made up my mind I did not want to stay on in Holland, and Rosenthal urged me to come to Paris, which he thought would be better for my son's schooling and where I would have friends I could rely on. But I did not want to be there either. I told him perhaps the best place would be somewhere Ludwik and I had never been, but I could not at the moment think where to go.

Rosenthal had told me that, if I did not mind, I would have two visits next morning. At nine o'clock Alfred and Marguerite Rosmer came, an elderly couple whom I was glad to meet. Rosmer, an old labour leader and one of the founders of the French Communist Party, was not a Trotskyite, but a close personal friend of Trotsky's. Later, when I was living in Paris and had got to know them very well, Rosmer showed me a letter Trotsky had written him from Mexico that ended: 'Whatever disagreements we might have, let us conserve our precious friendship.' For the sake of this friendship, the Rosmers helped Trotsky's son and his family, and Trotskyites could always stay at their house, hold confidential meetings and store papers there. They immediately offered to have me stay with them, and it was their kindness that eventually led me to return to Paris.

My next visitor was Sedov—a compensation, as Rosenthal said later, for what was to follow with Krivitsky. This very first meeting established a friendship I had learned not to believe in any more. When Sedov came in we embraced, as is the custom with Russian Communists, and Rosenthal then left us alone so we could speak Russian. To me Sedov was a Russian Communist, just like the ones we had left behind in Moscow. His gestures, his speech, even his very Russian aspect, made me feel immediately at ease with him. So did his compassion, his solicitude, his interest in my child. Naturally we spoke of Ludwik and his death. I learned how little Sedov had known about the arrangements for the meeting at Rheims. I asked him why he had not come with Serge to the meeting at the hotel, and had sent his secretary instead; had he in fact been ill? To my surprise he said he had not known I was in Paris, and had learned it only afterwards from Etienne. I was about to ask more when Rosenthal came in with lunch, and Sedov left saying he would return later that afternoon for the meeting with Krivitsky.

Rosenthal told me of the preparations for the meeting, at which, besides the two of us and Krivitsky, only three others would be present: Sedov, Sneevliet, and Pierre Naville. As they had not yet met Krivitsky, they had taken every possible precaution.[1] Naville was to fetch Krivitsky from an apartment where he had found shelter, and he would not know where he was being taken. Further, the French police had been notified of the time and place of the meeting. I did not fear any treachery from Krivitsky; if he was being hunted by the N.K.V.D. the meeting was far more dangerous for him than for me.

At about three o'clock Rosenthal took me into his office; on that rainy November day it was almost dark already. Krivitsky sat on the far side of the desk facing Sedov and Sneevliet; Rosenthal pointed me to a chair some distance away, beside Naville, and himself sat alongside Krivitsky. Though he did not look up when I came in, I had a clear sight of him: it was Krivitsky all right, but only a shadow of the man I had known. He had always been slight, but now he looked shrunken. His face was ashen and under the bushy brows his eyes were hollow.

Krivitsky was speaking Russian to Sedov, who translated into French for the others. This was natural enough, as Krivitsky's

---

[1] The Trotskyites had asked me for a way of positively identifying Krivitsky, and I had told them to ask him what he had taken along on his trip to Moscow in April and for whom it was intended. Krivitsky remembered the coat I had sent with him for Fedia's boy, and so established his *bona fides*.

French was poor, but I could see Sneevliet's face tighten. It was evident, too, that Krivitsky was addressing himself mainly to Sedov: like me, he saw in Sedov a young Russian Communist like so many he had known, and felt he could speak freely to him.

Sedov explained the precautions that had been taken, and apologized for his comrades' having searched Krivitsky before they let him enter the room. Krivitsky replied that he had not been surprised at this, and said: 'How can you trust me?' Sedov pointed to me.—'We trust her,' he said, 'and she vouches for you.'

Only then did Krivitsky look at me, as he said: 'I came to you. I came to warn you that you and your child are in grave danger. I came in the hope that I could be of some help.'

'Your warning comes too late,' I said in Russian. 'Had you done this in time Ludwik would be alive now, here with us.'

'What could I have done?' answered Krivitsky. 'What was there to warn Ludwik of? He knew as well as I did that they would kill him.'

'This is not the time or the place to discuss what you could have done,' I told him. 'You know best why Ludwik had to make the break alone, although you had agreed for so many years that you would go together. You let him go alone. He was sure you had gone back to the Soviet Union. If you had joined him, as you said you would and as he expected, he would be alive and you would be in a different position.

'I did not want to come here,' I went on, 'but I was persuaded to come, to introduce you to those who can help save your life. I think I have done all that could be expected of me.'

'Is that all you have to say to me after all these years?' he asked.

'Yes, that is all. You are safe with these people.'

I made a move as if to get up, but Naville gently pushed me back in my chair, saying, 'Stay. This is important.' Krivitsky turned to the others and said, 'Of all that has happened to me this is the hardest blow.'

He then went on to explain that a copy of the letter signed 'Krusia', which he had sent to me in care of Gérard Rosenthal, had been shown him by the N.K.V.D. 'It was in their hands before it reached Amsterdam,' he said. 'I denied having written it, and denied knowing who might have done so. From that minute on I broke off all my attempts to manoeuvre to save time, and went into hiding. But who had that letter? How did it travel? There is a dangerous agent in your party. This proves it.'

The copy of the letter had been shown him by Hans Bruesse, a close collaborator and trusted friend. Bruesse was the son of a well-known labour leader living in the Netherlands, whom Krivitsky had at considerable risk to himself saved from an assignment in Nazi Germany where he would very likely have been killed. He had got in touch with Bruesse by the same means he had used with us—an advertisement in *L'Oeuvre*—and met him in Paris. Apparently to gain his confidence, Bruesse told him the N.K.V.D. had compelled him to try to break into Sneevliet's house in Amsterdam; he had been told to get Ludwik's papers at all costs, not stopping even at murder. For a time it appeared Bruesse was willing to join Krivitsky in his break with Stalin; then he showed him the 'Krusia' letter, and Krivitsky knew he had been betrayed. Having got away from Bruesse through a ruse, after which he claimed the protection of the French police, he was now here demanding: 'How did this letter, which was sent in care of Gérard Rosenthal, get into the hands of the N.K.V.D.?'

Everyone turned to Rosenthal, who answered: 'I gave it to Victor Serge to post to Amsterdam.'

There was silence for a moment. I could see that Krivitsky was not aware of the tensions he had created. He must have believed, as I had earlier, that he was dealing with a single cohesive group, the Fourth International. He could not have understood, any more than I did, why Rosenthal, my attorney and a member of Sedov's group, should have shown the letter to Serge, who was not even a Trotskyite. And even if he had done so because, as I realized, he liked, respected, and trusted Serge, why had Serge shown it to someone else before posting it?

Sneevliet, already greatly irritated by Krivitsky's speaking a language he could not understand (though Sedov had translated everything he said completely and accurately), was trying to control himself. When Krivitsky repeated, 'You have an agent in your midst,' Sneevliet blew up.—'An agent? Why, you are an agent, and agents see agents everywhere! Why did you come to us? You are a miserable N.K.V.D. agent, that's what you are!' he shouted violently.

The others tried to calm him, but without much success. Finally I said to Sneevliet: 'No. It was you who insisted I come here, not to meet "a miserable N.K.V.D. agent" but a man in danger. I came to introduce you to a Communist who has broken with Stalin.' Pale, his features distorted, Sneevliet sat down again. This was the end of the meeting. Krivitsky took his leave in the company of someone who had come to fetch him. He did not look at me as he went out and we did not shake hands.

I had been very anxious about my son all the time I was in Paris, and once back in Amsterdam I was too happy to be reunited with him to ask Sneevliet some of the questions that were in my mind. But the visit to Paris, which I had dreaded so much, had broken my reluctance to go back there. I knew I could count on the Rosmers and valued the contact with Sedov and Gérard Rosenthal. I realized there were dangers, but also that no place was really safe. A few days later I broached the subject to Sneevliet.

He objected strenuously, insisting that Paris was unsafe and that as long as I stayed in his house in Amsterdam I would be secure. He did not believe the attempts to break in would be repeated. Finally he maintained that the contacts I would have in Paris with Sedov would lead to disaster, as there was an agent in his entourage.

I am convinced that in the time between the end of the meeting with Krivitsky and next morning, when we went back to Amsterdam, Sneevliet had seen Serge. He must have told him what Krivitsky had said[1] and taxed him with showing the 'Krusia' letter to someone, for when I asked Sneevliet now if he meant the agent Krivitsky had referred to, he answered: 'Yes. I do. There is an agent and it is that little Polish Jew, Etienne.'

The sentence has stuck in my mind all these years, and I can still recall the conversation that followed in all its details. 'It is obvious,' I told Sneevliet, 'that when Serge brought this

[1] Serge in fact vividly describes the meeting, as though he had been present, in his *Memoirs of a Revolutionary*, p. 343.

young man to meet me at the hotel he did not suspect him of anything. Now that you have told him about Krivitsky's letter having got into the hands of the N.K.V.D. it is easy enough to say that Etienne is the agent. What I want to know is why Serge showed him the letter in the first place.'

'I am not speaking about Serge,' answered Sneevliet. 'I say and I repeat that this secretary and right-hand man of Sedov's is an N.K.V.D. agent.'

'If you are convinced of this,' I said, 'then it is your duty to bring the matter up immediately with Sedov and insist on a full investigation.' Unfortunately, nothing happened. Sneevliet, then being accused by Trotsky of being responsible for Ludwik's death, may not have wanted to expose Serge's irresponsibility; by shielding Serge he was in a way protecting himself, thinking no doubt of things he had told Serge and the careless way Serge bandied everything about. He probably did write to Sedov about it, for by the time I returned to Paris Etienne was under suspicion—though not from Sedov.

2

Sneevliet remained violently opposed to my moving to Paris, but agreed that my son ought to continue his education in French. He therefore suggested we move to Brussels. The idea did not appeal to me but I agreed to see how it would work out. Sneevliet asked a friend, Georges Vereeken, a Belgian oppositionist, to arrange an appointment for me with the Socialist Foreign Minister, Paul Henri Spaak, to discuss the problem of establishing a legal residence in Belgium.

Spaak, when we saw him, was most attentive and kind, and thanked me for the confidence I had shown by coming to him. He was then an admirer of Trotsky, and may still be. However, though he was greatly in favour of my settling in Belgium, and offered to help my son enter a school there, he could not see how I could live in the country legally under a false name, as I would have to do. Belgian law, he said, would make that impossible. When Vereeken pointed out that the Habsburgs were living in Belgium under an alias, Spaak said this might constitute a precedent and he would look into it. But in the meantime I learned that all Belgian schoolchildren had to take courses in Flemish as well as French, which would have put my son, who knew not a word of Flemish, at a great disadvantage, so I did not follow up Spaak's offer of help.[1] When I met Vereeken again years later he told me he would not have approached Spaak on his own behalf, being then a political opponent of his, but had not hesitated to act on Sneevliet's advice for my sake.

When I returned to Amsterdam I found a letter from Marguerite Rosmer. She had found an apartment for me in a Paris suburb, very close to where she lived, and was busily furnishing it for me. We could move in in a few weeks. This settled matters for me. It was with great relief that I placed myself under someone else's protection and with the Rosmers' help overcame Sneevliet's objections.

Marguerite arranged to meet us in Brussels and go back to Paris with us by train. The apartment she had found was quite small, and sparsely furnished, but for the first time we had some privacy, and were glad to be away from the continuous agitation of the Sneevliet household. (By chance our next-door neighbour was a police official—an added guarantee against attempts to break in—though sadly this young man, not yet thirty, died of leukemia soon after we moved there.) Thanks to some friends of Marguerite's who were teachers, my son was admitted to a *lycée* under an assumed name, though it was by now late in the academic year.

I saw the Rosmers daily until I moved, sometime later, into the centre of Paris, and got to know some of the other people who visited them. One of these was the widow of the Spanish P.O.U.M. leader Andreas Nin; she was Russian, and her daughters were near my son in age so they played together. Another was Katia Landau, whose husband Kurt Landau, an Austrian oppositionist, had been murdered in Spain by the N.K.V.D.

Also through the Rosmers I met an Armenian named Tarov,

---

[1] After the war, when I was in the United States and Spaak was Secretary-General of the United Nations, I saw him to ask his help in getting a post at the U.N. Once again he was kind, but said frankly: 'You will never get one in spite of anything I could do and your obvious qualifications. Too many of your old friends are in powerful positions in the Secretariat and the various delegations.' He was quite right; I did not get the job.

who had performed the almost incredible feat of escaping from a Soviet prison camp. His history was rather fantastic and confused. According to him, he had first joined the Zinoviev opposition, but his views were closer to those of Rakovsky and Trotsky. In the mid-1930s he was arrested and sent to an 'isolator'. In the company of Eleazar Solntsev, a well-known oppositionist, Tarov succeeded in escaping; Solntsev was shot as they swam across a river on the border of Iran, but Tarov got away. The Mensheviks had helped him to get to Paris, where he met Sedov and his friends.

Tarov must have been in his forties, though he looked much older. He was obviously ill and very tense and quarrelsome. The Rosmers had helped him find a job as a mechanic, but he spoke harshly of them as 'petty bourgeois'; Sedov he treated as if he were a young puppy. One day Sedov said to me: 'I'm certainly glad Tarov made it, but isn't it too bad that if only one of them could get away it wasn't Solntsev?' Still, Tarov turned over most of his pay to the *Bulletin* of the opposition, and his revolutionary enthusiasm never abated. Once he asked me abruptly: 'And you, are you still grieving for your husband? When will you finally understand that he died as a revolutionary, with his boots on? I dread the thought that I might die in bed.' His fears were unjustified. When the Nazis attacked the Soviet Union he joined an Armenian Communist resistance group and was executed by the Germans, with all his comrades, in 1942.

Through Sedov I also came into contact with the Mensheviks, the Russian Socialists in exile in Paris, where they had settled when Hitler's rise to power made it necessary for them to leave Germany. This small, closely knit group continued to publish their bulletin *Vestnik* (The Messenger) in Russian, and to carry on their political activities, which consisted mostly of writing about and research into conditions in the Soviet Union: they were probably the best informed group on such matters. Although there were different political tendencies among them, they were united, and their solidarity extended to other opponents of Stalinism, including the Trotskyites. When Ludwik and Krivitsky had been planning their break I had suggested they might get in touch with the Mensheviks, particularly as they had considerable influence with the French Popular

Front government. They had refused, mainly because they knew little of the group and because in the Soviet Union the Mensheviks were always pictured as the arch-enemy. When I came to know them I saw what a tragic error this had been. They would have done everything in their power to help; moreover, as we were to find out, this was the one émigré group that did not have N.K.V.D. agents in its midst.

One Menshevik I came to know well was Boris Nikolaevsky, the historian and director of the Institute for Social Research. He was interested in meeting me, particularly as he had already talked with Krivitsky and wanted to check his statements against mine, as a matter of scholarly interest. From this initial contact a warm friendship grew up between us.

One of the most exceptional people I came to know among the Mensheviks was Lydia Dan, wife of the leader Theodore Dan and sister of Martov, who had been the leader and a close friend of Lenin. I really only came to appreciate Lydia Dan much later, in the United States after her husband's death. When she told me then of her efforts to get in touch with Trotsky's widow, in spite of the old and bitter differences between the Mensheviks and Trotsky, she answered: 'We have a great past in common, we struggled for the same cause, we shared prisons and Siberia. That can never be undone.'

Another Menshevik leader whom I came to like and respect was Rafael Abramovich. He was then still trying to find out what had happened to his son, Mark Rein, who had gone to Spain to cover the civil war for a socialist newspaper and vanished there. Abramovich had the support of the entire Socialist International, including the French, and of the Spanish Loyalist government, but had learned little when he went to Spain to search for his son. He knew that the head of the N.K.V.D. in Barcelona, where Rein had last been seen, had been a certain Orlov-Nikolsky, alias Shved or Lova, and was sure this man would know who had been responsible for his son's disappearance. As I have mentioned, I had met Orlov and could give a fairly accurate description of him, though Krivitsky and I were both sure he must have been ordered home to Moscow from Spain and shot there with the others. One day Abramovich asked me and Juan Andrade, one of the

P.O.U.M. leaders, to his apartment, where he questioned us about Orlov. Neither of us had any idea of his whereabouts. I stayed on after Andrade left and Abramovich again asked me to describe Orlov.[1] I realized he must think I knew where Orlov was but was too much afraid of the N.K.V.D. to tell him. Profoundly unhappy, I tried to explain: 'Comrade Abramovich, I am a mother and you have lost a child . . .' I never finished what I meant to say. Abramovich threw his arms about me and wept. This was how our friendship began.

After the Nazi invasion of France I received, in Portugal, an emergency visa for the United States. When I got there I learned that the visa, and the funds for the journey, had been obtained through Abramovich, who had vouched for me. I went to see him and thanked him. He insisted that he had done nothing and tried to change the subject. I too insisted, saying: 'I know very well what you did, but I don't know whether I would have done the same for you not so many years ago.' He laughed.—'I know you would not have done it then. But you see, we are socialists, not Bolsheviks.'

My contact with Sedov was brief, we knew each other only a few months, yet ours would I am sure have been a lasting friendship. In my own plight I had become attached to this man, several years younger than I, who had the maturity and compassion of a much older man. This was of course only natural: from his early youth he had known the terror and every death sentence pronounced in the Soviet Union affected him personally. The compassion he offered was genuine.

Sedov lived in a very modest apartment with his wife and his nephew Seva, son of his sister who had committed suicide in Berlin and of a Trotskyite named Volkov who had long since vanished in the U.S.S.R. Once or twice Sedov came to my place, bringing Seva with him; the boy and my own son were about the same age and soon became friends. A few times we went

---

[1] When Alexander Orlov, who had been with the Soviet commercial services in Valencia, began to publish articles about the Soviet terror in Spain, Abramovich and others at first believed him to be Orlov-Nikolsky. But when Abramovich met Alexander Orlov years later in the United States it was clear from the description I had given him that this Orlov, who was slight, fair-haired, and about ten years too old, was not the man I had met near Moscow in 1932.

to his apartment. The place was barely furnished and there was only one decent piece, an old Norman chest of which Sedov was very proud. He would prepare dinner, after which we would each smoke a cigarette. I noticed that if I did not stub mine out carefully he would do it for me. 'That's that much less spent on smoke,' he said; he used to smoke the butts in his pipe. He could not afford to spend anything on himself. He never knew where he would get the money to pay the printer for the next issue of the *Bulletin*. The three of them lived on his wife's salary, and it was easy to see there was barely enough to go round.

As a rule, Sedov and I met in cafés. We would sit for hours talking about the Soviet Union, of which he had kept a vivid memory. Though he had left it so young, it remained his country —indeed, he had left a wife and child behind—and he was interested in the most trivial changes that had taken place there. He was amazingly well informed about the U.S.S.R. and I learned many things from him.

One day I asked him who the 'Markin' was who wrote such remarkable articles for the *Bulletin*—articles I thought showed an insight into Soviet problems second only to that of Trotsky. Sedov smiled and said with some pride that it was he who wrote under that name. It was not an invented name; the real Markin, whose story Trotsky tells in his memoirs, had played a major role in Sedov's life. He was a sailor whom Trotsky's two sons Leon (Sedov) and Serge[1] met by chance during the Civil War, and who looked after them when their parents were too busy to do so. Sedov still loved to tell how Markin used somehow to get the two little boys sandwiches and drinks from the canteen reserved for government officials, and how he took them to visit museums and to political meetings. He was killed in the fighting, and Trotsky describes the night when he had at last to tell his sons of the death of their friend, and he and his wife 'long heard the boys sobbing in their room'. And now Sedov used Markin's name, in memory of his friend.

[1] When Leon Sedov followed his father into exile his younger brother Serge stayed behind, believing he could contribute something to his country by remaining in his job as an engineer. He never engaged in political activity, but apparently it was enough simply to be Trotsky's son: reports circulated abroad after the war that Serge had been seen in a prison camp, but when his mother wrote to the Soviet government to inquire about him she received no reply.

Sedov's real love was mathematics, but he seldom had time to work at it, for the cause he served required all his time and effort. Even when he was very young, in Germany before Hitler came to power, it was he who had had to deal with oppositionists coming from the Soviet Union; when Trotsky was away it was Sedov's responsibility to represent him. It is never easy to be the son of a prominent father, and Sedov must often have felt insecure, knowing people thought of him as Trotsky's son rather than a personality in his own right. I believe this was not true of the Trotskyites in Paris; those who knew Sedov and worked directly with him accepted him for his own qualities and respected him. Moreover, Sedov was much more than an obedient mouthpiece for his father's opinions; though Trotsky's authority weighed heavily on him, as it did on everyone who worked with him, he often disagreed with 'the old man' who, away in Mexico, knew less than his son about some aspects of European politics. This did not keep Sedov from being blamed for some of Trotsky's decisions.

His personal life was complicated by the fact that his wife, Jeanne Martin des Paillères, although devoted to him and to Trotsky, had sided with her former husband Molinier in a dispute which had split the Fourth International in France. A highly strung and rather authoritarian woman, she did her best to isolate Sedov from his friends, who were at odds with Molinier. And this in turn led those in his group not always to tell him everything. This may have explained why Gérard Rosenthal showed Krivitsky's 'Krusia' letter to Serge but not to Sedov: the Trotskyites had every confidence in Sedov but none in his wife. And although I am sure they were wrong, and that Sedov, who knew his wife, her character, and her political beliefs, would never have told her about a matter of such importance when to do so might have involved the rival Molinier faction, these strains must have made his private existence very difficult.

In the circumstances it is easy to understand how Etienne, the one person who always agreed unconditionally with Sedov and with his father, was able to gain his complete confidence, and why Sedov defended Etienne against the suspicion that was slowly growing in the group.

According to the story he had told the French Trotskyites,

Etienne (Zborovsky) came from a rather conservative Jewish family which fled from the Ukraine when the Bolsheviks came and settled in Poland. There he, the youngest, joined the Polish Communist Party, much to the disgust of his family. Soon parental pressure and police attention forced him to leave Poland and he went to Germany, where he looked unsuccessfully for work. After Hitler came to power he went to France and enrolled at the University of Grenoble, where he studied anthropology and earned his living as a waiter in a large hotel. He used to say that, although he was a convinced Communist when he went there, it was only in Grenoble that he learned to hate the bourgeoisie. He felt bitterly humiliated whenever he brought breakfast to the rooms of bourgeois ladies who did not bother to cover themselves when they opened the door at his knock, but looked through him as if he did not exist.

In 1934 he turned up in Paris and joined the Trotskyite group headed by Sedov. Trotsky's son was glad to have a new Russian-speaking member in what was essentially a French group, but the French Trotskyites, Pierre Naville in particular, were suspicious of Etienne from the start. He claimed he had left Poland to avoid being kidnapped by the N.K.V.D., and Naville, who took an instant personal dislike to him, wanted to have this story checked, but was overruled by the group. It was not long before Etienne had become a member of the groups' central committee, with access to all confidential meetings and information; indeed, Sedov made him his deputy at meetings he himself could not attend. Etienne soon knew all the clandestine addresses and had access to all the letters received by the group, including Trotsky's instructions to the party. With Sedov he edited the Russian-language *Bulletin*. Sedov's confidence in him was such that when Krivitsky came to the group for protection after his break, Sedov gave him Etienne as a bodyguard.[1]

Through the Trotskyites Etienne also became an intimate of Victor Serge, who had ties with the group especially through

---

[1] This was thought to be a dangerous assignment and Etienne was admired for his courage, but in fact the risk was not very great: the N.K.V.D. was not likely, after the kidnapping of General Miller, to undertake another adventure on French territory.

Naville and Rosenthal; it was he who had introduced them to Trotsky in Moscow years before. Sedov was rather cautious of Serge, feeling as we had done that there were suspicious features about his release in 1936, and the old French labour leaders such as Alfred Rosmer and Pierre Monatte did not like him particularly, though they respected him as an oppositionist and recognized his talents as a writer. But Etienne professed great admiration for the old revolutionary and Serge was only too happy to act as mentor for a younger comrade, and took him along everywhere—as he had to my hotel when I passed through Paris with the Sneevliets after Ludwik's death.

Although the circumstances of our first meeting had disturbed me, I rather liked Etienne as a person, and was glad to talk with him about events in the Soviet Union; he readily agreed with me about the dreadful things that were happening there. He was a devoted family man, and once or twice brought his child to my place. He obviously adored this little boy and would tell me, in his obsequious, flattering way, that he hoped he would grow up to be like my son. This was the one aspect of Etienne's behaviour that I did not like. The flowery praise he lavished on Trotsky I found tasteless, as I did the way he talked about Ludwik: 'I have not had the honour to know him.' We had always disliked and distrusted such panegyrics in the Soviet Union, feeling them to be false and intended only to evoke a reaction from others. I mentioned this to Sedov, who said: 'Yes, that's true, and I don't like it either. But Etienne is still young in the movement. He does not have our tradition; after all, all he knows is Stalinism.' This seemed to be the only thing Sedov disliked in Etienne.

Nevertheless Pierre Naville kept up his 'persecution', as Etienne called it, of Sedov's close collaborator. Unable to exclude him from confidential meetings, Naville made a point of fetching him in a car at the very last minute, so that Etienne never knew in advance where the meeting was being held. Naville wanted to know how he made a living, though Etienne was obviously poor and always shabbily dressed, and explained that he lived in a better-class building because his wife worked as the caretaker and they did not have to pay rent. He put up with Naville's abuse, though in turn accusing him of chauvinism and anti-Semitism, and complaining that the Frenchman's aim was to shake Sedov's and Trotsky's confidence in him, Etienne.

I myself thought Naville, whose zeal was fanatical, was exaggerating and thus hampering the group. He was not unlike Dzerzhinsky, whom he resembled physically, who used to see Okhrana agents everywhere and was always forcing the party to launch investigations. Naville could not produce anything tangible to back his charges, and Sedov not only continued to trust Etienne but blamed Naville for the vicious rumours then circulating in the group. 'I have to stand up for Etienne,' Sedov once told me. 'They don't like him and they don't trust him, but I know how devoted he is to me and to the old man. He would do anything for us and for the organization.'

Early one February morning Marguerite Rosmer came and told me Sedov was dead. I was stunned. I knew he had been ill, but not that he had been operated on; it seemed inconceivable that someone so young should die of natural causes. 'He *died?*' I repeated several times. 'Yes, *mon petit*, he died,' answered Marguerite. When I asked whether there might not have been foul play she said, '*Mon petit*, we will never know. We are writing to the old man and Natalia what we think, but that will never bring back their son.' The Rosmers soon after this took Sedov's nephew Seva with them to Mexico, and were living in Trotsky's house when the first attempt on his life was made.

Sedov had undergone what seemed minor surgery, for an ulcer, in a Paris clinic; the operation was apparently successful, but some days later he suddenly took a turn for the worse and died. Sedov's wife, at odds with his group, did not consult any of his French friends over the choice of either a surgeon or a clinic. Gérard Rosenthal, son of a doctor, could have advised her; instead she consulted two émigré physicians who had little contact with French medical circles. The surgeon they recommended had had a great reputation but in recent years a record of several fatalities after relatively simple operations. The clinic she chose—with such secrecy that not even Etienne knew where the operation had been performed until after Sedov was pronounced out of danger—was one that happened to have several White Russians on its staff. There was no evidence of Sedov's having died other than naturally, but intervention by the N.K.V.D., working through a White Russian organization as they had done in the case of Ludwik's death and General Miller's kidnapping, could not be ruled out.[1]

Etienne, whom I saw a few days after Sedov's death, seemed profoundly shaken. He said that now more than ever he must go on with his job and especially with editing the *Bulletin*. But Sedov's death had deprived him of his main support in the largely suspicious and hostile French group, so he wrote to Trotsky soon afterwards to ask his advice. He attributed the campaign against him to jealousy of his close relationship with Sedov, and pointed out that with Sedov gone he was the only one who knew enough to carry on the work of the organization.

Trotsky gave the only answer possible: that an investigatory committee of members of the International should carry out a thorough inquiry. If Etienne were cleared of suspicion he could continue Sedov's work. The Trotskyites were then preparing for their annual congress. Naville was unsuccessful in preventing Etienne from attending, but kept the place of the meeting secret as long as he could, and brought Etienne there— to Rosmer's house in Périgny, some twenty kilometres outside Paris—at the last minute as usual.

In order to acquaint all the members of the International with the problems to be taken up at this meeting, it had been decided to send the agenda, preliminary resolutions, and documents—among them Trotsky's instructions to the International to appoint a committee to investigate Etienne's case—to the foreign sections. A young German, Rudolf Klement (or Adolf), who had assisted Sedov in German matters, left for Brussels with the documents, which the Belgian section was to forward to the other groups. He vanished. A week or so later a headless corpse was fished out of the Seine near Paris. The police could not identify it, but Naville and another man who had worked

---

[1] A young surgeon, Jean Daniel Martinet, son of Trotsky's old friend the revolutionary poet Marcel Martinet, told me he was inclined to believe in a badly performed operation, adding that no French doctor would have recommended a surgeon with a record such as this man had.

closely with Klement for years, recognized the torso as his from a characteristic scar on one of the hands.

Though a police investigation produced no results, suspicion again fell on Etienne, who went on with his job in the now even more poisoned atmosphere. If the N.K.V.D. were responsible for Klement's death, as seems likely, it is not clear why they killed him when the documents he was carrying would have been accessible through other means, and when in any case there were other copies. One could only speculate that Klement must have found out something his comrades in Paris did not yet know.

Suspicion had meanwhile fallen on Etienne from another quarter, for he had been one of three people who knew where the Trotsky papers, stolen some time before from the archives of Boris Nikolaevsky's Institute for Social Research, had been stored. The others were Nikolaevsky himself and his secretary. Nikolaevsky had the utmost confidence in his secretary. But Etienne had moved some of the archives to another place a few days before the theft, and these had not been touched, which seemed to eliminate him.

As the signs pointing to the presence of an agent in Sedov's group increased, however, Nikolaevsky became more and more interested. He had always been fascinated by the problem of agents in revolutionary movements, and like all Russian socialists had been deeply affected by the case of Evno Azev, on whom he had published a long study.[1] One day, discussing the possibility of treason among the Trotskyites, he said to me, 'This is a new Azev case.' When I answered, 'Not quite,' he commented: 'Other times, other standards, but just as important.'

The episode of the 'Krusia' letter had provided such incontrovertible evidence of treachery that Nikolaevsky asked both Krivitsky and me to prepare detailed accounts of all we knew about the events that followed Ludwik's murder, and especially about the letter. In his report Krivitsky flatly accused Serge

---

[1] Azev was the leader of a secret terrorist wing of the Russian Social Revolutionary Party. He was also an agent of the Okhrana, and was unmasked by a member of his own party, Vladimir Burtsev, who as an old man had helped Nikolaevsky gather the facts for his study of the case.

of being the agent, while I limited myself to pointing out Serge's irresponsibility and stated my belief that he had been used by an agent. Both reports were eventually sent to Trotsky.[1]

3

Gradually my relations with Krivitsky had become less strained. Before he left France for the United States we often met at Nikolaevsky's Institute and also in cafés, though avoiding parts of the city where we had met in the past. Although we knew there was some danger in our meetings, we learned to take it in our stride. Krivitsky was being watched by the French police, of course, but even without this protection I think our loneliness would have made us disregard the risks.

Krivitsky felt bad about being protected by the French police, and especially about having to talk to the French intelligence services. He told me his wife could not understand his reluctance. 'After all,' he said, 'we too belonged to such a service. You know, for other people we too were police. In a way they are right—but by God, it is not the same thing.'—'No, it isn't,' I said, and touching for the first time on our common past reminded him of Fedia's advice to a young man in the intelligence services (actually it had been to Brun) to grow a moustache, wax it and make it bushy so he would look like a good Okhrana man. ' "You can't be a good policeman without a bushy moustache," he used to say.'—'Yes,' said Krivitsky, 'I remember. But the N.K.V.D. is not the Okhrana, they don't give you time to grow a moustache.'

As I talked with Krivitsky I began to ask myself how Ludwik and I could ever have thought he would join Ludwik in a break. He was more outspoken than Ludwik, but he was also much more easily swayed by the slightest sign of a change for the better in the U.S.S.R. In retrospect it is astonishing how a man so intelligent and so knowledgeable about Soviet politics could have been so mistaken. Did Ludwik, who had known Krivitsky from childhood, believe he would ever take the final step? I had heard so many contradictory statements from Walter I had ceased to take him seriously, but Ludwik always said he had full confidence in him, and I could still hear him saying, when I

[1] They are now in the Trotsky archive at Harvard University.

had suggested Krivitsky might be forced to join in the hunt for him, 'If Walter does that, then life is not worth living anyway.'

In fact, as I now know, Krivitsky was forced to join the hunt. He describes in his book how at the last minute he was ordered off the train that, in August 1937, was to have taken him to a Soviet boat and to Moscow. He thought this was a test the N.K.V.D. wanted him to pass, but actually it was because he was needed for one more assignment.

Later on I was able to piece together how the N.K.V.D. came to be informed so rapidly of Ludwik's plans and movements. Spiegelglas, who was in Paris and was to lead the hunt, had known for some time that someone 'important' had established contact with Sneevliet. The N.K.V.D. did not know who it was, but suspected either Ludwik or Krivitsky; clearly the person who reported that Ludwik had been in Amsterdam had not known him or Krivitsky by sight. Thus when Spiegelglas opened the letter to the Central Committee which Ludwik had handed to Lydia Grozovsky—and which she immediately handed on to the N.K.V.D., an act which later caused her to be expelled from France—he could tell Krivitsky, 'I'm glad it is not you who are the traitor.' And the hunt could begin at once.

But someone was needed to lure Ludwik to an appointment, and for this Krivitsky was given one more chance—though in doing so Spiegelglas himself took a big chance. Years later, our friend the Dutch 'blue-blood' whose arms-gathering exploits Krivitsky paints so vividly and so misleadingly in his book, told me of Krivitsky's visit to him that August. Knowing his friendship for Ludwik, Krivitsky asked the Dutchman to help him contact Ludwik to arrange a meeting. This is the answer our Dutch friend gave: 'If Ludwik asked me to do that to you, I might think about it for a minute. But he would never have done such a thing and my answer to you is no.'

I am sure now that Krivitsky went to our friend knowing he would refuse—it was one way of keeping Spiegelglas satisfied. And as it turned out Krivitsky's help was not needed, for the N.K.V.D. learned independently of the meeting Ludwik was to go to in Rheims. The person who told them—perhaps the same person who had told them Ludwik had gone to Amsterdam—was someone who knew Sneevliet and Serge, and Sedov, who knew of the plan. And it must also have been the person who told them of my passage through Paris after Ludwik's death. (Spiegelglas told Krivitsky they had planned an attempt on me and my child at the Gare du Nord as we boarded the train for Amsterdam, but 'There were too many police around,' he said. 'There was nothing we could do. I am just as glad. I am sure she won't tell the police anything.' No doubt he thought he had already done enough to me.)

Krivitsky stayed behind that summer, I now believe, simply because he had no orders to return home. He preferred others to make decisions for him. His own break came about as a result of inertia; if his half-hearted attempt, in the 'Krusia' letter he wrote to me in Holland, had not been intercepted and Bruesse detailed to betray him he might never have broken. From then on it was a question of technique; Krivitsky's was superior to that of young Bruesse and he got away. Through me he reached Sedov, through Sedov the Mensheviks. He was safe. I remembered what Krusia had said: Krivitsky was born lucky, he was born with a silver spoon in his mouth. It was through this luck, as I then thought, that he would be the only one of the friends from the little town to get away.

Before leaving for the United States Krivitsky showed me a letter he had received from the so-called Dies Committee of the U.S. Congress. I told him I had received a similar letter. He asked me what I intended to do about it. I said I would reply in the negative, as I had nothing to testify about. 'You're right,' he said. 'I have nothing to testify about either. I am by no means through with the Soviet Union or with Stalin either, but this is not the way to fight him. Right now I don't know how to do that. I am not ready to write anything either. When I am I will let you know beforehand.'

In the United States he had to make a new start in life, without knowing the country or the language. He did find friends, good friends, but among them he realized how frightfully alone he was. They persuaded him to write: it would help to break his sense of isolation and also to earn a living. When he agreed I am sure he did not intend to produce the series of articles that appeared under his name in the *Saturday Evening Post,* or the book that was published subsequently. But, unable to write in English, he had to rely on ghost-writers, and he knew nothing of the American press. Whoever wrote his book cared only for one thing : to make it as sensational as possible. I am sure he simply gave the writers the information and then looked on, as he had always done, while they distorted it. The errors and exaggerations I have pointed out are only the most obvious ones; the omissions from the book are almost as serious as the distortions. It did create a sensation—a sinister one, in Europe, and for me.

Krivitsky did several other things he cannot have intended to do. He did testify before a Congressional committee, and after the war began he made a trip to Britain to talk to officials there; on that occasion, once again, he took credit for someone else's work.[1] On his return to America he lived in relative security and even affluence from the sale of his articles. His family was safe and well cared for, he had friends, it seemed he could start a new life. But something else had happened. For the first time he had the leisure to see himself in his new situation. He had broken with his old life and had not built a new one. He went to a hotel in Washington, wrote a letter to his wife and one to his new friends, and put a bullet through his head.

His friends did not believe in his suicide. They could not understand why he should kill himself when he was safe and had no financial problems. Nor did suicide fit the character his friends had created in his book. They said unanimously that he had been murdered. The letters, they said, had been dictated at gun point. But to those who knew his handwriting, his style, his expressions, there could be no doubt that he had written them. The hotel staff testified that no one else had been seen going to his room. He was found fully dressed except for his shoes, on the bed with the gun by his temple, the letters on the table, the door locked from the inside. He died on the 11th of February 1941, the day I arrived in the United States.

---

[1] Krivitsky cannot have known that the misinformation he gave the British would be corrected, many years later, by the same Dutch 'blue blood' who has set the record straight on other counts.

Epilogue

THE UNITED STATES

The war and emigration to the United States might have seemed to Etienne a good way of escaping from his past. I do not know why he did not take advantage of the opportunity.

When I saw him in America, he asked whether I could put him in touch with the American Trotskyites, as he wanted to work in the movement. I said I knew few of them and that as far as I could tell they were not a particularly homogeneous group and furthermore seemed to concern themselves largely with internal American politics. He answered that this was not a good enough reason for a devoted militant, even though a foreigner, not to participate actively in their work.

I never thought much about his request, or whether he was involved with the U.S. Trotskyites or not, but I continued to see him socially from time to time. One day, I think in the spring of 1955, the F.B.I. came to see me and asked me some questions about Etienne. This did not surprise me particularly; I assumed he had applied for a position that required a government security clearance. One of the questions they asked was whether he had been a Trotskyite. I told them that when I met him in Paris he was Sedov's friend and secretary, which would lead one to assume that he was. This seemd to be all they wanted to know, and the whole matter a routine one.

I gave it no further thought, but when I met Etienne, as I often did on the campus of the university where we both worked, I told him the story and asked him what kind of job he had applied for. He seemed surprised and disturbed. He had not applied for a government post, and had no idea what the investigation was about.

Some time later, when I had almost forgotten about it, the

F.B.I. came again. They said they had been watching Etienne closely and that they had seen us together. Then they told me they had evidence he was an N.K.V.D. agent and cautioned me to stay away from him.

After that I did my best to avoid Etienne, but we did meet on two occasions. At a party given by an anthropologist I saw him among a crowd of students. I hoped he would not see me, but he did and sat down next to me. He said: 'You, too, seem to be affected by that virus of the emigration. The illness is not a new one in history, suspecting everyone of being an agent.' I was taken aback by his casual tone and could not help saying: 'There is enough evidence to make me stay away from you.' He said something offensive, got slowly to his feet, and walked away.

Our second meeting was not accidental Etienne rang me one day, saying he had an afternoon off and wanted to see me. When I opened the door he walked past me without a word. In the living room he said, looking at his feet, 'Do you know why I came?' Then, without waiting for an answer, he looked straight at me. 'I came to tell you that it is all true. I have been an N.K.V.D. agent for more than twenty years.'

His 'confession' did not produce much of an impact on me. I was more surprised at his coming at all. When I asked why he had come he said: 'Because I don't owe anybody any explanations except you. You may be able to understand me, the others cannot possibly.'

I knew it was up to me to ask questions, but I did not feel ready to face the truth and to go through everything again. He did not wait for me to ask him anything, however, but began to tell me how he had been recruited by a fellow worker, a Russian, in Grenoble, who had suggested he go to Paris where he could find friends and 'be useful to the Soviet Union'. The story of how Etienne had infiltrated the Trotskyite organization—where, in fact, very little that was of interest to the N.K.V.D. was going on—contained nothing unexpected, even down to his having had dealings with Russian Orthodox priests and White Russian officers, members of an anti-Semitic émigré organization, whom he must have hated as a Communist and a Jew. Somehow this did not seem to concern me at all.

There were only a few things I was interested in, and finally I interrupted him.

I asked about Sedov who, according to Etienne, had been the main target of his spying. 'Do you remember, when I saw you a few days after Sedov's death, what you told me then and how defeated you were? I understand what a blow that must have been, the loss of your closest friend. Do you remember?' Looking straight at me he said : 'Yes, I do, but it was the happiest day of my life.' This startled me. 'The happiest day?' I asked.—'Yes, the happiest. I did not have to spy on him any more, I did not have to denounce him. My job was finished, or so I thought.'

Then I asked him whether he had had any contacts with the N.K.V.D. in the United States. He answered that he had been approached by them while on holiday with his family but had refused to work for them. Remembering how he had asked me to introduce him to the Trotskyites in America, I did not believe this, but it did not seem very important.

I finally led the talk to questions which I knew he wanted to avoid. I asked him outright whether it was he who had informed the N.K.V.D. of the contents of Krivitsky's 'Krusia' letter to me. 'Did Serge show you that letter?' A wry, pitiful smile on his distorted face and a shrug of the shoulders were his only reply. It was neither a confirmation nor a denial, just that helpless smile of his. It was the same with all the questions I asked about Ludwik's murder. Only a shrug of the shoulders. I knew then without a doubt who had informed the N.K.V.D.

It was getting dark in the room, and there were only my questions. He did not make a sound, but even in the dim light I could see his smile and the shrug of his shoulders. I could have gone on for a long time but I wanted to make an end of it. I asked him about his role in the disappearance of Klement. This time he answered: 'I don't know.' I still do not know whether to believe him or not, but I took advantage of the fact that he had spoken to ask him: 'Do you remember telling me in Paris that you were indignant at Victor Serge for spreading the rumour that Sedov's woman secretary was the agent? You told me then that you went to see Serge, and I can still repeat your words: "Victor Lvovich, if it were not for your white hairs I would break your neck for this." '—'Yes,' he said, 'it was true. I remember it quite well and I did say that. I wanted him to stop spreading that rumour, though it was not really in my interest that he should stop. After all, I knew who the agent was. I was.' This, for some reason, sounded convincing and I believed him. Then I asked him point-blank: 'Were there other agents than yourself among the Trotskyites?' By now he had regained his composure and answered angrily: 'I don't know, but you ought to know that an agent is never told about another unless they are supposed to work together.'

It was time to finish the conversation. I got up and told Etienne I could not possibly keep what he had told me to myself, that I would get in touch with the F.B.I. and that I advised him to do the same. He said he would, but would rather see a lawyer first. Quite possibly he had already been to the F.B.I. when he came to see me.[1]

Some time later Etienne was arrested and tried for perjury, on the basis of evidence given the F.B.I. by a man then serving a term for espionage against the U.S., whom Etienne had denied knowing. At his trial the judge was determined not to depart from the matter of perjury with which he was charged, and all attempts on the part of witnesses to steer the testimony towards Etienne's political activities were ruled out of order. He was found guilty and sentenced to five years' imprisonment.

Many of Etienne's fellow anthropologists attended the trial and gathered round him during the recesses, ostentatiously demonstrating their friendship and faith in him. They knew nothing of agents or secret police, or of Soviet political matters; to them a Soviet agent and a perjuror was merely an innocent victim of political persecution. They were determined to apply their methodology of primitive cultures to modern terror, as I realized when a prominent American anthropologist said to me after the trial: 'In this country we are against human sacrifice.'

---

[1] An account of Etienne's activities in Paris, including the part he played in Sedov's death and the theft of the Trotsky archives, and in informing the N.K.V.D. of Ludwik's meeting with Sneevliet in Amsterdam and of the plans for the meeting in Rheims, was published in *The New Leader* (21 November 1955, 19 and 26 March 1956), and later by Isaac Deutscher in *The Prophet Outcast: Trotsky 1921–1940* (London and New York 1963), pp. 347–9, 390–96, 405–10.

Index

Abramovich, R., 258—9
Andrade, Juan, 258–9
Artuzov ('Sovietized Swiss'), 145
Azev, Evno, 266

Balabanova, Angelica, 61–2
Bardach, Marco, 138–40
Bazarov, Boris (Bykov), pseud. (Shpak).
 147–8, 151, 158, 205; stepson ('young
 Bazarov'), 148, 158, 198
Becher, Johannes, 190
Benario, Olga, 112
Berman, M. D., 182
Berzin, J. K., 120, 123, 127, 186,
 211–12, 213
Blumkin, Jacob, 146–7
Bolsheviks, 28–30, 43, 62, 70, and
 passim; old Bolsheviks, 1–3, 60, 150,
 172, 191
Borodin, M. A., 132; son ('young
 Borodin'), 132, 134
Borovich, Alex, 103, 111, 185–6, 194, 199
Bortnovsky, B. (Bronkovsky), 111, 113,
 120, 193–6, 212n.
Braun, Otto, 112
Bruesse, Hans, 253, 269
Brun, J. (Spisovich), 116
Brzozowski, Stanislaw, 12
Bukharin, N. I., 111, 201
Burtsev, V. L., 266n.

Cheka, see G. P. U.
Chicherin, G. V., 74
Comintern (Third, or Communist,
 International), 2, 30–31, 32, 33, 39n.,
 43, 54, 62, 66–7, 79–80, 85, 105–7,
 111, 120, 126–7, 183, 190, 218; intelligence networks, 21, 42, 43, 55, 57–8,
 109, 121, 154, 193, 207, 212; international liaison department (O.M.S.),
 53–4, 104, 105
Communist Party: Austrian, 140;
 Bulgarian, 66–7; Chinese, 78, 199;
 Czechoslovak, 73, 154; Dutch, 76–7,
 84; French, 250; German, 33, 53,
 104, 110, 133, 143, 169, 181, 223;
 Irish, 84; Polish, 26, 27–36, 40–42,
 43, 44, 50, 116, 126, 158–9, 169, 193,
 262; of the U.S.S.R., 30, 36, 75, 79,
 84, 85, 107, 109, 113, 118, 120,
 169–70, 204n., and passim; of the
 Western Ukraine 35; Yugoslav,
 102n., 111
Corpus, Lilly, 190
Crop, Hildo, 75–6, 77

Dąbal, Tomasz, 41–2
Dan, Theodore, 258; wife Lydia, 258
Dimitrov, G., 67
Drobnis, J., 2
Ducomet, Pierre Louis, 239–40
Dzerzhinsky, Felix, 43–4, 264

Efron, Serge, 238–40
Eisler, Gerhard, 64, 175
Etienne, see Zborovsky, Marc

Fedia (later Fedin) (pseud. Alfred
 Krauss), 12–14, 16, 19–20, 21, 22–3,
 25, 39, 53–5, 58, 71, 98, 103–4, 105,
 106, 107–10, 113, 121, 125, 129, 140,
 142, 161, 167, 168–9, 170, 172–8, 183,
 187, 191n,. 192, 194, 196–8, 200–201,
 202–3, 204n., 205, 208, 209, 251n.,
 267
Feuchtwanger, Leon, 3, 176–7, 178,
 198, 199
Field, Mrs. (mother of Noel and Herman Field), 144
Firin, S., 122, 178–9, 180
Fischer, Franz, 38–9, 41, 124–5
Fischer, Louis, 48n., 179–80, 245n.
Fischer, Ruth, 143
Fisher, Volodia, 111
Fourth Department of the Red Army,
 21, 44, 53–5, 58, 65–6, 69–71, 75,
 81–2, 85, 92, 93, 104, 105–8, 109,
 110, 111, 115, 120–25, 139n., 147,
 148, 179, 185n., 193, 212n.
Fourth International, 3, 246–7, 265
Frankfurter, Gerda, 144, 165, 248–9
Friedman, Max (Maximov), 75–6, 77,
 83, 113–4, 185–6, 194, 195, 204
Friedmann (Latvian Communist), 209

G.P.U., or Cheka, 43, 128, 146, 147,
 164, 186, 214–15, See also N.K.V.D.
Georgiev, General Kosta, 67
Gide, André, 176–7
Glan, Betty, 111–12
Gorkić, Milan, 111–12, 124, 160, 207,
 218
Gorky, Maxim, 16n., 22, 245
Gorski, Felix, 58, 66, 69, 87–8, 101, 111,
 122, 128, 145, 151–2, 156–63, 164,
 168, 170, 178–80, 185, 186, 189,
 190–92, 193–4, 195–6, 198–201, 202,
 204, 205, 207, 208, 223; former wife
 Justina, 101, 111, 112, 124, 159–60,
 194, 207
Gouzenko, Igor, 81–2

Gravpen (N.K.V.D. official), 163–5
Grinko, G. F., 140
Grozovsky (N.K.V.D. liaison man),
 152–3, 154; wife Lydia, 152–3, 221,
 228, 268
Gutchkov, Alexander, 238; Gutchkov
 Circle, 238, 240

Hanfstaengel, Putzi, 145
Henrykovsky, H., 193
Hirsch, Werner, 181
Howard, Roy, 2
Huberman, Stanislaw (Stakh Huber-
 Wrzos), 39, 202; brother Bronislaw,
 39

I.N.O., *see* N.K.V.D., foreign section
Inkov (Felix Wolf, Nikolai Rakov),
 pseuds. (Krebs), 53, 59–60, 69
intelligence services: British, 73–4, 145;
 French, 267; German, 139; Soviet,
 see Comintern; Fourth Department;
 N.K.V.D.
Isourin (N.K.V.D. employee), 217n.

Jacob, Berchtold, 138
Joffe, A. A., 62, 63, 78

Kaidan (Polish *gendarmerie* comman-
 dant), 5–6
Kalinin, M. I., 100
Kalyniak, 9–10, 15n., 24
Kamenev, L. B., 2, 150, 192
Kaminsky (N.K.V.D. employee), 188
Kandelaki, David, 210
Katz, Otto (André Simon), 142, 245n.
Kautsky, Karl, 69
Kedrov (N.K.V.D. interrogator), 165n.,
 181; father (M. S. Kedrov), 165n.
Kippenberger, Hans, 180–82
Kirov, S. M., 65n., 107, 150, 159
Kisch, E. E., 137, 140–42
Khvilovoi, M., 140
Klausen, Max, 106
Klement, Rudolf (pseud. Adolf), 265–6,
 273
Klinger, Galina, 117–18, 206
Kokhanski (Red Army officer), 116
Kondratiev (White Russian journalist),
 239–40
Kostov, Traicho, 67
Kotsiubinsky, J. M., 60–61
Kowal, Sophie, 37–8
Krasny, *see* Rotstadt, J.
Krestinsky, N., 74
Krivitsky, Walter, 11, 20, 22, 26, 40,
 65n., 69, 71, 75n., 107, 108, 110,
 124n., 139, 145, 146n., 148, 149, 150,
 151, 165n., 171n., 175, 181, 185n.,
 204n., 209–10, 211n., 218–20, 221,
228, 231, 245, 246, 249–55, 257, 258,
 261, 262, 266–70, 273; 'Krusia' letter
 from, 20, 249–55, 261, 266, 273
Krupskaia, Nadezhda, 41n., 172
Krusia, 11, 14, 19–20, 22, 44, 196–8,
 249, 269

Ladan, Pavlo, 111, 126–7, 140, 174
Landau, Kurt, 256; wife Katia, 256
Laval, Pierre, 2, 170–71, 240
Lenin, V. I., 3, 16n., 29, 31, 32, 39n.,
 41n., 55, 61, 62, 91, 115, 132, 165n.,
 172, 191, 192, 197, 258
Lenski, pseud. (Leszczynski, J.), 116
Levi, Paul, 59
Litvinov, M. M., 77
Locker, Jacob, 23, 44–6, 50–51, 186
Ludwik, *see* Poretsky, Ignace
Luxemburg, Rosa, 28–34, 38, 39n., 43,
 75, 78
Lykov, Alexander, 66–7, 68
Luft (pseud. Paul Ruegg, Noulens), 62–5

Maly, Theodore, 128–9, 146n., 151,
 157, 213–6, 228, 231
Manuilsky, D. Z., 185
Marchlewski, Julian (pseud. Karski),
 30, 31
Markin, N., 260
Markin, Valentin (Oscar), 122–4, 179
Martignat, Etienne Charles, 239
Martin des Paillères, Jeanne, 259, 261
Martinet, Jean Daniel, 265n.; father
 (Marcel Martinet), 265n.
Martov, J., 62, 258
Massing, Paul, 137, 150, 164; wife
 Hede, 164
Maurer, Emil, 68–9
Maximov, *see* Friedman, Max
Mdivani, Budu, 2
Medved, Philip, 65n.
Mensheviks, 28, 62, 257–9, 269
Messing, Anna Mikhailovna, 102, 113,
 162, 182–4, 202, 212; husband (S. A.
 Messing), 113, 162, 182, 183
Miller, General Eugene, 240, 262n.,
 265
Mirov-Abramov (O.M.S. official), 53,
 109
Molchanov, G. A. 200–201
Molinier, Raymond, 261
Molotov, V. M., 111
Monatte, Pierre, 263
Mrachkovsky, S. V., 2, 150
Mueller, George, 186–9, 203, 204–5
Muenzenberg, Willy, 64–5, 102, 136,
 191, 197
Muralov, N. I., 2, 200
Mussert (Dutch pro-Nazi leader), 247
Mussolini, Benito, 108, 137, 210

N.K.V.D., 20, 21, 26, 54–5, 58, 62, 65–6, 102, 105, 122–4, 125, 127, 132, 139, 140, 143, 144–50, 153, 157–8, 161–2, 163–5, 166, 179, 185n., 186–9, 192–3, 200–201, 203–5, 212, 215, 219, 221, 222, 223, 231–2, 236, 237, 241–2, 244, 248, 249, 251, 252–4, 255, 256, 258–9, 262, 265–6, 267–9, 272–4, and *passim*; construction department, 122, 178–9; foreign section (I.N.O.), 53, 55, 110, 122–5, 127, 128, 148–9; and the press, 53–4, 109

Nazis, 107, 130–35, 144–5, 178n., 210, 240n., 243, 247

Naville, Pierre, 250, 251–2, 262, 263–4, 265

Nebenfuehrer, 44, 186n.

Nikolaevsky, B., 258, 266, 267

Nin, Andreas, 2, 211, 220, 256

Okhrana, 15, 56, 266n.

Okudzhava, M., 2

O.M.S., *see* Comintern: international liaison department

Ordzhonikidze, G. K., 200

Orlov, Alexander, 259n.

Orlov-Nikolsky (pseuds. Lova, Shved), 163n., 193, 258–9

Panitsa, Todor, 67–8

Piatakov, G. L., 55, 57, 60, 198n., 200, 208

Piatnitsky, Ossip, 105, 106

Pilsudski, Marshal, 32, 40

Plessner family, 111, 174

Plevitskaia, Nadine, 240n.

Poretsky, Ignace (Ludwik) (pseuds. Ludwig, Hans Eberhard, Ignace Reiss): early life in Galicia, 7–11, 14–19; father, 8–9; mother, 7, 17, 25; brother, 8–9, 16, 17, 25–6, 219–20; schooling in Lwow, 8–10; boyhood friends, 11–14, 20–23, and *passim*; in First World War, 14–19, 24; visits Vienna, (*c*. 1917) 19, (1919) 39, 43, (*c*. 1920) 42; visits Germany, (*c*. 1917) 23–4; party work in Lwow, 37–9, 40–42; 'mandate' from Polish party, 39; becomes Soviet agent, 42–4; visits Moscow, (*c*. 1921) 42, (1927) 72, (1935) 107; as Comintern agent: in Lwow, 44–6; imprisoned, 46–51; escapes, 52; in Berlin (1923), 53–8; as agent of Fourth Department: in Vienna, 58–71; in Prague, 72–3; in Amsterdam, 73–84; asks for reassignment, 84–5; in Moscow, 86–120; training as an agent, 69–71; methods of operation, 81–84; Soviet decoration (Order of the Red

Banner), 3, 39, 72, 100, 109, 114, 122; declines offer to join Comintern, 120–21; joins N.K.V.D., 122–8; wife and son in Germany, 130–35; as N.K.V.D. agent in Europe: 135–50, 208–11; and assignment in U.S., 151, 205; decision to break with Stalin, 150, 209, 219–21; letter to the Central Committee, 1–3, 221, 228–9, 232, 242, 268; in Switzerland, 227–35; death, 235–42

Radek, Karl, 28, 34, 41n., 43, 55–7, 59, 60, 74, 146–7, 165, 185–6, 189, 198–200, 208–9

Rado, Alexander, 142–3

Rakovsky, K. G., 2, 74, 191, 192, 257

Raskolnikov, F. F., 56, 59

Red Army, 33, 41, 89, 91, 100, 116, 127, 167–8, 185, 194, 196, 212; military intelligence section, *see* Fourth Department

Redl, Colonel Alfred, 70n.

Rein, Mark, 258–9

Reisner, Larissa, 55–7, 59, 202

Reiss, Ignace, *see* Poretsky, Ignace

Ring, J., 101

Roland-Holst, Henriette, 75

Rosenberg, Lisa, *see* Zarubin, Lisa

Rosenberg, Victor, 146, 225

Rosenthal, Gérard, 250–54, 261, 263, 264

Rosmer, Alfred, 250, 254, 256–7, 263, 264, 265; wife Marguerite, 250, 254, 256–7, 264

Rossi, François (pseud. Abiate), 236, 237, 239–41

Rotstadt, J. (pseud. Krasny), 43–4, 108

Roy, M. N., 79–80

Ruegg, Paul, *see* Luft

Rykov, A. I., 201

Schildbach, Gertrude, 24, 143, 222–6, 231–2, 233–7, 239–41, 246

Second International (Socialist), 2, 13, 30, 39n., 78

Sedov, Leon (pseud. N. Markin), 147n., 149, 210n., 218, 238, 246–7, 250–54, 255, 257, 259–65, 269, 271, 273, 274n.; brother Serge, 260; mother (Natalya Sedova), 258, 264

Seghers, Anna, 207

Serebriakov, L. P., 2, 200

Serge, Victor, 244–6, 251, 253–5, 261–3, 266–7, 269, 273–4

Sevriuk (Ukrainian in Germany), 139, 144

Shliapnikov, A. G., 78

Shlikhter, Alexander, 61

Sichinsky (Ukrainian student), 15n.

278 *Index*

Skobline, General, 240n.
Slansky, Rudolf, 142, 245n.
Slutsky, A. A., 110, 122, 123, 124n.,
    125, 127, 128, 146n., 148–9, 161–2,
    180–81, 187, 188, 199n., 204, 209n.,
    211, 213n., 222, 228
Smirensky, Dimitry, pseud. (Marcel
    Rollin), 238–40
Smirnov, I. N., 2, 150
Sneevliet, Henryk (pseud. Maring),
    77–81, 83, 220–21, 231, 232, 233,
    241–2, 243–56, 263, 268, 269, 274n.
Sochacki, Jerzy, 33–4
Social-Democrats, 28, 131, 197
Socialists, 28, 30, 34; youth movement,
    13, 19. *See also* Second International,
    Youth International
Sokolnikov, G. Y., 157, 198n.; former
    wife (Mrs. Sokolnikov), 157, 182
Solntsev, Eleazar, 257
Sorge, Richard (Ika), 64n., 70, 82,
    103–7, 109–10, 121, 170, 175, 186
Spaak, Paul Henri, 255–6
Spanish civil war (1936–38), 112, 149,
    150, 153, 163, 178, 185, 192–3, 195–6,
    210–12, 218, 219, 256, 258–9
Spiegelglas (N.K.V.D. official), 187–8,
    278–9
Stachevsky, Arthur, 195–6, 211–13;
    wife Regina, 194, 195–6, 211, 213;
    daughter Lolotte, 195, 213
Stahl, Lydia, 148
Stahl, Willy, 11, 20–21, 38, 40, 54,
    87–8, 90, 96, 113, 129, 161, 167–70,
    171–4, 184, 185n., 196, 197, 201, 203,
    205
Stalin, J. V., 1–3, 33, 34, 85, 91, 105,
    107, 113–14, 120, 121, 124, 125, 134,
    141, 144, 145, 149, 150, 159, 161,
    172, 175, 176–7, 178, 180, 182, 183,
    184, 191, 192, 198, 199–201, 209n.,
    210, 212, 217, 219, 238, 240
Steiner, Renata, 233, 235–6, 237, 238–
    40
Swart, Jef, 83
Swierchiewski, K., 125–6

Tairov, General, 103, 121
Tarov, A., 256–7
Thaelmann, Ernst, 121, 169, 181
Third International, *see* Comintern
Tilden, Alfred, 124, 185n.
trials, Moscow: first (August 1936),
    1–2, 150, 172, 209, 223; second
    (January 1937), 2, 57, 157, 189,
    198–200; third (March 1938), 2, 65n.
Trotsky, L. D., 33, 56, 60, 64–5, 76, 79,
    120, 121, 132, 146–7, 149, 150, 185,
    203, 209n., 239, 246, 247, 250, 255,
    257, 260–64, 265, 267

Trotskyites, 250–53, 259–67, 271–4, and
    passim. See also Fourth International
Tukhachevsky, M. N., 211, 212, 217,
    240n.

Ukrainians, 9, 14–15, 24–5, 34–5, 47,
    50, 103, 127, 140, 188
Umansky, Berchtold (Brun) (pseuds.
    Ilk, Steiger), 11–12, 17, 21, 54–5,
    110–11, 136, 161–2, 168, 169, 170,
    172–4, 180–82, 183, 196, 197–8, 202,
    205, 267
Umansky, Misha, 11–12, 17, 21, 54,
    161, 168, 170–71, 172–4, 205, 231
Union for Repatriation of Russians
    Abroad, 237–9
Unshlikht, J. S., 43, 75, 102, 113, 169,
    183–4; Sophia, 113, 116, 183, 184;
    Stephanie, 116, 183
Urban, Paul, 136–8, 143–4, 189–93,
    194, 195, 202
Uritsky, S. P., 179

Vereeken, Georges, 255–6
Vlahov, Dimitar, 68
Volkov, Vsevolod (Seva), 259, 264;
    parents (Zina and Platon Volkov), 259
Voroshilov, K. Y., 103, 113–14
Vyshinsky, Andrei, 65n., 189

Warynski, Ludwik, 34n.
White Russians (émigrés), 65, 71, 111,
    146, 237–40, 265; in employ of
    N.K.V.D., 146, 165, 214, 237, 265,
    272. *See also* Union for Repatriation
    of Russians Abroad
Wirth, (Joseph), 139
Wolf, Dr., 190
Wolf, Felix, *see* Inkov

Yagoda, G. G., 65n., 178–9, 200
Yaroslavsky (military attaché in
    Vienna), 108
Yezhov, N. I., 1–3, 201, 219
Youth International, 12, 39, 44, 104,
    197

Zaporozhets, Ivan, 65, 68, 146
Zarubin, V. (pseud. Rudolph), 145–6,
    148, 219; wife Lisa (née Rosenberg),
    145–7, 225
Zborovsky, Marc (Etienne) (pseud.
    Friedman), 244–6, 251, 254–5, 261–7
    271–4
Zeromski, Stefan, 5
Zetkin, Clara, 41n., 79
Zinoviev, G. Y., 30–31, 107, 150, 223
    257; 'Zinoviev letter', 73